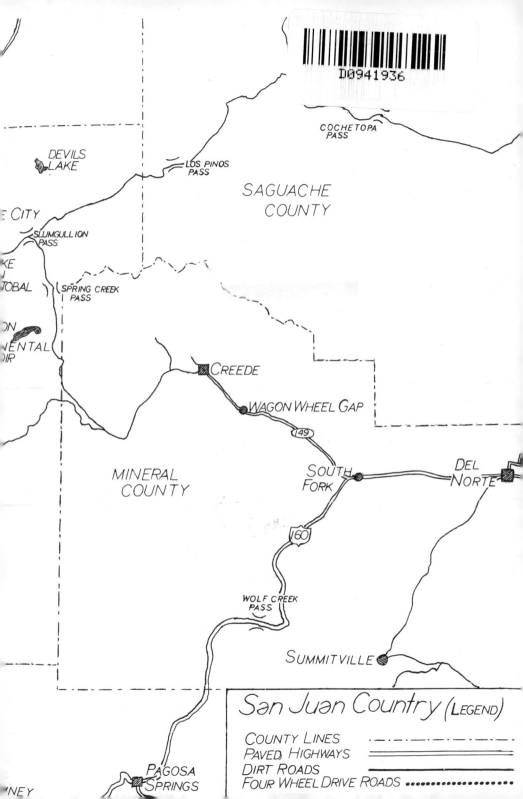

D0941936

COCHETOPA
PASS

DEVILS
LAKE

LOS PINOS
PASS

SAGUACHE
COUNTY

E CITY

SLUMGULLION
PASS

KE
TOBAL

SPRING CREEK
PASS

ON

NENTAL
IR

CREEDE

WAGON WHEEL GAP

149

MINERAL
COUNTY

SOUTH
FORK

DEL
NORTE

160

WOLF CREEK
PASS

SUMMITVILLE

San Juan Country (LEGEND)

COUNTY LINES
PAVED HIGHWAYS
DIRT ROADS
FOUR WHEEL DRIVE ROADS ●●●●●●●●●●

PAGOSA
SPRINGS

NEY

AN EMPIRE OF SILVER

AN EMPIRE OF SILVER

A History of the San Juan Silver Rush

By

ROBERT L. BROWN

ILLUSTRATED WITH PHOTOGRAPHS

The CAXTON PRINTERS, Ltd.
CALDWELL, IDAHO
1968

First printing November, 1965
Second printing December, 1968

LIBRARY

OCT 27 1975

UNIVERSITY OF THE PACIFIC

303370

© 1965 BY
THE CAXTON PRINTERS, LTD.
CALDWELL, IDAHO

Library of Congress Catalog Card No. 65-18665

Western
Americana

F
782
S19
B87

Printed and bound in the United States of America by
The CAXTON PRINTERS, Ltd.
Caldwell, Idaho
110938

For my Mother,
Mrs. Ardria I. Brown

Introduction

THE SAN JUAN COUNTRY is among the most spectacularly beautiful areas in all of Colorado. Its history, since earliest times, is a particularly fascinating and colorful one. Long before the founding of Jamestown, Spanish Conquistadores searched its rivers and their tributaries for gold. Intrepid fur trappers explored its streams and valleys in their relentless quest for beaver and other fur-bearing animals during the first half of the nineteenth century. Optimistic Anglo-Saxon gold seekers once more penetrated its vertical topography a full two decades prior to discovery of the white metal that brought its greatest fame, and ultimately its decline in 1893. Last of all came the permanent settlers who brought their families into the region, established lasting communities, and introduced agriculture.

The San Juans are located near the southwestern corner of Colorado. Here one finds the headwaters of innumerable well-known rivers, as well as the most startling mountain vistas in the West. But the silver seekers had little time for enjoying the scenery. Their job was the often difficult task of survival in a strange environment where nothing worked according to the rules that had applied back East. In this cold, arid, and intensely vertical world, it was necessary to learn how to conquer the long, steep, and rocky trails as well as how to build log towns from peculiar materials. What is more, they had to seek out alpine passes above timberline at twelve thousand feet and more, over the highest and most confusing topography in Colorado, wheezing and blinking every step of the way because of the altitude and the intensely bright light.

Since precious metals rarely occur at low altitudes, by far the largest number of paying mines were located high up among the peaks and in the alpine valleys, making access difficult. Wherever there was a mine, a town of sorts somehow evolved to shelter those who toiled there.

Wherever there was a rumor and a hole in the ground, men built a ramshackle settlement around it. They were christened with names like Corkscrew, Mineral Point, Burro Bridge, Smuggler, Matterhorn, Beartown, Eureka, and Red Mountain. With displays of almost unbelievable civic pride, each settlement claimed it was built exactly on the top of the mother lode and that its mud-encrusted streets would soon be paved with silver nuggets. Most believed that the San Juans were so rich that the combined rushes to California and Nevada were not even contestants in the same horse race.

Each new rumor sent hundreds of men up nameless creeks to wash away nameless mountains, a pound at a time. Consequently, most of the communities that were established during the silver excitement were situated far off the beaten tracks of today. One of the most striking comparisons that can be made between the San Juans, then and now, has to do with this disparity between where the population centers and roads were at that time, as contrasted with where they are at present. More often than not these out-of-the-way places are not even shown on contemporary maps. Finding some of these formerly important locations requires not only research but physical labor as well, since the old wagon roads and trails have seen little or no use, to say nothing of maintenance, since the turn of the present century.

Roughly a decade ago a close friend was kind enough

to invite me to accompany him on a three-day Jeep expedition that penetrated just deeply enough into the back trails of the San Juan country to excite my curiosity. This simple, uncomplicated introduction constituted the beginning of my fascination with this area, an interest that still persists. Since then, excuses have been found, or made, for much additional time to be spent in the San Juans each summer. In duration these visits have ranged from only a few days at a time to a full week on two separate occasions. Numerous interviews have also been pursued with persons who actually experienced the silver rush during the later days, in an effort to gather as much first-hand information as possible. Old manuscripts, newspaper files, documents, personal letters, business directories, and other kindred materials have likewise helped immeasurably to fill out the story.

In this book my purpose has been to bring together this diversity of information and to form a cohesive record of the area from earliest times through its period of optimum greatness.

Since I sincerely feel that photographs, like no other media, can parallel and supplement the printed page and are capable of conveying meanings far beyond the potential of mere words alone, matched pairs of old and contemporary pictures have been included to further the reader's comprehension and, I hope, enjoyment.

For the reader who is interested in photography, my contemporary pictures were made with a Leica, a Rolleiflex, and a Pentax "K" equipped with lenses of varied focal lengths. An occasional K-2 filter was used and the film was either X-L Pan or Plus X. Since many early photographers used lenses of relatively short focal lengths in order to include as much as possible in their pictures, wide-angle lenses, including one of twenty-eight millimeters focal length, were used far more than the so-called normal optics. It has often been difficult to correlate exact distances with long or short focal lengths in attempting to achieve identical perspectives with the older pictures. To further complicate things, trees seem to have a habit of growing up in such a way as to obscure the viewpoint from which the original picture had been taken.

On more than one occasion, after diligent research, comparison of old maps and herding our Jeep up some steep, rocky, half-forgotten trail, disappointment was our reward. Many of the towns are gone now, and nature is in the process of reclaiming its own. Only the mountains still look the same and inadvertently reveal the community's former location.

To the memory of all of the pioneers, of whatever stripe, who braved the wilderness and hacked out some semblance of a civilization in the San Juans, go my heartfelt thanks for providing these conditions that have truly turned this piece of research into a real labor of love. This book is an attempt to tell their story.

R. L. B.

Acknowledgments

DURING THE APPROXIMATELY three-year period of preparation for this book, quite a large number of persons, institutions, and sources of primary reference materials were consulted and are deserving of mention at this time.

First, a few words of very special gratitude to Mrs. Laura Ekstrom of the Colorado State Historical Society for locating copious quantities of old manuscripts, original letters, documents, and rare books. Many of these were completely new to me. Mrs. Enid Thompson, Librarian at the same institution, worked tirelessly on my behalf during many research sessions. Her associate, Mrs. Kay Pearson, also rendered invaluable assistance.

At the Western History Collection of the Denver Public Library, valuable assistance was rendered by Mrs. Alys Freeze and her staff, particularly Mrs. Opal Harber, who found a number of old and quite unexpected materials in the vault.

For assistance in locating and in overcoming the difficulties associated with actually getting to some of the old townsites and in their positive identification from old photographs, go a few words of sincere gratitude to the following people: to my wife Evelyn and our two children, Diana and Marshall, for spending countless days in the Jeep while we covered hundreds of miles of back trails in the San Juans; to J. G. "Pete" Heiney, who first took me to these beautiful mountains and who has since been my companion on many other trips in his vehicle or mine; to Jack and Erma Morison, good friends who spent several days with us in the San Juans; and to Dr. Gerald G. Coon for a number of four-wheel-drive excursions in the Cinnamon, Engineer, and Ophir Pass country. Robert M. Utley of Santa Fe, New Mexico, took time off from the writing of his new book to walk the Glorieta Pass battlefields with me, thus providing a far clearer interpretation of the crucial events that transpired at that location. My good friend, Arthur Abe, gave generously of his technical knowledge in the photographic department and provided most welcome assistance. Jack Thode made several old pictures available to me.

The following people provided valuable information through a series of letters and personal interviews: Claude Miner, Charles Parker, Randy and Morine Baisch, Mrs. Bertha Neal, John Joyce, Carl Bertram, W. C. (Bill) Little, and R. D. Dunagan. Paul Ton and Ronald F. Ruhoff gave valuable technical assistance in the photographic department. All of these people were most generous with their time and information.

A special word of thanks should go to Freda and Francis B. Rizzari and to my wife Evelyn, who did yeoman service by proofreading my final manuscript for oversights, errors, and omissions. Mrs. Evelyn Brown, Diana Brown, Harolynn Dyer, Lynn Ray, and Valerie Steinmetz labored tirelessly through the typing and necessary retyping.

Fred and Jo Mazzulla not only supplied a majority of the old pictures for this book but also came up with much technical advice, some rare books, and several personal contacts. I am also indebted to the following persons and institutions for other photographs which I have used: Francis Rizzari, Mrs. Bertha Neal, Randy and Morine Baisch, Claude Miner, the U.S. Geological Survey, and the Library of the Colorado State Historical Society.

Finally, the following references, in alphabetical order, were consulted during my research and proved to be particularly valuable: Atwood and Mather wrote Professional Paper Number 166 for the U.S. Geological Survey and called it *Physiography and Quarternary Geology of the San Juan Mountains.* This proved to be the most valuable single source concerning the origins and chronological development of these unusual mountains. Other helpful references were the following: the *Arizona Historical Review,* I, No. 2 (July, 1928); John B. Canfield, Publisher (no author listed), *Mines and Mining Men of Colorado* (Denver, 1893); the *Colorado Magazine,* September, 1945; Rev. George M. Darley, *Pioneering in the San Juans* (Chicago: Fleming H. Revell Co., 1899); the *Denver Times,* January 21, 1900; the *Denver Tribune,* July 26, 1872, November 7, 1881; the *Denver Weekly Tribune,* June 4 and October 18, 1873; the *Durango Herald-Democrat* of December 31, 1929; Frank Fosset, *Colorado: A Historical, Descriptive and Statistical Work on the Rocky Mountain Gold and Silver Mining Region* (Denver: The Daily Tribune Steam Printing House, 1876); Frank Fosset, *Colorado, Its Gold and Silver Mines* (New York: C. J. Crawford, Printer and Stationer, 1880); Rev. J. J. Gibbons, *Notes of a Missionary Priest in the Rocky Mountains* (New York and San Francisco: The Christian Press Association, 1898); Marguerite Moss Granger, personal letters in the files of the State Historical Society of Colorado; Don and Jean Griswold and Fred M. and Jo Mazzulla, *Colorado's Century of Cities,* published by the authors (Denver, 1958); Frank Hall, *History of Colorado,* four volumes published between 1889 and 1895 by The Blakely Printing Company of Chicago; E. M. Hamilton, *The San Juan Mines with Map* (Chicago: C. E. Southard, Printer, 1874); Charles W. Henderson, *Mining in Colorado,* U.S. Geological Survey Professional Paper Number 138 (Washington, D.C.: Government Printing Office, 1926); F. V. Hayden, *An-*

nual Report of the United States Geological and Geographical Survey of the Territories (Washington, D.C.: Government Printing Office, 1876); Ernest Ingersoll, *Knocking Around the Rockies* (New York: Harper & Brothers, 1883); Clarence S. Jackson, *Picture Maker of the Old West, William H. Jackson* (New York: Charles Scribner's Sons, 1947); Sidney Jocknick, *Early Days on the Western Slope of Colorado* (Denver: Carson-Harper Co., 1913); F. J. Kramer, *Catholicity in the San Juans* (no date); Arthur W. Monroe, *San Juan Silver* (Montrose, Colo.: the Author, 1940); the *Ouray Herald, Life of the Marlows*, Ouray, Colo., 1930; T. A. Rickard, *Across the San Juan Mountains, Engineering and Mining Journal* (New York and London, 1903); the *Rocky Mountain News* for February 15, March 27 and 31, April 4, 1877, September 5, 1879, and October 1, 1896; Lieutenant E. H. Ruffner, *Report of a Reconnaissance in the Ute Country* (Washington, D.C.: Government Printing Office, 1874); Sarah Platt Decker Chapter of the D.A.R., *Pioneers of the San Juan Country*, Vols. I, II, III, and IV, published in 1942, 1946, 1952, and 1961 at Durango, Colorado; the *Silverton Miner*, Silverton, Colo., September 27, 1907; the *Silverton Times*, Silverton, Colo., May 9, 1901; the *Trail*, March and June, 1920; W. B. Vickers, *History of Denver* (1880); Josiah M. Ward, *Missing Links in the Career of Captain Moss*, a series published in the magazine section of the *Denver Post* for April 10, 17, 24, and May 1, 1921; C. A. Warriner and Co., publishers (no author), *The San Juan, Its Past and Present Gold and Silver Mines* (Denver, Colo., 1876); W. Weston, *Ouray County, Colorado, in the San Juans;* Henry T. Williams, *Tourist Guide to the San Juan Mountains* (publisher and date uncertain, probably late 1870's). Last, but far from least, two superb books by Mrs. Muriel Sibell Wolle, of Boulder, *Stampede to Timberline*, first published in 1949 and still in print, and *The Bonanza Trail*, which appeared in 1953. Both of these books belong in the collection of all who love Colorado's past.

The most trying problems associated with the preparation of this book were encountered in endeavoring to separate fact from folklore. Accounts of early happenings, population statistics, and mine production figures —to name just three—vary widely from source to source. In each instance, my efforts have been directed toward finding out what really happened. In some areas the chronicles are so completely confusing that it now seems doubtful that the truth will ever be known. One example of this will be found in the chapter containing the exploits of Captain John Moss.

In no instance have I knowingly presented events as facts without good authority, or have I intentionally colored what happened by my own literary style or ideas of what should have been. Whenever a "story" has been included, it has been labeled as such. For all unresolved statements and figures that may have eluded careful checking, and for any other errors, real or imagined, that may vary from what the reader has seen or heard, the author apologizes in advance. In many cases within this story, the truth has been stranger than fiction.

R. L. B.

Contents

Illustrations

Page

AN EMPIRE OF SILVER

∽ 1 ∾

Mountain Building—How They Got That Way

THE ROCKY MOUNTAINS in Colorado lie generally north
and south, except in the southwest where they break into
several ranges and are called the San Juans, San Miguels,
and La Platas. Here they run in all directions. The San
Juan area is the highest generally in the United States,
and possibly in North America, containing hundreds of
peaks over thirteen thousand feet and nearly one fourth
of all the peaks in North America over fourteen thousand
feet high. Characterized by some of the most precipitous
topography and wildly rugged mountains in the world,
this remarkable district lies at an elevation of from one
and two thirds to nearly three miles vertically above
the level of the sea. The lowest point is at the southern
end, where the Animas River crosses the county line,
one and a quarter miles north of Needleton. Here the
elevation is 8,250 feet. The Needle Mountains are the
most precipitous, not only of Colorado, but of the United
States. They have long been the bane of explorers. Fremont called them, "The highest, most rugged, most im-
practicable, and inaccessible of the Rocky Mountains."
Drainage on the north, west, and south is toward the
Colorado River, and on the southeast toward the Rio
Grande.

The San Juan country forms a right-angle triangle,
approximately twenty-five miles wide at its base, or
southern boundary. The Continental Divide of North

America crosses the east portion of San Juan County, having a general southerly trend. To the west the Animas River, heading in the north extremity of the county, flows south and drains into the San Juan River, and then into the great Colorado.

The San Juan region has benefited from an esthetic standpoint by the names applied to its scenic features by the Spanish explorers. For example, "El Rio de Las Animas Perdidas" and "El Rio Dolores." The Animas River with its principal tributaries, Cement Creek, South Mineral Creek, and Cascade Creek, flows directly south with an occasional abrupt deflection to the southeast and southwest. The deep canyons are interspersed at points along the courses of these streams with flat gravel areas of limited size known as parks. The largest of these beautiful tracts is Baker's Park, in which the town of Silverton is situated. Eureka and Gladstone occupy similar but smaller parks. Silverton is at an elevation of 9,290 feet, Gladstone at 10,600 feet, Chattanooga at 10,250 feet, Eureka at 9,800 feet, Animas Forks at 11,200 feet, and Mineral Point at 11,750 feet. Summit, the point on the line where the Silverton-Ouray stage road formerly crossed the divide, is at 11,000 feet elevation. The land area of the San Juan country is just about equal to that of Massachusetts, Rhode Island, and Connecticut combined—about 15,000 square miles. The mountains are an integral part of the Rocky Mountain system spur. From it the ranges of the Rocky Mountain system have a southeast course, while the San Juans strike out generally to the southwest for about 250 miles.

The upness and downness of the San Juan country had its good side, as well as its bad, for the miner, its conveniences as well as its inconveniences. The whole region stands up on end, but the deep canyons leading in from all directions furnished access to the heart of it. The interior soon had adequate wagon roads and a great labyrinth of very good pack trails that were easy enough when you had learned how to navigate them and had a good trail horse to carry you. Because the mountains are very high and steep, the veins were well exposed on their sides. They were usually mined by adit tunnels (tunnels run in on the vein, draining the mines without the expense of pumping).

The San Juan country is heavily forested, including the Montezuma and San Juan National forests on the western and southern slopes of the mountains and the Uncompahgre, Gunnison, and Rio Grande forests on the northern and eastern slopes. The San Juan-Rio Grande primitive areas extending down from the Needle Mountains on the Continental Divide, are areas of rare wilderness, natural beauty, and ruggedness. There are many native varieties of pine, spruce, fir, and cedar, in addition to the deciduous trees such as the aspen, alder, cottonwood, and box elder. A number of larger shrubs, such as the mountain maple, willow, chokecherry, and white oak are found, and also a number of smaller varieties. The San Juans include extremes of temperature and humidity that range from the hot, dry, semidesert at the extreme south to the cold, snowcapped mountains that are in the maximum precipitation area of Colorado.

The San Juans are an esthetically beautiful group of mountains of generally volcanic origin, totally unlike most other ranges in the state. The peaks are trachytic, with frequent underlying schists. Literally hundreds of almost perpendicular rock walls rise to elevations of 1,200 to 1,500 feet, serrated with easily apparent quartz veins. Highest of all the San Juan peaks is Uncompahgre, with a summit that towers 14,306 feet above sea level. In form it is a truncated pyramid with a large triangular surface at the top. The Colorado area embraces about 12,000 square miles of towering summits of a domal structure. If we consider their extensions into surrounding states, a figure of 20,000 would describe their extent more accurately. Most of the actual mineral production has originated within a small 250-square-mile section divided among Ouray on the north, Ophir and Matterhorn on the west, the Silverton-Baker's Park area on the south, and Lake City on the east. So rugged and comprehensive are the mountains that San Juan County was once said to lack a single acre of soil that was easily adaptable for conventional agricultural purposes.

The name San Juan seems to apply equally not only to the mountains but also to the adjacent plateaus. They form an outlying group of the southern Rockies, well defined, extremely rugged, and nearly surrounded by plateaus and lowlands. Along their eastern slope, the San Luis Valley separates them from the eastern slopes of the Rockies. East of the valley lies the Sangre de Cristo Range, the so-called southern extension of the Rocky Mountains. To the west of them are three groups of peaks—the La Platas, the Rico Mountains, and the Mount Wilson group. On the northern side they are bounded by the Gunnison Valley, while they terminate at the valley of the Rio Grande on the southeast.

The jagged, sharp-pinnacled crests west of Ouray form the north front of the range and are referred to locally as the Sawtooth Mountains. The interesting variety of peaks surrounding Mount Wilson form the west side and are called the San Miguels. South of Silverton are the Grenadier Range and the Needle Mountains. The La Garitas lie between the Rio Grande and Sagauche rivers, while the Cochetopa Hills are to the north and east.

Due to comparatively recent glacial erosion, most of the valleys that are tributary to the Rio Grande have U-shaped troughs, while those with V shapes indicate a strong pattern of stream erosion at current levels of between five thousand and six thousand feet below the present summits. Most of the resulting canyons are deep, narrow, and rugged. The predominant plateaus stand between seven thousand and eight thousand feet high

Collection of Robert L. Brown
Teakettle and Potosi peaks dominate the skyline with Mount Sneffels. View is from the top of Engineer Pass.

Collection of Robert L. Brown
South Lookout Peak from the western side of Ophir Pass

with canyons that occasionally reach about one thousand feet in depth.

During earliest times the lower section of the San Juan area was covered at various periods by an arm of the vast inland sea that inundated several other portions of Colorado. As the land rose, the sea went down the drain to the west or southwest into the Gulf of Mexico. The waters, taking the path of least resistance, eroded away the softer portions, thereby creating river valleys. Only here in the West do we have the phenomenon of sunken rivers. The rivers are oldest and were here first. As the land rose up due to volcanic activity associated with a cooling of the earth's crust, the rivers actually cut their way down into the rocky surface. The rivers actually antedate the mountain ranges which were then in a process of generally slow and gradual elevation.

Certain of the higher portions of the San Juans remained as a part of the large land mass that protruded above the level of the sea. During the Devonian period, the so-called age of fishes, there followed a general submergence of the entire region. Limestone deposits, the fossilized remains of fish that lived in the ancient sea, provide us with undisputed evidence of what happened. As the land rose, the limestone deposits which were three hundred to four hundred feet thick in places, became exposed above the water level. In Permian times a continued movement of the earth's crust caused a further shifting of the waters and considerable erosion.

A prolonged gathering of sedimentary rocks occurred during the Mesozoic era. Only slight elevations would have been visible at this time except to the north where erosion was advancing aggressively in the Montrose and Uncompahgre regions. In Triassic times the portion east of Silverton and the Needle Mountains was thrust up and then compressed into a series of folds. All of these changes occurred in an extremely prolonged sequence, very gradually and slowly.

Within the Cretaceous, or chalk period, a stepped-up cycle of water erosion attacked the uplands of the eastern San Juans and wore them down almost to base level. The depth of the seas decreased greatly during the Montana epoch, only to deepen again later. Incredible as it may seem, the elevations we know now had not been deposited as yet.

Next came a tremendous regional uplift coupled with a domal deformation of about seventy-five by thirty-five miles in area and roughly ten thousand feet high. While the crust flexed, the first volcanic eruption came, creating the Animas formation. Still later came another long period of erosion which dug down through six thousand to ten thousand feet of the dome. The result was the formation and sculpturing of high and jagged peaks with, nearby, deeply etched canyons.

The next chapter ushered in a glacial period which resulted from a change in the climate. The region grew cold and piedmont glaciers were formed. At the end of the Telluride epoch, the first generation of San Juan mountains had completed the inevitable life cycle common to all mountains. Glacial erosion had reduced them to round hills with about two-thousand-foot-high gradual rolling elevations.

From deep inside the earth near present Uncompahgre Peak, violent volcanic activity vented itself once more through several openings and covered the northwest section of the San Juans with a massive tuff, two thousand feet deep. The sharp, fingerlike pinnacles so typical of the ranges around Ophir and Telluride, were carved from this deposit. Sneffels Peak, towering 14,143 feet above sea level, is composed of a dark-grained volcanic rock, identifying it as a great volcanic plug or what was at one time the center core of an active volcano.

The tremendous cliffs overhanging the deep valleys were created in the next period of erosion following the volcanic upheaval. Next came still another series of eruptions that in turn built up the Silverton volcanic series. Explosive outbursts and the creation of more volcanic cones were typical of the action at this time. Another period of erosion followed until an outburst of fierce volcanic activity near Potosi Peak stole the limelight and a huge volcanic plateau was created. The Silverton-Ouray region was buried under this pile which extended far off to the east. Depth at this time has been estimated at ten thousand feet. It should also be borne in mind that all of these initial volcanic forces and erosive actions upon the San Juan dome were being performed at a level well above even the tops of the present peaks. The pre-Cambian granite from which the current range was sculptured was still far beneath the surface.

Formation of the San Juans that we see now began with the Peneplain cycle of erosion. Very strong erosive forces began to cut away parts of the plateau and left the tops of some of today's highest peaks exposed. Vigorous action on the part of mountain streams cut into the surface and produced steep grades that average something more than one hundred feet to the mile. An additional period of uplift was coupled with a warping of the crust to add even more variety. The uplift was in the central and western portions, while at the same time the eastern margin and the San Luis Valley were sinking. The crustal warping was almost constant throughout the last geologic period. What is more, an almost perpetual cycle of mountain growth by continued domal uplift was also prevalent. Crustal deformation probably accounts for more of the deep canyons of today than stream erosion. Incidentally, this process, which is called the Canyon Cycle, is not only still going on but also is very young.

2

Early Exploration

ON MAY 27, 1867, President Andrew Johnson appointed
A. C. Hunt to be Colorado's fourth territorial governor.
The following year Governor Hunt negotiated an Indian
treaty that was to have far-reaching repercussions for
Colorado. Under the provisions of this agreement the
governor ceded the extensive San Juan country to the
Utes. The extent of this tract embraced an area of nearly
three hundred miles in length by about two hundred wide.
It was bordered on the south and west by the state bound-
aries of New Mexico and Utah respectively.

Nature, however, was not content merely to endow
the region with spectacular scenery. In addition, the
presence of gold, silver, and other deposits made the San
Juans one of the most heavily mineralized areas of the
state. With a stage setting that encompassed such props
and backgrounds as these, it became inevitable that the
rising curtain would reveal another reenactment of the
traditional drama in which the holy pioneer somehow
divests the savage of his acquired inheritance.

The first recorded prospecting expedition into the San
Juans was led by Don Juan Maria de Rivera, a Spaniard
from Santa Fe. The year was 1765, slightly more than a
decade prior to the outbreak of the American Revolution.
The party sought to follow up Indian rumors of gold
and silver in the north. Traveling up the Rio Grande
and Chama valleys, they rounded the Uncompahgre

slopes of the range and passed within a few miles of the undiscovered lodes that later paid off to the tune of millions in silver. Although they were realistic, hardheaded, and practical, the Spanish rarely tackled anything, like mining, that held out the promise of hard, arduous labor. They were successful in exploiting the riches of Peru only because they enslaved the natives and forced them to work in the mines. It will also be recalled that Coronado in 1541-42, introduced the hated institution of slavery to the Indians of the Rio Grande Valley—slavery, again, in the San Juans of necessity, but no hard work for the Spanish. Unless the gold or silver was seen suspended around the neck of an Indian maiden, the Conquisadores did not find it.

Consequently, the Rivera expedition never left the riverbanks. They failed since they did not invade the heavily mineralized cliffs. Moving farther north, they carved a cross on a tree near the Black Canyon of the Gunnison and returned to Santa Fe, lamenting upon the lack of gold or silver in the northern countries. Following the Rivera expedition, in the next eleven years, there were numerous other Spanish explorers who came into the San Juan Basin. It was at this time that many of the mountains and rivers received their musical Spanish names.

In 1776 our forefathers were occupied with signing their Declaration of Independence in a faraway city named Philadelphia. During that same year the Dominguez-Escalante expedition, with twelve men, left Santa Fe and came into Colorado near present Pagosa Junction. They crossed the San Juan, Piedra, Los Pinos, and Las Animas rivers and camped at the base of the Mesa Verde. They followed the Dolores south for some distance and later turned toward the San Miguel. Following down close to the present site of Placerville, they crossed Dallas Divide to the Uncompahgre and Gunnison rivers. Señor Miera, a member of the party, made a remarkably accurate map of the region. Their route became famous at a later time as the "Old Spanish Trail."

Although the fur trappers left few records, it is known that they were in the San Juan Basin in the early 1800's. One party is definitely known to have trapped in this region during the winter of 1832-33 and traded at either Santa Fe or Robideaux's Post on the Gunnison. In 1859 a Lieutenant Simpson led his geological party into the San Juan Basin, and in that same year a group headed by Captain J. M. Macomb climbed the north rim of the Mesa Verde.

Precious metal was probably first discovered in the San Juans around the Lake City area in 1848 by a member of the John C. Fremont party. The discovery apparently was not followed up at that time by any further search for mineral deposits. Following this discovery, an exploration was made in later years but no one, not even Fremont himself, was able to locate the place or even the stream from which the first small amount of gold was panned.

In 1848 Fremont had been leading an expedition of thirty-three men in an attempt to find a winter route across the Rockies. Always before he had availed himself of the services of Kit Carson as his guide; however, this time Carson was not available and Old Bill Williams was signed up to do the job. Sometimes called "Preacher Bill," Williams had come into the mountains back around 1820 to christianize the Indians but instead had gone native himself. He was sixty-two when the expedition started up Embargo Creek into the San Juans from the San Luis Valley during that bleak December of 1848. Williams wore the blackest, filthiest set of deerskins west of the Missouri and, being completely eclectic, he could bellow excerpts from half-forgotten sermons or take a scalp with equal facility.

Historians still differ as to who was responsible for the tragedy that followed. The disagreement between

Fremont and Bill Williams has since been the subject
of considerable controversy. It now seems that Fremont
ignored the advice of the only man who knew the country and stubbornly led his party into the teeth of a San
Juan blizzard from which eleven of them failed to return. The mules froze in their tracks and were eaten by
the half-starved men. Some say that "Old Bill" had a
few bites of something besides mule meat. The rumor
gave rise to a widely circulated suggestion that advised
men, "Never walk ahead of Preacher Bill when he's hungry." The much sought crossing was not found, and
Fremont never again considered driving a railroad survey across the San Juans in a blizzard. Whether or not
there was gold or silver in the range seemed a trifling
consideration under the circumstances. Efforts to relo-
cate the spot at a later, more opportune, time resulted
in failure.

So the first of several acts of the drama had already
been played out prior to the day in 1868 when the Ute-
Hunt treaty was agreed upon.

The initial exploration of the San Juans by Anglo-
Saxons, aside from the Fremont party, is generally
credited to a party led by Captain Charles Baker, a veteran of the 1860 gold excitement in California Gulch
near present-day Leadville. Baker was a typical frontiersman in the finest tradition of Frederick Jackson
Turner. Restless, adventure-loving, always seeking the
unknown will-o-the-wisp that might be found beyond the
crest of the next hill, he obtained the financial support of
his employers, S. B. Kellogg and Company, to pay for
his projected expedition along the San Juan River. In
July of 1860 he left California Gulch at the head of a
party of seven men. His occasional reports to Kellogg
described placer deposits that paid about twenty-five
cents to the pan. These reports caused Kellogg to em-
bark for the States before the first snow. In November
of 1860, he returned to Denver with his family. The good

news that gold had been found in the San Juans spread throughout the mushrooming Cherry Creek settlements like the proverbial measles in a kindergarten. The presence of rich placer gravels is usually indicative of richer veins or lodes upstream from which the minute dust particles have washed down. Judicious panning of a stream, while following it toward the source, has often been a richly rewarding experience. Consequently, no one was surprised to see a party estimated at one hundred and fifty treasure seekers following the Kellogg family on their departure from the settlements on December 14, 1860.

Other parties continued along the trail at different times until about three hundred persons were on their way to the San Juans. Many notable pioneer names appear to have participated in this migration, including Abner French and Noisy Tom Pollock, erstwhile early-day executioner of pioneer Denver. Pollock, incidentally, had just been married to Miss Sarah Chivington, daughter of the recently arrived Methodist clergyman, the Reverend John M. Chivington. Later commissioned a major, Chivington was to achieve a measure of fame at the battle of Glorieta Pass, and a reputation for infamy for his conduct at Sand Creek. The newly wedded Sarah and Tom Pollock started for the San Juans together.

The route of the party took them by way of Colorado City and Pueblo before crossing old Sangre de Cristo Pass. This passage, difficult at any time, became doubly treacherous under the added hardships incurred with a winter ascent. The necessity of road building in places and a lack of forage for their stock were among the difficulties that consumed a total of fourteen days in accomplishing their crossing. Upon reaching the San Luis Valley, their troubles were by no means over. There a severe winter storm poured wind and snow down upon them and scattered their stock. In March they passed through Conejos, Colorado's oldest town, and then proceeded west through Pagosa Springs. The first of April found them in camp at a location where Cascade Creek flows into the Animas River south of Silverton. From this point a scouting party made contact with Baker, who had been living in a broad, beautiful, sheltered valley twenty-five miles to the north. The spot has since become known as Baker's Park and is the present-day location of Silverton.

A series of crude, brush, lean-to shanties had been erected to provide shelter against winter in the park. The actual gold diggings found by the party were being worked at a point nine miles farther up the Animas River. Surprisingly enough, this same spot was to become the center of another great rush a mere two decades later with the impending discovery of silver, not gold. This identical location saw the founding of Eureka, which grew into a busy and thriving mining town in the seventies and eighties, only to decline in the nineties. Only faint traces of Eureka remain to be seen by today's visitor. The area is rapidly returning to its natural state.

Baker himself had, of course, been closely watched and was followed by the usual crowd of restless men, ever on the lookout for anything that even remotely promised gold. Stories about the San Juans were heard from time to time through trappers and hunters from 1860 to 1869. They all told the same stories of its great wealth in mineral veins, but at the same time they gave such accounts of its lofty peaks and deep canyons that it was looked upon as a district, without a doubt, incomparably rich in great fissure veins, but so out of the way as to be practically valueless. Then, too, the mineral districts more to the north, such as Central City and Georgetown, almost entirely occupied the attention of mining men in Colorado at this time.

In June of 1861, discomforting rumors concerning the outbreak of the Civil War were carried into the camp by migrants from across the range. Several of the wives pooled their white goods, blue bonnets and red petticoats to sew up a rough approximation of an American flag. The tallest pine, stripped of its branches, became the staff for the first flying of our national colors over the San Juans.

The summer of 1861 also saw the erection of whipsawed sluice boxes along the banks of the Animas for a more efficient recovery of gold. The diggings were worked throughout the summer but with rather disappointing results. Like many a later mineral rush, the optimism of early reports grew with each telling until the promises held out far exceeded the actual values to be derived. During that summer the best results never exceeded fifty cents per day to the man and frequently failed even to meet expenses or to pay for the workings. At that time the presence of silver was still unsuspected.

Some of the other members of the party made numerous exploratory trips into the nearby mountains, following the rivers and gulches. Their searches were restricted to looking for placer or gulch gold. Some prior knowledge of lodes or vein formations or the presence of a trained geologist in the party could have made for a far different outcome. As it was, their searches yielded little or nothing.

The Cascade Creek camp broke up about the first of May. Most members of the group moved along the Animas River to about the site of present-day Durango. Here they founded a community known as Animas City. Early in July, after more abortive attempts at prospecting, Animas City, too, was abandoned. The disgruntled settlers made their way back across the divide toward civilization. Failure is never a pleasant reality to be faced.

Meanwhile, Baker and a small nucleus of his original party remained at Eureka Gulch until fall. Before the snow fell, they had made their way out by way of Fort

Garland. Here, the rumors that they had previously heard of the Civil War were confirmed. Baker, a native son of Virginia, returned to his state and fought with the Confederate forces until their surrender at Appomattox.

Notwithstanding the fact that the Baker parties had practically abandoned the San Juans, grossly exaggerated reports of their meager discoveries were being spread in South Park and in the mining camps of the upper Arkansas Valley. As the summer of 1861 progressed, several hundred men were en route to the San Juans. In the days before established transportation systems, travel was slow and arduous. Consequently, wave after wave of migration converged upon southwestern Colorado. Fall passed and a fearsome winter moved in to catch many of the unwary still in the mountains. Many others never crossed the ranges. Half frozen and often starving, they straggled into scattered military posts in southern Colorado and northern New Mexico throughout the winter. A minor gold rush had started.

In January of 1861, the *Rocky Mountain News* reported that many inquiries were being received from the East about gold prospects in the San Juans. At that time most of the immigrants were purchasing their supplies in Denver, and it was the principal outfitting point for the San Juans. The *News* further reported that the success of prospecting in that region was not a foregone conclusion. The stories were very conflicting and readers felt that until something like a unanimous favorable proof of the district's richness was forthcoming that a stampede to the San Juans would not be a formidable one. A number of miners who returned from the San Juans in 1861 gave the impression that the gold excitement had been started by traders, who had large stocks of goods on hand that had found a very dull sale among the natives for the past two years. They thought that by inducing the ingress of a large American population they could dispose of their goods and get their country prospected at the same time.

Not everyone who went to the San Juans struck it rich. The *Rocky Mountain News* reported in March of 1861 that: "The tide of pilgrims flowing through here a few weeks ago on the way to the San Juans has now been reversed. A number of them may be seen in the streets. One such party consisted of six men with well ventilated feet and shabby clothes and such matted beards as were seen by many of those who faced the returning Pike's Peakers in '59." Their reports were confirmed by the more fortunate class who returned, as they had gone, with money and good outfits. They were forced to believe the accounts. Though partially true, glaring misrepresentations were sometimes made.

In June of 1861, a man named George Gregory wrote a letter to the *Rocky Mountain News* which was published under the title of "The San Juan Humbug." Mr. Gregory's letter cried out like a voice in the wilderness. He stated that he would rather travel from Denver to the Missouri River and back six times than to go to the San Juans and back once. The hardships of travel that he experienced were vividly described. He complained of the altitude and that the snow remained in the gulches much longer than in other districts and that the San Juan season was too short for profitable mining. He further complained that the agricultural potential was almost nonexistent and that sustenance of life would be difficult. He said that the valleys were not suited for grazing and that the entire district was, in fact, inferior in everything. Gregory reported that the Baker party was running a sluice which was paying them only thirty-seven to forty cents per day to the man. Gregory described Charles Baker as being, in his opinion, "almost a lunatic."

Since provisions were very high in price, most of the prospectors were living on the game they could kill and even that was very scarce. The Gregory article concluded with advice which said that if you cannot make a living in the Gregory district near Denver, you should not think of going to the San Juans. He said that he had never gone through as much hardship in his life as he experienced on a trip there, and he saw many men who were far worse off than he. Gregory said he had plenty to eat all the time but that he saw many who had not had a bite of bread for a month. In April of 1861, two men named Graham and Green completed a new road to the San Juans and opened it to travel by migrants who approached the region from Canon City.

The Civil War caused a significant decline in the state's mining fortunes and the San Juan district was no exception. Many of the early argonauts held strong convictions and felt duty bound to return home, North or South, and enlist. Since a predominant number of the early strikes were made by Georgians, there was a large Confederate segment in the population.

Territorial Governor William Gilpin's first census revealed that about one in four Coloradoans was a Confederate sympathizer. In Denver itself the proportion was much higher. Being a close friend of President Lincoln, Gilpin was quick to declare the State's support of the Union. Quite apart from the fact that they constituted a minority, several attempts to organize a "Secesh" militia were made; and one such group formed and paraded openly in Denver. They were later captured in Kansas while marching south. At least one duel was also fought by proponents of the opposing viewpoints. Editor Byers of the *Rocky Mountain News* condemned the "bogus Confederacy" and carried on a running feud with the *Mountaineer*, an openly pro-secession newspaper in Gregory Gulch.

Since the North possessed 71.7 percent of the railroad mileage, 84.8 percent of the factories, and a startling 91.1 percent of the wealth produced, the South was in a severe bind for money and supplies even at the outset. Several European nations stood ready to furnish arms to the Confederates, but only on a cash-and-carry basis for pretty obvious reasons. Consequently, at least four separate, and equally desperate, attempts were made to capture the output of Colorado's gold fields in order to supply ready specie payment.

The first attempt was led by a Captain Madison, who terrorized southern Colorado with a series of hit-and-run raids for a time during the summer of 1862. The second effort deviated radically from the previous guerrilla raids. It was an official, highly organized, full-scale Confederate attempt to take the mines of Colorado, Nevada, and California. The Second Texas Cavalry, under the command of General Henry H. Sibley, advanced up the Rio Grande Valley in February of 1862. They were victorious at the battle of Valverde and took Albuquerque and Santa Fe after the latter city's Union defenders fled in terror. Their next target was the Northern supply depot and headquarters at Fort Union.

A frantic call for help brought the Colorado Volunteers, an unauthorized and highly irregular group that Gilpin, with fortunate foresight, had brought into being. A remarkable forced march of ninety-two miles in thirty-six hours put the First Colorado Volunteers at the eastern end of Apache Pass, New Mexico, on March 26, where they won the first of three skirmishes when they and the Texans surprised each other in a narrow defile. The second, and major, battle was fought two days later at Pigeon's Ranch in a broad meadow near the crest of La Glorieta Pass. Simultaneously, Major John M. Chivington led a hardy detachment of mountaineers across the ranges where no trails existed and dropped down on the enemy's wagon supply base behind the lines. All Confederate military equipment was burned, including seventy wagons; and thirty mules and horses were bayoneted. Without supplies the Rebels were lost and their grand scheme had failed. What is more, the remaining Confederates were sent scuttling back to Texas on foot.

Then there was Charlie Harrison, former proprietor of Denver's Criterion Saloon, who wangled the Confederates out of a commission as a colonel with the promise that he could deliver an insurrection in Colorado and capture the mines. The date was May 14, 1863. He led a sizable band of hand-picked Rebels which got only as close as western Kansas. There the Osage Indians ambushed them on general principles and inadvertently did the Union a favor. However, the traditional scalping ritual presented a problem in Harrison's case, since he was bald. In the end, Osage ingenuity triumphed and they settled for taking his beard instead.

The final effort was an abortive Confederate guerrilla raid by the Reynolds gang in their attempt to take the output of the better mines in South Park during 1864. After robbing the Buckskin Coach near Fairplay and committing a few other minor depredations, they led three separate posses on a merry chase in the gulches around Kenosha Pass. Allegedly, when the pursuit got too hot for comfort, the loot was buried near the top of the range in either Geneva, Deer Creek, Genesee, or Handcart Gulch. Since that time, the more gullible have been perpetually deluged with "authentic" Reynolds maps, "drawn on the deathbed" by one or another of the gang after they split up. Each purports to show the location of a buried forty thousand dollars which has never been found and may never have been hidden in the first place.

While the war undoubtedly retarded a full realization of the potential riches of the San Juans, a few intrepid souls still continued to make sporadic journeys into the country. As a generalization, it could safely be said that conditions during the war had changed not at all since the exodus of the Baker party. Due to the isolated position of the country and the fiercely vindictive hostility displayed by the Utes, the miners and explorers found it nearly impossible to develop their strikes. In most cases the rich treasures remained unmolested.

Six persons commanded by a Captain Smith left Santa Fe in December of 1862. They crossed the Rio Grande River, explored the heart of the San Juan Range and found what came to be known far and wide at that time as the "San Juan Mines." Being excited at the idea of a speedy fortune, they constructed a log cabin and began prospecting with some success. All went well until the night the Utes descended upon them, killed two of their number and forced the rest to flee for their lives. In their haste the miners left behind all their silver and gold, provisions, and mining implements. This event is felt to be quite unusual, inasmuch as the Utes regarded it as unwise to fight at night. In common with most other tribes, the Utes believed that an Indian killed at night would remain in perpetual darkness in the hereafter. Finally making their way back to Santa Fe, the survivors told marvelous stories of the riches they had discovered. The men extravagantly described the mountains as being absolutely honeycombed with silver-bearing quartz. They told of the hostility of the redskins, until no one who heard their tale cared to repeat the experiment.

Following the cessation of hostilities, many restless young men experienced difficulty with the process of fitting into the main stream of life in the old hometown. Having become accustomed to a constant diet of suspense and excitement, however grim and unpleasant, many sought to fill the void by joining the postwar, westward migration.

Once again the thoughts of prospectors, and others who paid attention to such matters, turned to southwestern Colorado. Having survived the war, Charles Baker again returned to Colorado in 1868 and camped for a time south of present Buena Vista. With a small party of associates, he ultimately moved out toward the southwest. Exploring and prospecting along the principal rivers, the party gradually dwindled down until only Baker and two others remained. Hostile Indians dogged their progress all the way into northern Arizona. There, near the junction of the Little Colorado with the main stream, they sought escape by constructing a driftwood raft. Before it could be launched into the turbulent waters, Baker was killed in a furious exchange of gunfire with the hostiles. His two companions strapped themselves to the raft and escaped down the rapids.

August of the next year, 1869, saw the organization of another party, led by Calvin Jackson, at Prescott, Arizona. The twenty-nine men who comprised the Prescott party joined forces on the Salt River with a comparable group under the leadership of a Captain Cooley. The combined forces numbered fifty men, well armed in anticipation of Indian depredations planned to keep the whites out of their favorite hunting ground. During the day, smoke signals between Indian bands were visible and nighttime revealed the presence of signal fires high on the mountains.

While the party was attempting to prospect on a small stream, which they nostalgically named Cherry Creek, Apaches began rolling stones down the narrow canyon walls. The attackers wisely remained beyond rifle range while completely dominating the situation with a relatively inexhaustible supply of natural ammunition. After abandoning their camp, eight members of the party elected to continue, the others to return to Arizona. A peace treaty with the Apaches allowed the men to cross this territory, provided they did not stop to dig any more holes or search for gold in any way. In spite of their having agreed to the terms offered by the Indians, an Apache escort was assigned to follow them. The Arizonans were then able to move on through Zuni and Navajo country without serious incident.

In October the party entered the Mancos Valley. A snowstorm of five days' duration, typical of the unpredictable San Juan weather, forced their retreat to a lower altitude. With only their inadequate Arizona-type clothing and blankets, they withdrew, shoveling their way out through the drifts over the Dolores Range. Ten days of arduous labor enabled them to reach the Animas Valley and the protection afforded by the empty houses of Animas City which had been erected and abandoned by the Kellogg-Pollock expedition of 1861.

A side trip to Santa Fe by a few members of the party restored their supply of provisions and also brought news that the Utes were aware of their presence. A Ute council led by Chiefs Ignatio and Sopath extracted a promise that they would do no plowing, build no cabins or fences, and never forget that the land belonged to the Utes. The winter was passed in some abandoned government buildings at Tierra Amarilla where C. E. Cooley, one of the original leaders, rejoined them with three other men from Montana.

During April of 1870 the journey was resumed. At that time the San Juans were a part of Conejos County. The party split, with one group going up the Dolores. The second group prospected around Baker's Park and eventually discovered the "Little Giant" and "Mountaineer" lodes in Arastra Gulch. Winter saw their return to Santa Fe once more to await the next spring. When warm weather returned, a majority of the expedition moved up to Baker's Park again. After some futile attempts at prospecting, they settled in the park and continued to live there for many years, quite apart from their promises to the Utes.

To the Baker-Kellogg-Pollock party and the Jackson-Cooley expedition, as well as to the numerous unrecorded individual prospecting attempts, must be accorded the credit for opening up the San Juan country to fuller production of its vast stores of mineral wealth and its subsequent development after 1871.

3

Indian Country

FROM EARLIEST TIMES the Utes had lived in and traveled about over the Colorado Rockies. They were often referred to as "Mountain Indians" or "Black Indians" by their enemies, the Arapahoe and Cheyenne of the Plains. The Muache and Capote bands belonged to the so-called Southern Ute group. North of their territory, in west-central Colorado, was the land of the Tabegauche people. The Northern Utes resided in the north-central part of the state.

Early in the fourteenth century, the Utes and Apaches arrived in Colorado from the southwest. Many scholars credit their appearance as being one of the reasons for the hasty departure of the Pueblo Cliff Dwellers from the Mesa Verde. Since that time the Utes had regarded the larger parks and valleys of the Rockies as their home. Adequate shelter and an abundance of game made this an attractive place to live. Prior to 1863 they claimed almost all of the Colorado Rockies.

South Park was one of the favorite hunting grounds in all of North America. Here the Utes hunted the buffalo and were provided with food, clothing, and shelter from this single source. Many pitched battles were fought for the privilege of hunting in this desirable location. Even today, ranchers still turn up arrowheads and spear points, providing mute testimony to the extent of these encounters. Since there is no flint obsidian in the area, its source becomes reasonably simple to deduce; and in the process the Ute migrations up Eleven Mile Canyon may likewise be followed.

The treaty of 1868 set aside nearly all of present Colorado, west of the Rockies, for the exclusive use of the Utes. The actual territory was bounded on the east by the one hundred and seventh meridian and on the north by a line fifteen miles above the fortieth parallel. In this same treaty the government elevated and recognized Ouray, a Tabegauche, as chief of all the Utes. The "forever," so glowingly described in the treaty, lasted a mere four years.

Upon discovery of valuable gold and silver deposits within the Ute Reservation in the San Juan and Uncompahgre mountains, the prospectors rationalized that because the Indians had no use for gold or silver they should be forced to migrate elsewhere, so that they would not stand in the way of white men who desired a chance to acquire quick wealth. The Los Pinos Agency became the scene, in August of 1872, of a council to effect a peaceful settlement of the constantly recurring land disputes. The actual purpose was that of inducing the Utes to cede this mineralized portion of their lands. Chief Ouray put the government negotiators to shame by exposing numerous violations of previous treaties that had been signed, agreed to, and ratified by the Senate of the United States.

The unenlightened aborigines refused to move. A company of Federal troops under General McKenzie was sent in to remove the trespassers. But it soon became evident that a small-scale civil war might be the result.

On the nineteenth of September, 1873, the following year, Washington sent Felix Brunot, chairman of the Peace Commission, west to work out a treaty under which the Utes would give up about four million acres. The San Juan Cession of 1873 is sometimes referred to as the Brunot Treaty. Brunot's task was to rescue the prospectors from their awkward situation as trespassers.

The Utes expressed no objection to yielding the mining region, but under no circumstances would they give up the agricultural valleys.

Finally Brunot turned to Otto Mears, long regarded as a trusted friend of the Utes, the only man available who could talk and reason with them. One account tells us that Mears spoke fluent Ute, with a Yiddish accent. In any case he performed yeoman service and his intercession for Brunot doubtless turned the trick. Mears' success in his various dealings with the Indians was once reported to be due to the fact that he was able to "hunker" himself down on a buffalo robe in the filthiest of lice-infested Ute lodges, smoke with them and negotiate as an equal, without giving any impression of a feeling of superiority or revulsion.

A section covering about sixty by seventy-five miles, which included the principal mines, was ultimately agreed upon and the talks continued. The miners were only mildly embarrassed by the fact that the territory had belonged to the Utes. The land was to be purchased from the tribe for the startling price of about twelve cents per acre. During this same time, the United States General Land Office was charging homesteaders at the rate of a dollar and twenty-five cents per acre for less valuable Western lands. This time, however, Ouray accepted the inevitable and persuaded his people to give up the mining region. Annuities to the tribe were increased and Ouray was allowed to draw a salary of one thousand dollars per year. The treaty thus negotiated was ratified by the Senate on April 22, 1874. The Southern Ute Indian Agency moved, about 1875, to a position in the Umcompahgres where it could keep an eye on both the Utes and the miners. Mears went on to build roads for the San Juans, took out toll charters, and made a small fortune on them.

In their new homes the Utes were told that they would be permitted to hunt upon the lands, "so long as the game

Collection of Fred and Jo Mazzulla
The caption on this old picture described it as an "ox team caravan in the San Juans, loaded with supplies for the Utes." The town, possibly Del Norte, was not identified.

Collection of Robert L. Brown
The lower, more recent portion of Summitville, one of the earliest camps in the San Juans.

lasts and the Indians remain at peace with the white people." A more honest appendage might have been added, making provision for another Anglo-Saxon take-over "just in case" valuable ore deposits are discovered in the new location.

In the spring of 1870, Nathan Meeker, debt-ridden visionary follower of Horace Greeley, founded the Union Colony in northern Colorado. This experiment in communal agriculture eventually evolved into the present-day city of Greeley. Through highly placed Republican friends, Greeley secured for Meeker an appointment as agent to the White River Utes. Being thoroughly sold on the inherent virtues of agrarian life, Meeker immediately sought to replace the migratory hunting existence of the Utes with a peaceful, settled farm life. Meeker tried to educate them, to teach them to cultivate the soil, to live in houses, and to adopt Caucasian ways.

Since Ute women have traditionally done all tilling of the soil and most other hard work, this amounted to about the same thing as a conqueror invading our shores and trying to reverse the traditional male and female roles in our culture. Meeker's ideals were splendid, yet he comprehended very little of the basic nature of the male Ute whose only desire was to be left wholly free to do as he pleased. Ute men despised every form of manual labor as constituting an intolerable degradation. Their highest ambition was to be left unfettered to hunt, fish, fight, pursue the mysteries of religion, and drink whiskey.

When Agent Meeker attempted to enforce his demands, some of the Indians ran away while others fired from cover on the white agency employees as they worked in the fields. Steadfastly refusing to plow, the men let it be known that they preferred to spend their time in horse racing, long a favorite Ute recreation. In reprisal, Meeker ordered their racetrack to be plowed up. Resisting frequent threats and warnings of an uprising, Meeker refused to assure his own safety by accepting advice that he leave. Troops from Fort Steele, Wyoming, moved south to protect the outpost as conditions at White River moved from bad to worse.

The ultimate and inevitable result was the notorious Meeker Massacre of September 29, 1879, when Meeker and nine other male agency employees were murdered on the spot. Three white women, including Mrs. Meeker and their daughter, Josephine, were kidnapped. The rescue party from Wyoming, led by Major T. T. Thornburgh, was ambushed on Milk Creek and held at bay for six days. Thornburgh and thirteen of his men were killed. The fight ended only when a message was received from Ouray, ordering the Utes to stop. The remaining troops pushed on toward the agency.

They were the first upon the scene and soon found that all the white men had been killed and the buildings burned. Meeker's body was found, with a logging chain around the neck, about two hundred yards from his house. A barrel stave had been driven through the mouth and out the body. Another account has it driven through the mouth and out the back of his head into the ground. In either instance, the finality cannot be disputed. All bodies had been stripped and some were mutilated.

These incidents provided the necessary excuses for expulsion of all the Utes, not just the guilty ones; and therefore, free and legal access to all of the riches of the San Juans. "The Utes must go" became the battle cry of the prospectors and farmers who sought to profit from Indian misfortunes. The Utes, with no political influence, had no voice in the affair. The whites, with their votes, sought and secured the influence of Washington.

When news of the Ute expulsion was received, the Del Norte newspaper printed this poem:

> Then shout the glad tidings,
> Triumphantly sing;
> The San Juan is opened,
> We've busted the ring.

On May 24, 1873, General A. J. Alexander arrived from Fort Garland with tidings of the suspension of the "Most Unholy and Obnoxious Order." The news spread like magic in the crowds, and groups of eager and anxious prospectors were soon collected, listening to someone who was eagerly disseminating the information as he had received it from second or even third parties. The miners would no longer be interfered with, but could go and come when they pleased.

A kidney infection brought about the death of Ouray in 1880. Some say that he was mercifully spared the final indignity of seeing his people expelled from Colorado. All Northern Utes were driven from the state under pressure of arms and confined to the Uintah-Ouray Reservation in Utah. The Southern Utes were allowed to stay, provided they agreed to confinement on a long, narrow strip of land bordering on northwestern New Mexico. The Consolidated Ute Reservation still contains the descendants of this original group.

In most respects this Indian treaty was no worse than most. At one time Sitting Bull summed up the situation quite well when he said, "I would have more faith in the Grandfather in Washington if he did not have so many bald-headed thieves working for him."

Prospectors lost no time in taking over the mountains while sheep and cattle growers moved into the lush grazing country north of the reservation. The mines of the San Juans attracted settlers to southwestern Colorado as never before. The chief obstacle to settlement disappeared with the removal of the Utes. All that remained now was to make the country more accessible.

⌒ 4 ⌒

The Rush Begins

FROM A PHYSICAL STANDPOINT the San Juan silver excitement was one of the most difficult migrations ever chronicled in Western history. The rugged nature of the San Juans with their jagged peaks, steep sides, deep canyons, and sheer rock walls, made access to the region an extremely trying challenge. Even in the present century, many parts can be reached only by a four-wheel-drive vehicle or on foot. Frequent rock slides, early snows that became deep drifts and remained well into summer, plus the highest general altitude in Colorado, all combined to retard growth and progress in this potentially rich region. All goods and supplies had to be carried in on the backs of pack animals, over rough and frequently dangerous ledge trails.

Being located so many hundreds of miles away from the rest of the world and lying under the many disadvantages caused by hard winters and almost impassable mountain barriers, the San Juan mines had few markets for their ores. Nevertheless, much was accomplished during the first few years notwithstanding the great distance from railroad communications, the inaccessibility of the country, and the want of capital for the development of new mining camps.

And so the rush began and emigration progressed from the various older mining districts of the high Rockies. Tumbling down into the Western river valleys, the would-be argonauts, ne'er-do-wells, the unemployed, and the curious hurried to the San Juans. In this time of a scarce labor supply, there was work for all and the chance for a fair living to be made. In case one failed to uncover a paying lode, there was always the opportunity to work for others at six dollars a day. In many ways this was a poor man's rush and success was not so much a matter of intelligence as of knowledge or luck. Many prospectors knew only one rule: "Gold or silver is where you find it."

In the early days, not many of the people who settled here actually thought seriously of making their homes in the San Juans. They came for immediate gain and expected to go away as soon as their objective had been attained.

They lacked most of the conventional customs and institutions that had been familiar at home, such as schools, granges, adequate government, and legitimate courts. Such deprivation resulted in substitute behavior which had as its outlet activities such as crime, a highly emotional variety of religion, increased sexual tensions among the more mobile, and far more political participation than they had ever engaged in at home. The mines would not last forever, and the heritage of the soil was not thought worthy of consideration. Very few ever came in the early years who did not hope soon to be able to return home and leave Colorado to its natural citizen— the Indian.

Those who came were not all legitimate miners by any means, or were they always motivated by legitimate intentions. It has been estimated that 30 to 50 percent of the incoming argonauts were misfits, the first to be unemployed in the great nationwide panic that followed the Civil War. Since statistical estimates during this time were frequently gross inaccuracies, so high a proportion of misfits in relation to the total population is certainly a figure that would be open to question. There were no door-to-door psychiatrists with folding couches to diagnose the ills of a migratory population.

Many others were mere fortune hunters; and not a few were common criminals, seeking new fields of adventure and a safe refuge from crimes past and greater prospect of immunity for future infractions of the law.

In this typical pioneer environment, people generally did not feel the restraint of socially defined rules; and many, consequently, became involved in conflicting situations from failure to establish satisfactory social relationships. Unity of the family was often broken, with the breadwinner migrating west to seek the family fortune and promising to send for mother and the kids "as soon as I make my strike." This inevitably resulted in a society where men were men and women were either a rarity or a bargain. Among the family units that did come, those that had been the most mobile were also the most likely to leave.

During 1871, the San Juan country was visited by about twenty-five to forty men who located some one or two hundred veins and dug into a few of them with picks and shovels. They carried out probably three to five hundred pounds of ore and built a narrow trail over some of the worst places down to the Rio Grande. In the fall they laid out a town called Loma. Most of the prospectors stayed there or in Saguache during that first winter. Some old-timers used to contend that "Saguache" could be pronounced properly only by a Ute with the hiccoughs.

The town of Loma was one hundred and forty miles from Pueblo and thirty-five miles above Fort Garland on the Rio Grande River. It became a logical jumping-off point toward the San Juan mines. Pack animals had to be used to get from there into the mountains, however. Although the original town was on the opposite side of the river, most authorities today agree that Loma became the present-day city of Del Norte.

From early reports that were published, it was often believed that a murderous Ute stood concealed behind every shrouded rock to take the scalp of the first pale-faced invader. Consequently, during the winter of 1870-71, little had been done except some quiet talking and writing of letters.

Some of the ores were sent to New York and Chicago that year. Such peculiar gold samples attracted much attention because gold had never been found in like formation with the possible exception of one case, which was said to have been in Siberia. The San Juan mine from which it was taken was very appropriately called the Little Giant. Some prospecting was done there; and an arastra, a primitive crushing and amalgamating device run by water, was put up on the Little Giant property. In less than six weeks, nearly four thousand dollars of the "finest quartz gold in the world" was taken from ore broken from the outcropping vein.

A small community called Bullion City grew up in the vicinity of the Little Giant. The number of houses there did not exceed thirty at any time and all supplies were said to have been priced very high. Judge Gargan was there and when his presence was not required in court, he baked bread which he was able to sell at one dollar per loaf. Several other holes from two to fifteen feet deep were sunk on some of the first-to-be-discovered lodes; so that when fall arrived, the miners came out of the high country again for the winter and brought with them some remarkably fine ores, primarily silver-bearing. Not a single gold vein, other than those at the Little Giant and those up at Summitville, was struck that promised well. Several samples, however, showed traces of gold. During the following winter, news of some of the richer mines was noised all over the country, and some new capital was invested. A rush was confidently expected as soon as spring opened.

The spring of 1872 saw the first acceleration of the

impending stampede. By that summer, enough people had migrated into southwestern Colorado to warrant organization of a number of new mining districts. The incoming population was made up of individuals as rugged as the fourteen-thousand-foot peaks of the San Juans themselves. One source has estimated a census tally of between three and four hundred souls at this time, with location of two or three thousand claims, many of which did not develop. Despite such a flurry of activity, there was still little actual development during this early era.

From the standpoint of weather, 1872 was a terribly bad season. There were almost continuous rains during the months of August and September. Nevertheless, the first train of wagons, loaded with a quartz mill for the Little Giant, was successfully taken in over the range.

Considerable blasting and sinking of shafts on various lodes was also done. The road in was made passable and several other roads were started. To be realistic, probably a total of one hundred and fifty miners did work on as many as fifteen hundred to two thousand claims, and when fall came they again took out several tons of ore. By these figures we may deduce that by no means all of the people were engaged in mining, or were all claims worked.

No one wintered in the San Juan country during 1870, 1871, or 1872. In many of what later turned out to be the prime locations, deep snowpacks built up in the high valleys. Some, like Animas Forks, often recorded a depth of twenty-five feet, with traces that remained into the following July. In the spring each year when the miners returned they elected someone to serve in the capacity of recorder with pay of one dollar for each claim recorded. Each fall the book was taken to Conejos and the entries copied into the records of that county. Most of the early mills were only about 60 percent efficient until introduction of the flotation process which was able to claim an efficiency closer to 90 percent.

Everybody who had mining interests elsewhere said that this was in such an out-of-the-way place that no machinery could ever be moved in; and so when it was known that a mill had been brought across Stony Pass for the Little Giant, capitalists felt that they could wait until that enterprise either failed or succeeded and then be guided accordingly. The mill was installed and the problem of a road for wagons to the San Juan mines had been solved, and this during the worst season known for years all through the mountains. It was, however, accomplished too late for returns that year.

When crossing Stony Pass, it was the rule to hitch as many teams as could be harnessed to one wagon and then try to go up the mountain. When the top had been gained, the descent on the other side was so steep that the wagons were likely to be turned over. Meanwhile, miners had flocked in as anticipated; and times in the mines were becoming quite lively. Men were there from all parts of the territories, and the universal opinion of the district was, "Never saw anything like it anywhere."

The autumn of 1872 came and though few practical results were achieved, the miners once more came out to the settlements rejoicing, each man with one or two donkey loads of ore from veins that he had located. Considerable money was invested at this time and the country was thoroughly advertised. Whenever one went among mining men, the San Juan country was discussed and information was eagerly sought.

The spring of 1873 opened and before the snows were off the range, the mountains were hazy with smoke from miners' camps. Everybody was eager to be in ahead of the other fellow. By the first of May, many more of them were on the scene.

The Little Giant Mill was soon up and working, despite a lack of nearly every convenience and the scarcity of labor. On the nineteenth of July its whistle blew for the first time. It must have startled the Rocky Mountain sheep and grizzlies as its shrill sound echoed from peak to peak. The Little Giant sent to market some of the finest quartz gold ever found and proved itself capable of yielding from three thousand to five thousand dollars per week to its fortunate owners. The optimistic proprietors felt that this capacity could be increased in the coming years.

George Green and Company, in 1874, erected a thirty-ton smelter on Cement Creek. It made one run on ore from Arastra Gulch but the process was a failure. After remodeling, the smelter was opened for operation once more the next August and ran until November with an output of twenty-five thousand dollars but with expenses of thirty-three thousand dollars. Despite having been tried out for several years it was never a real success. It was later dismantled and moved to Durango. A smelter built in the early 1880's, called the Martha Rose, stood at the south end of Silverton. After remodeling, it became the Thomas Walsh Smelter and handled concentrate ore from the Red Mountain District. The San Juan Smelting and Refining Company smelter, better known as the Ross, was built in 1900 on Boulder Mountain.

The spring of 1874 was an early one, and many prospectors again came into the district on snowshoes. The population during the summer was about five hundred, consisting of prospectors and parties employed in claims located the previous season. The next year many buildings were erected, and several parties engaged in the business of furnishing mining materials. Most winter supplies were laid in early for many of the producing mines in the San Juan country. These included flour, beef, potatoes, canned fruit, candles, powder fuse, cordwood, charcoal, drills, and so forth. All of these mines would soon be blockaded from the outside world by huge masses of snow, except for those operators who were proficient in snowshoe navigation. Since there were few wagon roads to these almost inaccessible spots, cattle and sheep were driven up over the trail from Cement Creek, for example, and killed at the mines.

By 1874 more work had been done and the richness of the silver in the deposits began to be even more apparent. Del Norte continued to assume a position of considerable importance as a point of departure for the San Juan mines. At about this same time the town also went through a small fever of real-estate and trading speculation.

The road to Lake City from Del Norte was reported to be lined with great freight outfits loaded with machinery for the mines. Mule skinners appeared to be rough but took good care of the animals. In places the trail was boggy and logs were laid crisscross on the road in corduroy fashion.

The eyes of the world were focused again upon the San Juans when gold was discovered on the shores of Lake San Cristobal in 1874. The winter of 1874-75 was the last before the opening of the fabulously rich gold and silver mines at Lake City. Rich ore had already been discovered at the site of the Ute-Ulay Mine and a toll road was being built into the Lake City country by Otto Mears and Enos Hotchkiss. Their intention was to extend their route up through Burrows Park and past the site where Sherman was to Silverton.

While they were employed as laborers on the road past Lake San Cristobal, the two Hall brothers prospected on the side and found an outcropping of ore and decided to do some more looking. That winter they loaded eighteen sacks of precious metal on wagons and started toward Denver with them. The snow was deep and the horses could not pull the wagons. They finally put all of the bags on one wagon, doubled the team, and reached their destination. These eighteen sacks of ore brought one thousand dollars each, or a total of eighteen thousand dollars at the old Grant Smelter in Denver. Enos Hotchkiss personally located the Hotchkiss Mine, which was later renamed the Golden Fleece. This mine, in a few weeks, changed Lake City from a group of four or five cabins to a town of five thousand people, all trying to locate a rich lode. The mine broke Hotchkiss and was sold on default of assessment work.

Hinsdale County was organized in 1875 and Lake City, its seat, was founded that same year on the shores of Lake San Cristobal. At that time the closest post office was still 125 miles away at Del Norte.

In 1876 heavy snows retarded opening of the mining season. Despite this, many prospectors came in on snowshoes to await the moving of the water. The Little Annie Mill employed about a dozen or more men in hauling the quartz down to their establishment on hand sleds.

Quite apart from the regular, approved methods of locating a valuable mineral deposit, many other borderline techniques were also employed. Chief among them was the divining rod. Such devices took a variety of forms, but in operation all followed the same basic principle. In theory, the device was suspended from the operator's hands and would turn and point in the direction of concealed veins of silver or gold. Since the accepted fiction was that they could only be depended upon in the hands of people possessed of spiritual qualities, and since the cooperation of the "spirits" was essential, not everyone could operate such devices. Dave Wood, a freighter who lived at Dallas Divide, believed ardently in the powers of divining rods. He once fired an employee for making so much noise that the spirits were frightened away. The Reed Drift on the Camp Bird Mine was drilled on the advice of a clairvoyant.

The Lake City *Silver World* reported on May 6, 1876, that emigration to the San Juan country was beyond the calculation and expectation of those who had tried to create a public interest in that country originally. The large majority were from Kansas at that time and the exodus from the state would probably have run up into the thousands. The interest and excitement there were the result of work by the Hon. Sidney Clark, who visited the mines in 1875 and had been urging people to migrate there. During several weeks in May, the departures for the San Juan mines were estimated at two hundred weekly.

Many people approached the San Juan district by railroad as far as the end of the track. From there they crossed the San Luis Valley and then traveled over the primitive roads to Silverton and Lake City. The San Juan country also received a large amount of publicity from the Kansas Pacific and the Atchison, Topeka, and Santa Fe Railroad Company.

The San Juan Guide, published in Topeka, Kansas, in 1877, stated that there were three things that were essential to the success of any San Juan miner. These were: courage, patience, and strength; courage to encounter hardships, patience to overcome difficulties and wait for success, and strength to wrest the gold and silver from the mountains in which they were imbedded. *The San Juan Guide* was published for the Atchison, Topeka, and Santa Fe Railroad company for the purpose of furnishing those persons who wanted to visit the San Juan country with "accurate, reliable, and statistical information." This guide reported that there were not less than one hundred mines in Burrows Park along the Lake Fork of the Gunnison. The road from Lake City to the forks of the Animas passed directly through this park. The town of Argentum, at that time was located in the park, and was one year old. It was reported as having had a post office, five stores, two hotels, a butcher shop, and quite a number of dwelling houses. Some very high assays were obtained from the mines in this park and the testing of ores in quantity proved to be very successful, so said *The San Juan Guide.* The Atchison, Topeka, and Santa Fe also ran frequent emigrant trains from the depot at Pueblo to the end of the line for a fare of twenty dollars.

Some other guidebooks were also published at this time by the *Silver World* of Lake City, the *Chieftain* of Pueblo, and the *Gazette* of Colorado Springs. One of the most useful of all such publications was George Crofutt's *Grip-Sack Guide of Colorado*, published in Omaha during 1881. In this remarkable volume, now a collector's item, the traveler could find not only distances between points, but post road numbers and schedules. The *Grip-Sack Guide* was published in both a hard-cover and a paper-backed edition for sale on the railroads. In addition, a publisher at Buffalo, New York, issued a *San Juan Gazette*.

The reputation of the San Juan mines spread throughout the length and breadth of the United States. A number of scientific men who had previously visited Colorado with the Wheeler Expedition resigned their positions with the government to come to the San Juans. Mr. A. D. Wilson, who had been first assistant on the Hayden Survey, resigned to return to the San Juans. Between ten and eleven thousand tickets to Colorado were sold in England alone.

By way of encouraging still more new migration into the San Juan country, *The San Juan Guide*, in its later editions, reported that "Any person who was a citizen of the United States or who had declared an intention to become a citizen, might locate, record, and hold a mining claim of fifteen hundred linear feet along the course of any mineral vein or lode, subject to location." Any association of persons meeting these same conditions might make joint locations of claims up to fifteen hundred feet, but in no event could the location of a vein or lode exceed fifteen hundred feet along the course, or be more than three hundred feet wide, regardless of the number of people in the association.

It was further stated in the law, according to *The San Juan Guide*, that the miners in each district might make their own rules and regulations so long as they were not in conflict with laws of the United States or of the state of Colorado. Actually, mining laws governing the location, manner of recording, and amount of work necessary to hold possession of a claim varied quite widely in practice.

Although the "Bandwagon" and "Transfer" techniques are widely recognized, well-documented and thoroughly misused persausive propaganda devices today, perceptive individuals were quick to exploit others by these means long before sociologists discovered how they worked, stood up and described them and subsequently took the credit for them. Consequently, the astute publishers of *The San Juan Guide* further reported that the general population of the San Juan country was made up of people from all parts of the world. They said that good order prevailed, and that life and property were as secure as in any of the Eastern states. Beneath the roofs of those mountain cabins and in all San Juan mining camps, the visitor was said to have found the banker, merchant, statesman, man of letters, physician, lawyer, clergyman, and gentleman of leisure. Allegedly these people, when not mining, spent their time discussing finance, commerce, literature, politics, religion, or any other sufficiently intellectual subject. *The San Juan Guide* further reported the climate of the San Juans as being "delightful."

A popular route to the San Juans at the time of the Hayden Survey involved taking the Rio Grande Railroad from Denver to Colorado Springs. At this point the traveler was obliged to obtain his own conveyance, since there was no public transportation from there to Saguache or Del Norte. The road from Colorado Springs led through the mountains by way of Manitou, crossed South Park at its southern end, passed the Salt Works by way of Trout Creek to the Arkansas River. From here the trail changed direction and followed the Arkansas

River to the South Arkansas River. At this point the road joined with the one from Canon City and continued over Poncha Pass to the San Luis Valley. It then skirted along the western border to Saguache. The road from Canon City passed through the north end of the Wet Mountain Valley where it turned north.

One road led through Sangre de Cristo Pass and struck the valley at Fort Garland, from which a road led to Del Norte. The ultimate route crossed Mosca Pass and then dropped down into the San Luis Valley to Del Norte. The Mosca Pass Road was the shorter by some miles. It was also somewhat easier since there was less sand to contend with. Hayden also recalled encountering the construction party in the process of building its road over Cinnamon Pass.

An early report described the needs of the Summit District at that time in this fashion:

What we need most is a road that can be traveled during the winter months. The present route does very well when there is no snow, although a portion of it is quite boggy at any time when not frozen. As you enter the Summit District it crosses the range at nearly five hundred feet above timberline. The best men in the district are fully appraised of the necessity of a change which may be effected this year. It would require grading and some good bridging, but good judges who have since examined the route are unanimous in the opinion that the road could be built for less than ten thousand dollars. The distance through Fort Garland by way of the proposed route across the Summit District is only about sixty-seven miles thus saving about twenty-five miles over the road by way of Del Norte.

The town of Summit, or Summitville, was the most prominent mining camp to grow up in the range to the southwest of the San Luis Valley. It was situated about twenty-seven miles from Del Norte and was actually comprised of three smaller camps called Iowa, Sunnyside, and Summitville. The latter name was adopted because of the Summit Mine which was located there and developed by Dr. Richard F. Adams in 1875. Actually, Summitville is rated by many as being the second oldest camp in the San Juans. The claim is supported by the mining activities of James and William Wightman, which date from 1870, and which were the basis for early migrations into the district.

The post office went into operation in the town on April 1, 1880. A triweekly mail service was carried on between Summitville and the lower settlements. In 1888 the town had grown to the point where it was able to support thirteen saloons. Prominent among the mills at Summitville were the Annie, the Golconda, Aztec, and Rio Grande, fed by a large number of good mining properties. A fairly large town grew up around Summitville and the mineral output was quite large. The Summit district was essentially a gold-bearing one.

In 1870 prospectors went south from Del Norte, and in June of that year they discovered gold in the Summitville district. The party consisted of William and James L. Wightman, E. Baker, J. Carry French, Sylvester Reese, and William Boran. James Wightman himself got the first prospect; but all of the party, with the exception of Wightman and Reese, had left by the middle of September. These two stayed on and engaged in sluicing until the ninth of November when they carried out heavy pack loads through waist-deep snow, reaching the Rio Grande in three days.

In the spring of 1871 a large number of people flocked into the Summit district, hundreds still arriving while the snow was very deep and work was impractical. These early men became quite disgusted, and by the last of August there were only three remaining in the area. This trio stayed at the camp until about the twentieth of October. They took gold, realized by sluicing, to Denver and had it refined at the mint, dividing $170 among them after paying all expenses of the season's operations.

Collection of Fred and Jo Mazzulla
Although the original was undated, the presence of tents and the
limited number of frame structures mark this as a rather early
view of Summitville.

Collection of Robert L. Brown
The deserted remains of Summitville in June 1964. This pair of
pictures shows the older section. A larger number of buildings of
later vintage are out of the picture to the right.

This was not a particularly encouraging yield for a hard summer's work. Several other lodes had been found in the meantime. These discoveries led to the opening in 1872-73 of the Little Annie and other lodes. A total gross production of gold, silver, lead, and copper from the Summitville district has been estimated at $2,556,909.

In 1872 a few other new locations were made, and 1873 witnessed a new surge of immigration into the district. In that same year the richest mines of all were located. During 1874 a number of new locations were made and the attention of the owners was turned to the matter of getting in machinery. Dr. Richard F. Adams, having become satisfied that his mine would pay, located a site and ordered a mill which was brought in and placed in operation in May of 1875. Also during the spring of '75, permanent mining operations were started at Summitville. In the latter part of May, the machinery for the Little Annie and the Golden Queen mills reached Del Norte from Chicago and was drawn by mule teams on a road cut for the purpose over Del Norte Mountain, thirteen thousand feet high. Cost of this unusual transportation was over four thousand dollars. The machinery for the two mills weighed over fifty tons but was successfully transported above the lower cloud belt and placed in position before the close of September. The Little Annie had more development than any other mine in the district, some twelve hundred tons of ore having been taken out. Population of the Summit district rarely exceeded two hundred souls at any given time.

One of the most notable persons to be associated with the fortunes of the Summitville area was a jurist from the South. Judge Tom Bowen came to the San Juans a poor man from the state of Arkansas, where he had once lived as a wealthy planter. For seven long years he prospected, always in debt and getting in deeper. Each month and year he invested every dollar of his earnings in prospect holes. His legal talent served to keep the wolf from the door, but prospecting had become his real love.

During the days he was a judge in this district, he was too poor to own a horse and plodded on foot over the mountains from county to county. He was overwhelmingly in debt when he made his strike in the Ida Mine. Bowen kept up his nerve and confidence and was able to hold the trust of his men and get them to work with promises to pay when the great bonanza was struck.

Gold fairly rolled into his account and in an incredibly short time he had money enough to pay off all scores and have a surplus in the bank. The Ida, out of which all this gold was being taken, was one of a group of claims belonging to the San Juan Consolidated Mining Company. Judge Bowen owned three fourths of the stock. He also held all but four shares in the Odin Company and had many attractive offers from Eastern and English capitalists of the day to buy him out. No farther back than the previous winter, shares of the San Juan Consolidated Mining Company, valued at twenty-five cents each, were used as stakes in poker and to buy drinks in Del Norte and other places. Judge Bowen had bought $300,000 worth of the stock eighteen months before, for one-fourth of a mill on the dollar. An old man named Walker, who kept a boardinghouse at Silverton, held another $75,000 worth of the stock, which he also bought for nearly nothing.

Judge Bowen once said that only a small portion of the newspaper reports about his properties had been correct. Much exaggeration had resulted; and some entirely false stories were printed because of the newspapers getting information from the wrong sources, according to the Judge.

The Little Annie was reportedly sold for $410,000. Numerous other claims were also taken up on the same mountain. Unlike most other mining districts, these claims were worked without the least regard for direction. By 1875 a total of ten stamp mills had been erected on the mountainside. They were each capable of treating about ten tons of ore daily and were turning out between seven hundred and one thousand tons each week. In value, the ore averaged about twenty-five dollars to the ton in gold. The Golden Queen Mill was completed too late to go into operation during the previous year, but it did start up in 1876. Senator Jerome B. Chaffee erected a twenty-stamp mill at Summitville on the property of the San Juan Consolidated Mining Company. It was widely rumored in the early days that because the air at Summitville was so thin, it was not safe to believe more than 10 percent of what you heard. Summitville's decline was as rapid as its rise. It went down very quickly about the year 1890.

However, by 1876 the first large migration was well under way. It would continue throughout the period with varying degrees of intensity. The Utes were gone, the first trails had been cut, several mills had been located, and enough strikes were made to justify the white man's optimism. The chief characters were already on stage or lurking in the wings. Our next act was ready to commence.

ᴄᴀ 5 ᴀ~

Life Among the Miners

PEOPLE IN FRONTIER SOCIETIES were neither the happiest, nor the most contented in the world. Lack of social control and regulation was as unnatural then, as now, for individuals trained and reared in group living. Many a man on the San Juan frontier drank himself to death who would have practiced a measure of sobriety in a better regulated society. Others who would have lived to successful and peaceful old ages in a community of effective civil government, died at the point of a gun or danced their lives away on the end of a rope in those trigger-happy towns. While social controls can become too rigid, they are generally as important to an individual as to the group.

Despite many seemingly trying conditions, a genuine spirit of camaraderie existed, a sort of "code of the hills" for the isolated regions. For example, according to those who took part in the San Juan rush, there was a general "gentlemen's agreement" between the miners that all cabins were to be left supplied with both food and wood in case of a severe storm. The agreement further stipulated that if these facilities were used in a blizzard or other emergency, the fuel would be replaced for future use by the owners. Generally speaking, people were very hospitable in the early days. A stranger was always welcome. Most houses were of the simple two-room type, but there would be space to make a bed on the floor. A stranger could always eat and stay all night.

One of the most serious conditions of life that had to be endured was the weather. From June through September, a majority of the days were comfortably warm, although the snowpacks sometimes lasted into July around some of the higher camps, such as Carson or Engineer City. Nights were always uniformly cool, and many Easterners were surprised to find that heavy bedding was a year-around necessity in the San Juans. As a general rule, it was comfortable to sit by a fire at night. The atmosphere was arid and little rain fell except in the months of August and September. The nights, as a rule, were clear and bracing. Spring and fall were unpredictable, but usually of a temperate character.

Because of the altitude, snow in the summer was not unknown; and preparations for heavy weather were in order anytime after the middle of September. Some San Juan winters were particularly severe, while others were comparatively mild. Due to the extreme dryness of the air, cold was never felt as much in the San Juans as in sections of the country where the difference between summer heat and winter cold was greater. Nevertheless, the temperature often fell several degrees below zero. Month after month, from late in the spring into the latter part of August, the snow melted slowly and mountain torrents poured down gulches and over the valleys irrigating farms and ensuring good crops. For this reason, farmers watched the winter storm with joy —while the miner, fearing the snowslide, dreaded its approach.

The winter of 1890 was long and bitter. The rocks and mountainsides were covered with deep snow, and the tall pines with their fleecy coats of white looked small. Most roads were blocked and often impassable. Moses Liverman, manager of the Silverton Railroad, was pushed to the utmost to keep the line open until Christmas. A large number of men had been at work since October, and the banks on both sides of the track were so piled with snow that no more could be thrown over. The Silverton Railroad was one of the highest in the world. One day, during this particularly bad stretch of weather, a locomotive pulling only two cars was derailed at least six times between Ironton and Silverton and all hands had to assist in removing the snow and in prying the little cars back onto the track.

Wages in the San Juans were higher on the average than those paid in other mining districts. The average pay was $3.50 a day, until the unfortunate reduction in the monetary value of silver took place. Such a high wage can be justified when one recalls that it was once claimed by ambitious chambers of commerce that there were more individual mines in San Juan County worth a million dollars or more each, than in any other section of equal area in the United States. Whether this is true or not, several properties passed this mark in commercial value. Among them were the Silver Lake, Highawa-Tiger, Contention, North Star, Gold King, Sunnyside, and Mogul.

After 1893, despite conditions of perpetual poverty, the miners often held that some things were more precious than ready money. When a small mining property was up for sale, the prospective purchaser sometimes found that the price of the claim went sky high. Many who lived in the mining country in the early days also noted this phenomenon but were at a loss to explain it. Some people today feel that it was due to a sentimental attachment, resulting from extreme isolation, operating within the same emotional framework as a hermit's fondness for a dog, cat, or goat.

In the springtime, pneumonia was frequently prevalent in Colorado mining camps, and the San Juans were no exception. Many of the men crossed the range for the last time. Deaths and funerals became so common one

spring in the 1880's that, according to the Reverend J.
J. Gibbons, "Many a hardened sinner who might have
scorned the advice of even dear friends, harkened to the
counsel of clergy in the eleventh hour."

Electrical storms were another hazard of life in the
San Juans. The Hayden Survey party recorded graphi-
cally their experiences with such inclement weather while
on the top of a mountain. They first noticed a tickling
sensation along the roots of their hair caused by the electricity in the air. By holding their hands above their
heads, a ticking sound was produced which was still
louder if they held a hammer or other instrument in their
hands. As the clouds approached, the tension of the electricity increased more rapidly. They observed a bolt of
lightning strike a peak across the canyon of the Lake
Fork of the Gunnison. At times a portion of the stormy
mass seemed to be moved by an upward current which
carried it several hundred feet above the general level
of the mountains. Then, as the force ceased, it would
topple over and slowly fall back and lose itself in the
canyon. When the Hayden party rose up, their hair
stood on end. Each of the sharp points of the hundreds
of stones above them emitted a continuous sound. The
general effect of it all was as if a heavy breeze were blow-
ing across the mountain. The lightning flashes were now
coming thicker and faster, being separated by not more
than three minutes at a time. The party realized that
their peak would soon be struck. They started to walk
down from the crest over loose rock. They had hardly
moved more than thirty feet from the top when it was
struck. Hail and sleet began to fall freely making it
highly dangerous to cross any prominent point, even
though it was much lower than the peak itself. They
were well drenched with rain even before reaching their
mules. In these high altitudes after a storm, Hayden
noted that there was scarcely any twilight and darkness
quickly followed the setting of the sun.

Several of the San Juan camps followed the example of mining towns in the earlier rushes and lost little time in erecting some sort of community structure which they labeled an opera house. Such buildings were pointed out with pardonable community pride as positive evidence that culture had arrived and that theirs would be a permanent camp. Most opera houses served a multiplicity of community purposes. Chairs were rarely fastened down in order to facilitate their removal for the inevitable Saturday night dances. On Sundays the chairs would be replaced to provide the essentials for a church service, conducted by any circuit rider who happened to be in camp. Sectarian denomination was not a factor. Pianos were frequently borrowed from and returned to the saloons and dance halls following the conclusion of the services.

During the week the opera house often doubled as a community school during the daylight hours. At night, various fraternal orders, miners' protective associations, unions, or mineowners' clubs might assemble there. Traveling shows often set up their equipment and played to appreciative audiences for one- or two-night stands. At Ouray the celebrated Tom Thumb and his troupe once played at the two-story Opera House. The tiny ponies used by these diminutive performers are said to have had some difficulty getting up the stairs to the second-floor hall. Occasionally, two-story opera houses were erected, but most of them were single-level buildings.

From time to time, groups of local talent pooled their resources and collective musical abilities to produce "amateur night" productions which were always well attended. Hometown talent was a popular source of entertainment in nearly all pioneer societies. In the later days, when camps became more settled and prosperous, dance halls sometimes stayed open around the clock. Many of them provided a bill of variety acts at several different times each night. According to one veteran of

the San Juans, "Everyone went to the dance halls except
the preachers, who went in the back doors."

Some other people just forgot the whole thing and
went to a ball game. A surprisingly competitive and
quite unofficial baseball league developed in the San
Juans with keen rivalry among the camps. Baseball
teams were backed and sponsored by those saloonkeep-
ers who could afford it. It proved to be an excellent
means of advertising and a good time was had by all.

The early theatres were not merely show houses. Plays
were usually put on as an attraction to the bar. No admission fee was charged and the operators expected to
make money from drinks sold to customers or patrons.
Beer was served in the boxes, generally for one dollar
per bottle, of which the girls selling the drinks received
from ten to twenty-five cents. Occasionally, the theatres,
in addition to a bar, might also have a poolroom. The
Grand Central Hotel at Silverton, located on the present
site of the Federal Building, was one such establishment.
It had a small bar and an adjacent poolroom. One day a
miner named Dison Eskridge rode his horse through the
door and began shooting at the ceiling. He wasn't angry
but was just having a good time and did not hurt anyone.
The proprietor was behind the bar and was not only
angry but frightened because he feared what might hap-
pen. Sheriff Bob Dwyer stepped through the door and
said, "Dis, I'll take those guns." Eskridge handed them
over. After things quieted down, Bob returned the guns.

The Clipper Theatre was erected where the Salvation
Army Hall now stands. Most of the professional gamblers refused to consider any other means of livelihood
and got by on cold nerve. A fellow who dealt games
for pay wasn't considered a gambler in those days. The
"sucker" never made any money on such games. He was-
n't supposed to. Jim Raynor often ran the Beehive game
in the Clipper Theatre. Beehive is a game in which a
ball strikes a series of pins and may then be deflected

Collection of Mrs. Bertha Neal
Greer Street at Silverton in 1888 from half of a stereo pair

Collection of Robert L. Brown
Greer Street now

into any of several slots. The player is paid accordingly. When the booster, a hired decoy, played the game,
the ball used often entered the grand prize slots but
when the "sucker" played, a slightly larger ball was
used and the victim never had a chance to win. One
night Raynor, who was running the game, could not
find his stooges, so he hired a couple of strangers. They
won fine gold watches, capital prizes, and then disappeared. Raynor crabbed until the town sheriff told him
to be satisfied, that after all this was the only time a
"sucker" ever won on the Beehive.

Wyatt and Jim Earp operated in Silverton for a while
in those days. Most men of that type came in from Dodge
City but they did not often stay long. The Earp boys
were gunmen but they did not bother anyone at Silverton. One night in the Great Northern Saloon the games
had quieted down and the dealers were around a table
where Wyatt Earp was dealing faro bank. One of the
boys said to him, "You have killed quite a few men;
doesn't your conscience bother you?" "Well, listen," said
Earp, "my conscience does not hurt, but you notice I
always go out a door backwards." His killings were always said to be on the level—he never murdered anyone.

The *San Juan Prospector,* a pioneer Del Norte newspaper, was first published on February 9, 1874. During
the first few years the columns were printed from hand-
set type upon a Washington handpress, which had been
hauled across La Veta Pass by freight teams from Pueblo. At that time, mining was practically the only re-
source of the county. Through poor foresight, the importance of Del Norte as a mining center was greatly
lessened when the railroad was constructed over Cum-
bres Pass instead of through Del Norte and up the South
Fork of the Rio Grande into the San Juan Basin. At
that time the newspaper carried a heavy subscription
list among the mining camps of southwestern Colorado.

When railroad construction began, business firms and citizens made a grand scramble to desert the sinking ship. Stacks of merchandise, household goods, families, and individuals left Del Norte bound for the San Juans. The *San Juan Prospector,* with a new owner and editor, installed a completely mechanical outfit. With the mining resources for Del Norte knocked into a cocked hat, the *Prospector* then took up the cause of stock raising and farming by irrigation. Its columns began to be filled with articles extolling the advantages of stock raising in the sunny San Luis Valley.

Del Norte in the early days was made up of three different points or communities. Loma, the first location selected for a townsite, was north one mile and a half across the river from the second location which became the present town. West Del Norte was a continuation of the main street to the west. Here were located many of the pioneer wholesale houses, livery and feed stables, and a stagecoach station. Intermingling among these institutions were hotels, rooming houses, saloons, dance halls, and every kind of business that went to make up a hustling, wide-awake, western-pioneer community.

The Barlow and Sanderson Stagecoach and Express Company had a large headquarters here and some immense warehouses. Freighting outfits used oxen as well as horses and mules, maintaining great corrals where the huge freight wagons were stationed and the stock fed and cared for. Express, mail, and passengers were whizzed through the surrounding country and over the roads to the San Juans in Concord coaches drawn by four horses. The animals were kept at a steady gallop and were changed at relay stations after each twelve miles.

The bank at Del Norte was the only such institution in the whole of southwest Colorado. They had large accounts from Ouray, Mineral Point, Animas Forks, Eureka, Howardsville, Animas City, and Parrott City. Most business was done by mail. The demands on the bank for loans were numerous. This institution was later moved to Alamosa and, subsequently, to Animas City. When highwaymen made it unsafe to send currency by mail, the bank resorted to individual carriers. There was no express service at the time. On one occasion, a Mr. Camp wrote for currency and asked to have every effort made to get it over to him in order to supply his payroll demands. The bank president found a Durango man named Casey Kiethley and asked him if he would carry five thousand dollars in currency at their risk. He said that he would if it could be fixed so that it would not be noticed. The bank president told him that this could be managed and asked him to leave his vest. A seamstress opened the lining in the back and sewed in the packages. Keithley arrived at his destination safely with the currency but said he would never do it again.

At this time Del Norte was called the most wicked city in the world by globe-trotters who were qualified to make comparisons. These were strenuous times in which every walk of life had its representative. It was a time when men worked from dawn to darkness, and it was during the midnight hours that many men were found at their recreation. Dance halls and "red-light" institutions flourished in Del Norte and gambling tables were numerous. "Poker Alice," who ultimately died in Wyoming, was a character frequently seen in these infamous places and among notorious gamblers. She often walked out with the spoils of the night's games.

Gamblers, liquor dealers, and dance-hall proprietors dictated the policies of the *San Juan Prospector,* as was evidenced by the following news taken from its columns at that time:

A new cricket arrived on the stagecoach Wednesday morning and took up her abode at the Red Front Dance Hall. Two fresh grasshoppers came in Monday, direct from Pueblo and are domiciled at Dave Sponsiler's pleasure resort. Both are belles from the metropolis of the Arkansas and are not hard to look at. The boys will be out tonight to mingle with the new society.

Transportation from Pueblo to Del Norte was uncertain and dangerous as roads were mere trails and the trip, under ordinary circumstances, covered about six days with teams and light vehicles. Ox trains took double the time, and there were also long trains of ox-pulled wagons moving back and forth over the road into the San Juans and out again. At one period there had been no mail for three weeks so a collection was taken up to send to Pueblo for it. Twenty dollars was raised to pay for transportation. Major Lafayette Head was petitioned to grant the contract to Scarff and Miller for carrying future mail.

Reverend John Richards, who was to be the first Methodist pastor at Del Norte, arrived in town on the first stagecoach on October 7, 1873. He held the first Protestant service on the upper Rio Grande on the following day. The first Presbyterian church service was held in the old Del Norte town hall over what was then the jail. The pastor was the Reverend Alexander Darley, who became widely known later as an evangelist and worker among the Spanish people all over the state. By no means all of the miners, teamsters, and road builders spent their every off hour in the saloons and gambling halls courting the solace of "spiritus fermenti." Many held deep religious convictions and worked ardently toward the founding of church congregations in even the more remote communities. Lacking the competition of movies, TV, bowling alleys, and drag strips, church-sponsored activities filled a very real need in the lives of the people. The traditional church "social" was a commonplace event, occasionally supplemented by community singing and stereopticon shows which sent appreciative audiences outside, coughing and wheezing from the fumes so liberally expelled by early oil- and gas-illuminated projectors.

Father Hayes, a Jesuit priest, was the first to say Mass in the San Juans. A public hall was donated for his use in Silverton. This Mass was the only one recorded at Silverton in 1877. Following his appearance in the town, a priest managed to visit the San Juans nearly every year thereafter. In the early days when a priest arrived in some small town, Mass would be said at the house of a Catholic or in the parlor of the hotel. There were always more at Mass, however, than went to Confession and Communion. When Father Brady preached at Silverton in 1880, the greater part of his large audience was Protestant.

In 1876 Parson Hoge arrived in the San Juans from Texas and held Protestant services at Animas City during 1877 in a log cabin. One day Hoge went to a lumber dealer in the town and got some boards which he carried to the church lots on his back. He immediately started work on the Episcopal Church. Hoge was well liked by all elements in the settlement. He had been a gambler at one time and, therefore, knew about and sympathized with the troubles of the sporting element. His work among them was effective. Many times he went into a saloon or dance hall and told the proprietor he would like to talk to the boys. He was seldom if ever refused. On the wall of one gambling house was a box with a sign which read, "Don't forget Parson Hoge." The players often dropped in chips which the parson cashed for their game value. When Hoge's church was first completed it had a sawdust floor and plank benches for seats. At the front there was a low platform on which he stood. The congregation was mixed, as the gamblers and sporting people always gave him their moral support as well as donating money.

With the coming of the railroads, religious life in the San Juans changed. Every town of any size soon had a church, and religious hospitals were also established in

Collection of Fred and Jo Mazzulla
Rev. George Darley labeled this picture "Early Preaching Station on the Upper Animas." It is actually an extremely early photograph of Animas Forks, showing the first log cabins, before the fire.

Collection of Robert L. Brown
Animas Forks, from the same angle, photographed in the rain during August of 1964.

Durango and Ouray. In Lake City Rev. George Darley worked long hours toward the establishment of a miner's library, which became a reality in 1877. Since most of the surrounding mines closed during the winters large numbers of unemployed miners spent the cold months in town. Enterprises like libraries or free reading rooms helped to fill a genuine moral and intellectual void for the serious-minded transients, as well as the townspeople.

In the early days, Ouray, too, had a literary society that met during the winter months. It was described as small and the members preferred to keep it that way since individuality of character is often lost in bigger groups. The aim of the society was practical, and questions—moral, social, and economic—occasioned lively debate. The proceedings of the meetings, held once each week, were orderly and little time was spent on constitutions, bylaws, the minutes of the previous meeting, or personal explanations. Little time was likewise wasted in mere rhetorical display. It was, in a word, a club of sense, not of show.

A sense of humor was by no means absent from the grim conditions of life among the miners of the San Juans. One night at Howardsville, a miner came into the saloon and reported that the Indians had massacred everyone in the Animas Valley. He said he was on his way to get troops. He got some money and a few drinks and left. The Highland Mary shut down, sent the horses over the pass; and the men went into the tunnel and stayed there, prepared to repel the Indian attack. The savages never came; the report was like most of the Indian troubles, just a fake, or an excuse for a free drink and fun at someone else's expense.

At one time Mr. Henry M. Teller stopped at the Shaw Hotel in Animas City. He left early in the morning and failed to shut the door. A drunk came along and wandered into his room, lay down, and fell asleep. Shaw thought that Mr. Teller had changed his mind and decided to stay over for a while so he allowed the sleeper to rest comfortably undisturbed. On learning that Mr. Teller's horses were gone, Shaw investigated and found the slumbering drunk had perpetrated a hoax so he proceeded to awake and evict the sleeper. Indignation was high on both sides.

Watching wild animals has long been a favorite pastime of us human beings and it matters little whether we are in an isolated mining camp or spending a Sunday afternoon at the zoo. With very few organized or commercially inspired activities to fill their leisure time, residents of the San Juan camps spent many an hour at this popular spectator sport. In the early days at Ouray, both mountain sheep and elk frequently were forced down into town by inclement weather and lack of forage in their natural habitat. Since the residents thoroughly enjoyed seeing them and always provided feed, these migrations became a habit. In later years the sheep even reached the point where they recognized the sound of the bells used on the team that belonged to the local feed store. Regardless of the weather, they recognized its sound as an invitation to dinner and would come down and follow its rounds to the mines.

On summer afternoons in the early days, Ouray residents often used their spyglasses to watch the leader of a band of Rocky Mountain sheep as he stood guard on one of the nearby high points of rock while the other members of the herd took their meals. These animals lived near timberline like the chamois of Switzerland, far from the haunts of man, feeding upon small bunches of grass that shot from the crevices between the rocks. They were very timid and only an expert could come within range of them. When pursued, they would not hesitate to jump twenty-five to thirty feet down onto solid rock. Coyotes, wolves, and eagles, as well as sportsmen, preyed upon them so that only a few now remain.

Not all animals were friendly, and an occasional pioneer had this fact pressed upon him with considerable force. During the early mineral rush, bears were still fairly numerous in many parts of the San Juans; and the solitary prospector often had a feeling of loneliness, if not dread, when in the thick timber or on isolated paths most likely to be frequented by these animals. While crossing the trail between Rico and Durango, one miner had an encounter with a bear that deserves mention here. He was making his way over the shortcuts and trails away from the main road and lacked a jackknife or even a good stick with which to defend himself. Leaving the road to shorten the way, he plunged down gulches, over wooded hills, and through the dense growth of underbrush, following a cattle path. Upon looking around in response to a noise, he saw a large cinnamon bear with two cubs. For a moment he was seized with fright. Before he could resolve the situation, she turned and raised on her hind feet and came toward him with open jaws and outstretched paws. There was no opportunity or place to run and the bear attacked him at once. For a few moments the miner parried the blows as best he could, but always with a loss of a part of his clothing, which was being torn away by the long claws of the beast. Finally, having lacerated his arms and chest with one stroke, the bear opened his scalp to the back of his neck, knocked him down and placed her huge paws on his breast, ready to devour him. Instinctively, and fortunately, she turned to look for her cubs. As they were not in sight, she left her bleeding victim and ran after them in the direction they had taken. The miner fainted. How long he lay there was never known. At last he revived and to his horror heard the bear crashing through the brush at a distance. Gathering his remaining strength, although staggering from loss of blood, he dragged himself to his feet and fled along the trail as well as he could. At length he reached a farmhouse and was taken at once to Durango where a physician sewed up his torn scalp and body.

A number of people in the San Juan district soon discovered that there were means other than with gold and silver by which a fortune could be made. Farming and stock raising became very profitable businesses. The greater portion of the cattle brought to the San Juans was driven in from eastern and northern Colorado, with some herds from New Mexico and Texas. One livestock supplier who took animals into the San Juans recalls a time when he used a total of sixteen wagons, some two- and some four-horse teams. An oxteam ordinarily consisted of five yoke of oxen. Coming over the range they were able to make only two or three miles a day. It was necessary to take one wagon a mile or two and then come back for another, keeping the whole group together. They had a large bunch of cattle and also hauled both hogs and chickens. They often carried enough supplies from Denver to last for a year. The miners bought sheep from them occasionally along the road for seventy-five cents per head. Where the hillsides were steep, they took out a plow from their stock and plowed a furrow for one wheel and lashed poles to the wagon. Then a bunch of the men rode the end of the pole to keep the wagon from tipping. Progress at this rate was extremely slow. Such packtrains rarely made more than ten miles a day.

At various times there was said to have been over twenty thousand head of livestock in the San Juan country, exclusive of horses and mules. All had free access to the open ranges. Although beef on the hoof was always low in price, it could be made to pay under the circumstances. The Grimes brothers drove in seven hundred head of cattle one fall from Texas. When the spring roundup came around, only two hundred of them could be found. Flour sold at fourteen dollars per hundred pounds, coffee at forty cents per pound, sugar three pounds for a dollar, and dried fruits at twenty-five cents per pound. Some women in the San Juan country parched chicory and barley to make a cereal drink which served as a coffee substitute. Before the winter was out, some men expressed a feeling that it was better than coffee.

The vegetable situation was not quite as favorable, although a fairly good assortment of canned items such as corn, peas, and tomatoes could be purchased. Dried fruits were available with monotonous frequency and most miners came to dread their appearance on the table. For some unknown reason there were few jellies on San Juan menus. Naturally, there were no fresh vegetables available during the long winters. Parsnips were often buried in snowbanks and some said that the longer they were frozen, the sweeter they tasted.

Along about February the farmers in the San Juan country had begun to cut the eyes out of potatoes. They were saved for seed because potatoes were so hard to get. Some soaked them in the community water dish for a couple of days before planting because they had, of course, dried out. In March shipments of lettuce and radishes began arriving from Grand Junction. From truck farms to the north of Ouray came fresh vegetables of all kinds as the growing season progressed. Each fall brought wagonloads of fresh fruits from Paonia. Four horses were required to get each load over the passes to Silverton.

From the foregoing information, one might logically conclude that the dietary situation among the San Juan miners was not as monotonous as some writers have led us to believe. The fare was reasonably varied and generally wholesome. Since there were several labor shortages, men often left to seek work elsewhere when the food was not good. There was considerable competition among the mineowners for the services of good cooks. Biscuits, hot cakes, pies, potatoes, and roasts were common. Steaks were somewhat scarce. Cereals of several varieties were plentiful, and milk was almost always abundant. When fresh milk was not available, canned or condensed milk was mixed at the ratio of two cans to a large pitcher of water.

Food in the San Juans, unless one happened to be an intimate of Alfred Packer, did not differ materially from that consumed in other mining districts. Meat and potatoes made up the staple backbone of most diets. When not baked or boiled, they were fried in lard. A variety of homemade breads and pastries were available to the married men, while bachelors purchased such "goodies" from the limited number of women who reaped small fortunes operating bakeries and eating houses. Bacon, eggs, "salt side" (pork), and chickens were readily available. Ham brought sixteen cents a pound while a hind quarter of beef, which would keep through the cold of winter without refrigeration, could be purchased for only eight cents a pound. Some chose to vary the fare with a hind quarter of pork. Many of the permanent settlers kept cows, hogs, and chickens for their own convenience.

The shortage of women constituted a formidable problem indeed. Few of the miners who took part in the early San Juan excitement were married. Of the six hundred men employed at the Revenue Mine, most were foreign-born and nearly all were single. As a direct result of their isolation and loneliness, not a few answered the "lonely hearts" ads, to be found in such profusion in the periodicals of the times. Best known and most popular of the lovelorn agencies was one called "Hand and Heart," which earned a reputation for success among San Juan bachelors. Although the practice of securing "mail order brides" was widespread, the facts surrounding such alliances were hastily covered up and vehemently denied once the nuptials had been performed. Nevertheless, there was much covert whispering behind hands about how Olaf or Wladislaw got his wife through Hand and Heart.

One eyewitness account recalled the arrival of a "catalog bride" from the Midwest. After one look at her intended, a large and homely Swede, she was ready to get back on the train. At this point, friends of the intended groom took over, talked about the long ride home and how, despite appearances, the man was sober and a good provider. To make a long story short, she reconsidered, decided to remain, married the man and raised a large family. Several of their children still reside in the area today.

Actually, the San Juan excitement became a family migration in the late seventies. Prior to that time it had been pretty much of an all-male show.

In the early years, the twelve-hour work day was common in the mines. Next came the ten-hour shift which persisted until the strike for an eight-hour day by smelter workers in the late eighties. Many of the larger properties worked three or four shifts of miners around the clock. The only exceptions to this schedule occurred when the mines closed each year for Christmas and the Fourth of July. In the larger towns preparations were made for big celebrations. Those from the 7:00 A.M. to 4:00 P.M. workshifts began pouring into town the evening before. Others, who worked the "graveyard" schedule, drifted in during the predawn hours. From 1:00 A.M. on July 4, festivities were generally declared to be legally convened. The celebration of "National Wine Week" began quite unofficially on July 4 and many of the "delegates" were seen lying about in doorways. Other celebrants, who had worshiped less copiously at the shrine of the grape, spent the day in gambling halls, losing their accumulated pay of the last several months.

For the more civic-minded, there were parades in the morning with flower-bedecked floats sponsored by leading businessmen, the larger mines, local unions, or fraternal groups. Some were so heavy that eight horses were required to move them through the streets. Prizes for the

Collection of Francis B. Rizzari
Photo by George Porter
The body of a miner, killed in a snowslide, was brought down to Sneffels on a sled. George Porter took this photograph in front of his studio in the town.

Collection of Claude Miner
Here are some decorated floats and a uniformed band during a Fourth-of-July celebration at Ouray. The old flagpole is shown at the left.

most beautiful and the most original floats were given, and competition was keen.

During the afternoon, burro races were among the most popular events. Boys' and men's footraces were always great favorites in the mining camps, with a fair amount of money changing hands at the outcome. One of the most amusing contests was the three-legged race. Still on the lighter side, one could always anticipate the inevitable greased pig, smeared with the filthiest axle grease available, which could usually be counted on to run between the legs of the man wearing the best suit. Hordes of small-fry in hot pursuit of the slippery "porker," turned the reigning pandemonium into utter chaos. Another bit of good clean fun was climbing the greased pole which had a five-dollar bill attached to its top. Ouray always had a second pole, somewhat taller, with a ten-dollar note suspended from its apex.

Shortly after the turn of the century, one year's afternoon Fourth-of-July celebration at Ouray was interrupted by a one-hundred-yard dash of such uncommon origins that it is still discussed. It seems that a colored lady had stabbed another woman with a hatpin and now sought to elude the consequences. Ouray's sheriff pursued her through the crowd until she emerged into the flower-bedecked upper end of the main street, now cleared for the footraces. Finding herself in the open, she struck out down the course to freedom, with the law almost at her heels. Observing that the sheriff was about to overtake her, the miscreant pulled up her skirts to allow for more speed. The crowd roared its approval and cheered its favorites as the two runners sped down the track. Some old-timers, with a sparkle in their eyes, still insist it was the finest race of the day.

Late in the afternoon came the rock-drilling contests with purses as high as eight hundred dollars offered as first prize. The competitors worked as two-man teams, with one holding and turning the drill while the other rained blows with an eight-pound double jackhammer. A skilled drillman could change to longer drills between strokes of the hammer as the hole grew deeper. A further shift occurred after a specified period when the hammermen and drillmen changed places. An eight-by-eight-foot block of granite was hauled into the arena or street for the contest. One man from Cripple Creek, who was imported for the occasion, really threw the betting pools into a cocked hat when he struck one hundred and twenty blows a minute and defeated all of the local favorites.

Wearing apparel was high in price, but clothing worn in the San Juan country was not appreciably different from items of apparel found in other camps of the period. At one time there was a rumor to the effect that the miners were in dire need and Easterners collected boxes of clothing, some of which arrived in the district. Generally speaking, carpenters, and other town artisans wore bib overalls; the miners rarely did. Their preferences ran to overall pants or blue jeans with laced, hobnailed boots and broad-brimmed hats, usually smeared with candle grease from their miners' lights. The only distinctive tendency of dress indigenous to the San Juans was a habit that developed among foreign-born miners. Instead of wearing their shirttails in the usual way, they tucked the tails of both their under and outer shirts inside their undershorts. The elastic was usually exposed above their belts, a caste mark that served to identify the group.

Tramp mule skinners developed their own peculiar eccentricity of dress. When buying jeans, they purchased sizes that had legs that were far too long. This enabled them to wear deep cuffs as a badge of their profession. A man who drove only a six-horse team wore only a six-inch cuff, while his eight-horse-team companion was entitled to an eight-inch upturn.

Rubber boots were a common item of footwear in the deeper mines where groundwater was a problem. At one

time, rubber boots with leather, hobnailed soles caused
a small flurry of popularity but since they were prone
to leak, miners generally returned to the conventional
models. At another time, white rubber boots, impregnated with zinc, were tried but were also abandoned because they failed to insulate well.

The "Cousin Jacks," so common in Gilpin County, were
much in demand as excellent timber men for notching
and fitting logs into the shafts of many San Juan mines.
Welshmen, Italians, and Austrians were also commonly
found among the men who worked in the tunnels.

Prominent among those professional persons who migrated to the San Juans to care for the miners was Dr.
W. H. C. Folsom, a dentist, who reached Durango on
March 30, 1881, and opened an office in the First National
Bank Building. His equipment included a kitchen chair
with a headrest attachment. He wired the chair to a
packing box so that it would be high enough to work at.
He also kept a spittoon on the floor. Occasionally, the
customers hit it—but most of the time they did not.
There were three thousand people in Durango at that
time, but there was no dentist until his office was established. On opening day he was busy immediately. During the first day's work, several cowboys came in and
told him how they had beaten up the last dentist; but,
fortunately, they tried nothing of the kind with him.
There was no railroad to Silverton at that time, and
Folsom often rode up there on a horse to do dental work
during the first summer.

On one of his trips into the surrounding countryside,
Dr. Folsom recalled having approached the tollgate near
Rockwood. At the same time, a group of desperados,
known as the McCoy gang, were on the way over to Rico.
Their trail also brought them to the tollgate where they
promptly objected to paying the fee. There was quite
an argument. The gangsters had violent tempers and it
looked as if there might be some serious trouble. Finally,

one of the McCoy boys whipped up his horse and rode through the gate. When the rest followed, Dr. Folsom slipped through also and no one paid any toll.

Early-day fire-fighting equipment was anything but adequate. In Durango the fire-fighting system consisted of a small steam pump on wheels, with a single hose. Two cisterns were built, one at the intersection of Ninth Street and the other at Tenth and Main. These were not cemented and would not hold water. By the time one was filled, the other would be empty. When a fire broke out it burned eight blocks. The fire engine was also burned.

In 1876 the first star mail route was established. It ran from Del Norte to Animas City, a distance of one hundred and fifty miles. The route led over the divide, crossing at Cunningham Pass. There was one forty-mile stretch of high, snowy range where men often carried the mail on snowshoes. One of the carriers, a man named Grinell, was lost during the first winter in a terrific blizzard on the summit of the pass. It was many days before his body and the mail were found and dug out of the drifts by his companions. From Animas City, the route ran eastward by way of Pine River to Pagosa Springs where Charlie Johnson and his family had taken up a homestead.

The Johnson place came to be known as the general headquarters for the whole countryside on Saturday nights. On Sundays, cowmen and ranchers were there in force. The mail service was only weekly and came in for a lively patronage. Postmaster Johnson was a quiet, reserved individual. He had never learned to read, so when the mail arrived the crowd would rush him. In the absence of his trusted assistant, Poney Pollock, who might at that time be sitting in on an important poker game in the rear, Uncle Charlie would be obliged to function in his own behalf. Since he could not read, some means of improvising was essential. Postmaster Johnson, when forced to officiate, would climb to the top of the counter, reach for a big cracker box on the shelf, and with a bang bring the whole post office installation upside down. "Now, fellows, help yourselves and hurry; I can't wait here all day," he would say. In the end the delinquent assistant would usually turn up and relieve his chief. All flushed and beaming, he would insist that all hands take just one on him, for there was never a lack of old rye thereabouts. So it came to pass that firewater, poker players, gun toters and "Uncle Sam's" post office were all, sadly, housed under one San Juan roof.

Due to their location, some San Juan cabins incorporated special features in their construction. One particular structure that was built at Animas City in 1877 could be described as being reasonably typical. It was about fourteen feet square, had only one window and no stove —just a fireplace. The floor was dirt. During that time, Indians frequently came around and got sugar and some flour. Sometimes, if the settlers had it, they gave food to the Indians to keep them friendly; but that worked a hardship on the people since supplies were hard to get and they never kept too large a stock on hand. One day the man of the house decided to dig a cellar. He moved a bed and dug the hole big enough to get into and then scooped out a tunnel and made a room about six by eight or ten feet. He worked at night and his wife and son helped to carry the dirt out and throw it in the grass away from the cabin so that the Indians would not notice it and look for the cellar. After it was finished, they kept their food supplies down there and only got enough at night to use the next day.

The father of A. J. Chitwood, whose house this was, made a cover for the cellar, swept dirt over it, and put the bed back. If the Indians came along before the family had eaten their dinner, they sometimes took whatever was in sight, which meant that the Chitwoods had nothing to eat until after dark. They were never ugly or mean but just took whatever they could get.

In some of the outlying San Juan communities, springtime signified a period of possible trouble with the Indians. Since their rations were running low at that time of the year, some of the ranchers would kill and dress cattle to feed and pacify the Utes. This seemed to be the only known way to quiet them. The Indians would eat until full and then practically force the food down— after which they would be in too good a humor to fight. Nevertheless, portholes were built in the houses from which the settlers could watch the Utes dance around their homes.

Since these settlements were some distance from any established towns, the people would frequently hear mountain lions at night. These animals could smell the food and would hang around because they were hungry. Bears and coyotes would often fight during the night and would wake the settlers while squabbling over the meat. One settler told how a bear caught his cow at the corral and came back the next night to eat it. They shot at the sound but could not see him. Some of the men tracked him into the mountains but were unsuccessful in finding the animal.

This story, reported by Frank Blake of Durango, appeared in a first-person account in the files of the State Historical Society, and is illustrative of the great cultural void that existed between the Indians and the whites. Following expulsion of the Utes from the San Jauns, many of them took up residence at the Ute Agency near Ignacio. When food was to be distributed, ration tickets were given to the family. The tickets were then presented at the agency by the squaw, whose job it was to carry the supplies. One squaw came in with seven tickets. The ration issuers stood behind a counter as the woman passed along receiving flour, coffee, sugar, or whatever was called for on the ticket. Mr. Lake was issuing meat and occupied the last station on the counter. This particular squaw passed along seven times, one ticket at a time. She took her supplies outside and piled the meat on a blanket. There were always dogs around, but they did not touch the meat or allow it to be molested by other dogs or Indians. When she had received all of her rations, following the general custom she took a knife and cut the bones out of the meat. About ninety pounds of meat was carved out. The bones were thrown to the dogs. Then there was plenty of noise, snarling, and biting.

Ignatio's squaw always drew the regular meat ration and in addition received a whole round of beef. The Indians always gorged themselves on meat. Beef was killed on Tuesday, six or seven animals, and by the following Saturday no Indian would have a bit of meat. When the animals were killed, the squaws waded into the entrails, washed and ate them. Mr. Lake once told of having seen a squaw eat an entrail between two and three feet long, raw. He took his doubting brother outside to see it also. The brother later told him that if he had merely heard the story he would not have believed it; and after he saw it, he was still not sure it had happened.

Following the passage of the customary tent-city phase, most homes built in the San Juan country were of log construction. Big logs, squared off with an adze or broadax, were notched and stacked in the conventional manner. Frequently, a foot of earth was piled on the roof in a manner reminiscent of the earlier Kansas sod houses. When sawmills became more common, buildings of dressed lumber gradually replaced the log structures in all but the most remote camps. Very few brick houses were built, partly due to the poor quality of insulation of brick in a cold climate and partly because these materials were not generally available. A few mud bricks were made near the fish pond at Ouray, but the quantity and quality both fell far short of expectations.

The later types of frame houses employed either shingles or the much utilized batt and board siding. Their inside walls were almost never plastered. Two-inch strips of wood were nailed horizontally across the upright wall joists and a layer of muslin or canvas was tacked over the whole assembly. One or more layers of wallpaper completed the job.

In most San Juan communities education was a catch-as-catch-can proposition with little organization and even less incentive to attract and hold the prospective teacher. One example will suffice. The first school at Mancos was held in a cabin. Miss Lisa Allen, a sixteen-year-old girl who was staying in Parrott City, was the teacher. The cabin was too small, so several of the men went to work building a new one. The latter part of Miss Allen's term was held in the new building while a stockade of pine poles was being erected around it. This log cabin stood behind what was later the Bauer Mercantile Company Store. It was used for all public gatherings until 1887 when a new high school was built. One day two Indians arrived at the school. A Mr. Rich, who was hauling a load of hay, saw their horses outside and took his pitchfork and drove them out of the building. Miss Allen was frightened and the Indians were angry. They later told around the town that a man with a pitchfork had attempted to kill them. The seats in Lisa Allen's school were blocks of wood sawed from a pine tree. It had no blackboards and the books were those that had been brought in by the various families.

In many of the more remote mining districts, the men lived in bunkhouses built by the company according to the needs dictated by the size of the mine. Some of these were large, open, army-type structures while others were partitioned off into a number of rooms, each of which contained from nine to twelve wooden bunks, stacked up in vertical units of two or three high. The large old bunkhouse at Sneffels is typical of this latter type. Mattresses were furnished by the company, but each man was responsible for his own bedding.

For those men who toiled far from the established centers of population, any period of leisure was eagerly anticipated. On their days off, miners frequently left Red Mountain Town at 4:00 A.M., headed for Silverton. The early time of departure was dictated by the fact that large mining properties were situated with great frequency along the right-of-way, thus assuring that they would be invited in for several breakfasts.

No attempt to chronicle life among the miners would be complete if it failed to mention that most dreaded of all San Juan catastrophies—the snowslide. Although mentioned elsewhere in this book in connection with specific geographical areas, the phenomenon of the slide must nevertheless be considered as a condition of life indigenous to the San Juans generally.

Early in 1963, Coloradoans were shocked to read of the unfortunate demise of the Reverend Marvin Hudson, of Ouray, and his two daughters. The tragedy occurred when the Riverside Slide ran unexpectedly on the northern approach to Red Mountain Pass. The Riverside was always a particularly treacherous slide, since it has been known to run simultaneously from both sides of the canyon.

Unfortunately, slides on this pass are nothing particularly new. The following account describes the struggles of another clergyman in the early 1890's with slides in this same area. At 2:30 on a stormy winter morning, the doorbell rang at the residence of Father J. J. Gibbons, the Catholic priest for both Silverton and Ouray. He was asked to come at once to Silverton on an urgent sick call. At six in the morning, he and a companion started south. At Bear Creek Falls the toll gatherer, who had been there for years, came out to take their tickets and warned that they might run the risk of being lost in a slide or in a blinding storm which was advancing.

Despite the difficulties of the situation, the two men decided to start out for Silverton anyway. Bear Creek Falls was described as being fringed from top to bottom with a delicate embroidery of snow which clung to bridge, rock, shrub, and to the mountainside for hundreds of feet down. Within a half-mile of the second bridge, the priest and his companion were compelled to get out of their sleigh to shovel snow.

During the preceding fall, the Ashenfelder Packing Company had lost one team and a load of merchandise at this same place. Coming up a little rise in the road, the collar choked one of the horses. It fell, dragging the other horse toward and over the edge of the cliff. The driver saved himself in the nick of time by jumping from the wagon in the direction of the wall; but the outfit went down two hundred feet.

There were several known places where the two travelers might also be caught in the slides. Coming to the first of these spots, they were pleased to find that the snow had not come down and that it was not particularly deep on the incline. The year before, Father Gibbons recounted that he had nearly been caught at this same place and that large chunks were breaking loose above and gathering in volume as they rolled down. At that time as he sat in the saddle of his horse, viewing these suspicious advance guards, a great mass became detached above and, like a flash, carried everything before it. It was a close call.

When they came to the Mother Cline—a strange name indeed for a snowslide—they found the passage safe. This infamous slide had come down many times before and usually bore everything away in its track, recoiling from the bottom of the gulch and breaking off the trees up the mountainside for two hundred feet. The snow was from sixty to seventy feet deep on the roadbed and in the gulch. The mass of wrecked matter was a conglomeration of broken trees and huge boulders, some of

which weighed two or three tons. As long as the weather
was cold, a team could readily cross on the top of the
slide; but when the snow melted, the county was obliged
to cut a tunnel, which was one of the wonders of the
Ouray Toll Road during much of that next summer. This
tunnel was usually five hundred and eighty feet long
and high enough for a Concord stage. By late fall, the
roof of the tunnel was thawed out but some of the walls
remained standing for two years.

On their arrival at Ironton, the two men permitted
the horses to take a short rest, after which they went on
to Red Mountain. As they approached the greater altitude, the storm almost blinded them and they found it
difficult to keep on the road. Above the Yankee Girl
property, they met a sleigh coming from Silverton and
the men who were in it informed them that the sick man
had died. The priest at once changed sleighs and started
back. After an overnight stop at Guston, he set out for
Ouray the following morning in one of the most severe
storms of snow and wind. They were caught in the blizzard for ten hours at a time during which the cold was bitter enough to freeze one to death. At times it was nearly
impossible for the horses to move. The men got out of
the sleigh and waded hip-deep through the soft snow,
feeling for the road in broad daylight, creeping along
the wall to be certain they were not rushing headlong
into the canyon. After four hours of stumbling and
falling, digging a way for the horses, they emerged and
appeared at Ouray at five in the evening, and, incidentally
celebrated Saint Patrick's Day, or rather night, as it had
never before been celebrated.

While Father Edmond Lay was pastor at Silverton,
word was brought to him that a dying woman at Ouray
was calling for a priest. At half-past eight on Saturday
evening he started on horseback for the northern city,
having hired an animal for the purpose. A snowstorm
was already raging, and Ouray was over the range

twenty-six miles distant. This not only meant a long, cold ride—it meant a dangerous one. A good horse, in great measure, meant safety from stumbling off the road down the sides of the canyon, for even on a stormy night a horse usually knows the way. However, being on a good horse did not mean safety from snowslides, and the road between Silverton and Ouray is still a formidable one.

During the long night, Father Lay toiled over the difficult and dangerous road. Toward morning he arrived at Ouray. Here he found the woman in a wretched condition, an inmate in one of the worst brothels in the town. He had her removed to a better place, after giving her the Sacraments for which she had pleaded. On Sunday Father Lay said Mass before beginning his trip back to Silverton on Monday morning.

The roads were in bad shape after the snowstorm; and during that day, only one third of the distance back could be made. At this point he was compelled to leave his mount with a horse herd, as it was impossible to get the animal through the snow and still seek lodging for the night. On Tuesday morning, on foot, he again started for home. It was night before the little town of Chattanooga was reached, about two thirds of the distance from Ouray to Silverton. Before he entered the town, a snowslide came rushing down the mountain in front of him. Father Lay stayed at Chattanooga Tuesday night and the next day started south once more, this time on snowshoes. Hardly a mile out of town one of his frames broke. It might have been a serious matter for him if his accident had not been seen from Chattanooga. At nine o'clock on Wednesday evening, completely worn out, he arrived home in Silverton. The unfortunate woman, whose cry for the priest had been the cause of the trip, recovered from her sickness and immediately began again her infamous career.

Another of the more perilous slide areas was the previously noted Mother Cline, which came off the side of Mount Abrams a few miles south of Ouray. A second avalanche frequently hissed down from the steep slopes of Mount Hayden, near the twin bridges. Since this often filled the canyon with snow, the highway was ultimately relocated along higher ground above this point.

Around Silverton, especially near Howardsville, snowslides often played havoc. In a wild wreck of rocks, railroad ties, timeworn boulders, and broken trees, a slide on one occasion nearly carried away the depot at Silverton. It was, therefore, one of the first considerations of the wise miner to observe and mark well the lay of the mountains before building his cabin in the high San Juan valleys.

In the fall of 1883, a snowslide ran between the blacksmith shop and boiler house at the Highland Mary Mine. It hit one corner of the shop. The wind, made in passing through, opened the door of the boiler room. It piled snow over the mouth of the tunnel, and it was necessary to make another one about three or four hundred feet long to open the mouth of the first tunnel so that the mine could be worked again.

Quite apart from the more obvious hazards and drawbacks, most of the individuals who cut their pioneering eyeteeth on the San Juan rush, recall it with considerable pleasure and not a little nostalgia. At least two "San Juan Pioneers" societies have been organized within the state in order to facilitate the process of keeping in touch. Being rather closely-knit groups, it seems logical to assume that these organizations will eventually be superseded by similar groups of Sons and Daughters of San Juan Pioneers. As the years continue to take their toll, veterans of the silver excitement have now taken widely to letter writing as a convenient vehicle for reliving the great days and for thrashing out old controversies. In the intervening years, bonds of friendship have been strengthened among those who are still able to recall and write about the rigors of their exciting, unusual, and rewarding way of life among the high peaks. Geographical circumstances will not likely create another era from the same pattern in our lifetime.

6

Crime and Justice

AMONG THE BRUTALLY SEVERE realities attendant upon
the organization of any new society is the phenomenon of
crime. The initial injustice, against the Utes, had gone
unpunished and veritable hordes of people were literally
pouring in over the ranges. Unlike the more orderly migrations of the twentieth century, there were no agencies
set up to cope with the growing problems engendered
when masses of people were suddenly thrown into brutal
contact with one another, without benefit of such traditionally accepted institutions as courts, law officers, or
jails.

Even today, with all our pseudo-scientific approaches
to human behavior, the problem of crime is still with us.
Each year we Americans spend more money on crime
than we spend on the education of our young people.
The fact that it costs us between $2,000 and $4,000 annually to keep each and every male criminal behind bars
is profoundly shocking. Yet this astronomical sum accounts for only a minute fraction of the total cost. Even
more shocking is the fact that between 60 percent and
70 percent of our criminal population is made up of re-
peaters. In this particular area we have made little
social progress since the days of the mineral rushes.

The men who sought the white metal in the San Juans
were much like those who had participated in the seven
gold rushes and the numerous silver and copper migra-

tions. They were a mixed lot, but so were the men who journeyed across the ocean with Columbus. Many were pioneers and builders. A few were destroyers. Most of them were dissatisfied; the contented ones had stayed in the East. Some came in a search for greener and unmortgaged pastures. Others frankly sought the fatter fish to be found in less troubled waters.

In many early Colorado communities there were only three classes of punishment. First was public horsewhipping, which was reserved for minor crimes. For more serious offenses against good taste, the culprit might suffer banishment from the district for a stipulated period of time or, occasionally, he was excluded permanently. Last on the list was the most traditional of all trademarks of Western justice—the hangman's noose. In scope, the hanging covered a wide range of felonies that included most varieties of robbery at one end and murder at the other. Horse stealing, because it frequently deprived a man of his means of livelihood, was considered a particularly heinous offense.

In retrospect, all three reflect a cultural and material lack. Without adequate enforcement, courts, or probation officers, the variety of punishment that might be prescribed was severely limited by reality. Also reflected was a general lack of pioneer concern with current theories that would reform rather than punish the criminal. The immediate problem of the vigilante committee was simply quick removal of the source of irritation in order to preclude any possibility of a repetition of the act. Under such conditions, the rate of recidivism for lesser crimes was understandably high.

Since most of the men were far from home and their wives and sweethearts, they were generally unwashed and unchurched. In the more remote camps, the law consisted of five cartridges in the cylinder, while justice was the one in the chamber. Claims were protected in two ways: by lever action and by legal action. This was sometimes described as "Winchester Justice." Other kinds of law and justice were often enforced by officers of the "midnight court," "Judge Lynch" presiding. In such cases the victim often received a "suspended sentence."

Since it was the chief means of "blue chip" transportation in the seventies and eighties, the stagecoach suggested an infinite variety of possibilities to the nineteenth-century criminal mind. Despite the optimum advantages offered by stagecoach travel, there was also a number of very real hazards attendant upon the traveler.

In 1879 the Slumgullion Pass Wagon Road had served as the principal route from Lake City to Del Norte. When the Denver and Rio Grande reached Gunnison, it effected a change and stagecoaches, freight wagons, and most mail deliveries were shifted to the Lake Fork route.

One of the men drawn to the San Juans about this time was Billy Le Roy, an escaped convict from the Detroit Penitentiary. He was about as desperate and dangerous an outlaw as the West had sheltered. Le Roy was joined at Del Norte by his brother, who went under the name of Frank Clark. These two, with one other man, attempted to hold up the Slumgullion stage out of Del Norte.

The date was May 18, 1881. The time was 8:15 P.M. Barlow and Sanderson's coach was met by Le Roy and his gang, who not only rifled the mail but also robbed the passengers of their money and watches. Unpredictably, the lead horses were frightened by the sudden movements of the three men hidden beside the road ahead. The ensuing runaway baffled the robbers.

It was a characteristic of the Le Roys to return to the scene of their crime a few days later, successfully rob the same stage and its passengers, and give the horses a scare as a send-off. Often they would fire a volley into the coach as it whirled away. A reward of $1,400 was offered and, in the finest Hollywood tradition, a scouting party set off in hot pursuit. Sheriff L. M. Armstrong, with James P. Galloway, undertook the job of trailing the gang. Having apprehended the culprits in the mountains, the posse decided to take them to jail. They were successful, although they had to shoot Le Roy in the leg to capture him. He was game to the last; but Armstrong was one of those efficient old-time sheriffs and brought all three men back to Del Norte. Under cover of darkness, Sheriff Armstrong slapped the Le Roys into the Del Norte jail sometime after midnight. Being exhausted from having been on the trail for three nights with little sleep, the peace officer made his way home and tumbled into bed.

A hastily formed lynch mob had other ideas. The citizens of Del Norte were determined to put an end to lawlessness on their stretch of the road. It was they who had put up the reward of $1,400 for the arrest of the robbers. The price placed on the heads of the Le Roys did not indicate their true value to society; there was considerable discount on that. The citizens looked over the situation, determined that the Le Roys should not escape. Since Billy had a well-earned reputation as a jailbreaker, they first approached the home of the slumbering Armstrong. He was rudely awakened by the armed and masked mob who forced his return to the jail. Taking his keys, they removed the Le Roys from their cells. The bewildered sheriff was tied in bed at the jail, where it was hoped he might resume his interrupted slumber. Next stop was a clump of tall cottonwood trees, growing conveniently on the banks of the Rio Grande. Following a properly conducted necktie party, the lifeless bodies were cut down and returned to their respective cells at the jail. The mob dispersed to their homes with no effort being made to apprehend them. It was said that the Le Roys died because of a "stoppage of the breath," occuring while they were the guests of honor of the local "Uplift Society." One concrete result was a decline in such activities along the Lake Fork and Slumgullion routes for the next several months.

Nothing could stop a citizens' committee when they got the lynching bee in their heads. The jail—if there was a jail—could easily be kicked through, and the cottonwoods were quite close to the town. Many a miscreant was reported to have died of a fall when the platform on which he was standing suddenly gave way.

Two sets of stage robbers were so active in Durango that they were known by distinctive titles. These were the Stockton and the Allison gangs. Their code of morals was the honor of thieves. Ike Stockton was leader of the Stockton gang. He was a refugee from Lincoln County, New Mexico, where the bloody Chisum-McSween feud was carried on for years, and in which Billy the Kid and scores of other killers of his stripe participated. Stockton was sometimes described as a humble but useful saloonkeeper who was always careful to see that the weight of the miners' money didn't burden them on their way home.

Charles Allison, who headed the other gang, was not much better than Stockton; but he did possess courage. Convicted of horse stealing in Nevada, he had escaped from the sheriff by making a hazardous leap from a moving train while being conveyed to the state penitentiary. In 1878 he showed up in Colorado and demonstrated so much cleverness as a posse and emergency man that Sheriff Joe Smith unwisely appointed him deputy of Conejos County. Five successful stage robberies were traced to him in a brief road campaign; and, the trail becoming hot, he escaped, without the train this time, and landed eventually in Durango.

He was described as a cheerful, openhearted man, a sort of crude and undigested Robin Hood. He favored depending on his quickness with a gun for escape. The Stockton gang generally was composed of men who stuck pretty close to Durango. City life made it easier to ac-

Collection of Fred and Jo Mazzulla
A variation on the usual technique employed by "Local Uplift" societies to rid themselves of undesirables. Exact location of this picture has not been established.

quire material wealth, communicable diseases, and culture. They were petty larcenists as compared with the Allisons. Picking out a victim in a saloon, one or two of the gang would trail the man after he left, knock him senseless (adding several bumps not present on his phrenological chart), and rob him at their leisure. Occasionally, they cracked a thin skull and killed one or two. In such cases, there were usually no other witnesses and the next day a body would be carted to the cemetery for the unknown dead. Yet, although there were no witnesses, everyone suspected that each offense was an instance of Stockton gang workmanship.

The gang resented all summary proceedings that tended to interfere with their business. They sometimes started hostilities by shooting up the town. The event that precipitated their downfall was the killing of Bruce Hunt, son of former Governor A. C. Hunt, by a waiter who worked after hours in a restaurant as a second-story man. The only savings institution in the town, the Daniels-Brown Bank, was housed in a flimsy outer structure that boasted an interior vault of brick. The burglar, acting either alone or as the instrument of Stockton, set about digging a hole through the brick wall and extracting the money. It was an easy job. Being carried on while the noises of the saloons and dance halls were loudest, it should have been successful; but, several persons heard the opening of the vault and interrupted the waiter—among them was Bruce Hunt.

The culprit ran for his horse which had been hitched close by. With the pursuit becoming hot, he fired at the nearest rider. The unlucky shot struck and killed Hunt. The burglar fled into the night with retribution close at his heels. In the darkness his horse fell into a deep railway cut and broke its legs. In the fall, the rider's back was also broken. He was taken to Durango, where he died in agony.

In the middle of the excitement caused by this incident, a young fellow named Burt Wilkinson, a known member of the Stockton gang, killed a man and fled from the scene. "Enough is enough," said the citizens. With public indignation running high, all the other members, including Ike Stockton, quickly left town. Durango's loss, however, was Silverton's gain. Stockton easily trailed Wilkinson to his mother's ranch near Rockwood in the Silverton district. Wilkinson had a hole in the hills near her home, where she supplied him with food. Mother and son, however, did not reckon on the presence of the treacherous Ike Stockton. When Silverton offered a reward of five hundred dollars for the arrest of Wilkinson, Stockton saw in this the opportunity to make his own escape with the five hundred dollars in his pockets. He went first to Wilkinson's mother. Since she was aware of his friendship with her son, the hiding place was revealed. Taking along a Texan named Jim Sullivan, he sneaked up on Wilkinson, got the drop on him, and took him in irons to Marshal Watson. "See what I have here," said Stockton. "Give me five hundred dollars and I will skip out." It made little difference what Watson thought should be done; the citizens took the case out of his hands and summarily executed both Stockton and Sullivan by the good old cottonwood route. That ended the Stockton gang and the reign of lawlessness in both Durango and Silverton.

Citizens who would otherwise not have considered it good form or conducive to the public welfare sometimes fell into the habit of carrying guns, a custom which always led to trouble. Although street shootings, recently popularized in twentieth century pseudo-Western films and stories as a settlement for all differences, were never actually too common, an occasional "Reach for your gun!" was recorded with the inevitable result. Two physicians who became rivals for a certain woman's affections, were unduly inflamed against each other. When they met on the street, each habitually felt for his gun.

Such action, of course, meant warfare; and, once committed to a foolish course, neither could withdraw without being called a coward. When the smoke of the conflict cleared away, both their bodies were lying in the street.

Soon the people who had other things to do than loiter about stores and saloons became restive over the continuous reign of lawlessness and the growing bank account of the coroner. The coming of the railroads had brought in outlaws, desperados and thieves of every type, description, and kind of operation. Although the vigilante committees functioned well up to a point, progress almost inevitably dictated the hiring of a full-time sheriff and one or more deputies.

The task of being a law officer was not an easy one in any of the Colorado mining camps. Common criminals were by no means the only difficult people a sheriff was expected to handle. In 1892 the question of gambling and liquor divided the town of Silverton. One night while the city council was meeting in a saloon on Blair Street, they thoughtlessly passed an ill-considered ordinance requiring all saloons to close at midnight and put up the shades so that the people outside might have a view of the barroom. In a second ordinance passed that evening, they agreed to send out a regular patrol of two members at midnight to report on violators of the new law. An attorney, Mr. George H. Barnes, offered to prosecute violators without charge. Surprisingly, there was not much opposition to the reform. One night, however, two men on patrol were passing the Hub Saloon. A shot was fired at them from the opposite side of the street. They were not hit but the bullet shattered the plate-glass window of the barroom.

Few people were surprised when a delegation of a dozen cultured and refined ladies called on the Silverton sheriff, Bob Hines, the following morning and asked him to close gambling. He was indignant at the presumptuousness of an attempt to interfere with the duties of his office and, rising to his full stature, denounced the ladies in unequivocal terms as "busybodies." They demanded, however, that he enforce the law. Exasperated, he said, "It were those fellows who elected me and I'm not going against them now. I'm running this office." The ladies left in indignation, threatening to have him removed.

At another time, the incredibly talented Bat Masterson was hired to "clean up" Silverton, particularly Blair Street. Although he performed yeoman service as a law officer, he did not attempt to close down the multiplicity of questionable establishments that made life merry along Blair. It was, in fact, widely reported that he never intended to actually cope with the problem, since he personally enjoyed spending his off-hours in the "joints." Masterson was so highly regarded by his cronies in Silverton that it was assumed by most that if he had ever been thrown into the Animas River, he'd just naturally float upstream. Except with cards, he was no quick-draw artist. "Take your time and don't miss!" was one of his favorite maxims.

In September of 1893, a letter reached Silverton warning that a holdup of their bank was being planned by the notorious McCarthy gang. The cashier immediately placed armed guards in and about the building. The marshal was stationed in the back room with a shotgun. Upstairs, the bank's lawyer stood as a lookout with a gun in hand. Across the street was another guard, and many citizens were also armed and on the alert. The bank seemed well prepared to receive the robbers, who did not come. They passed by Silverton and headed for Delta, where they held up the bank and killed the cashier. As they fled on horseback, two of them were shot and killed and the bank's money was recovered. When it was all over, it was said that the Bank of Delta was visited by the firm of McCarthy and McCarthy—their purpose being to close out several large accounts. When the transaction was completed, they had been paid in full with interest compounded.

At one time a large portion of the Gold King lease at Gladstone was held by a man who kept a saloon at Silverton. To assure himself of some extra income, the barkeeper hired a number of high-graders to work in his mine. The purloined ores were, of course, sold to him. More often than not, the employees drank up their ill-gotten gains on the premises, thus assuring a tidy profit from playing both ends against the middle. The bartender's name, although known, is withheld to avoid embarrassment to his descendants, some of whom still live in the area.

The saloons could always mine the miners. Often their only business was rowdyism. Quietly, patiently, they waited for the miners to be paid off. Wide-open towns furnished a proper environment and ample inspiration for the "shearing of the lambs."

When the railroad came to Silverton in 1881, the inevitable bandits also arrived and two of them robbed a mine superintendent at Howardsville. Surprisingly, they chose not to leave the camp. They just began spending the money and having a high time. When the superintendent sobered up, he found the pocketbook of one of the bandits; and a delegation of citizens started the two thugs down the trail to Silverton. As often as possible someone kicked the rears of the two criminals. Here was a posse that really got to the seat of the problem. They were literally kicked all the way to Silverton and did not return to Howardsville.

Sometimes stagecoach robberies in the San Juans displayed a personal touch. On June 2, 1881, the western-bound stage was held up about three miles west of Pagosa Springs. They took about three hundred and fifty dollars from one passenger and seventeen dollars from a young man. They later decided that the youthful passenger was less able to stand the loss than his wealthy companion, so they returned two dollars of the original amount to him. The only other passenger was a lady. She was not molested. They broke open a couple of trunks but took nothing from them except some ladies' stockings, which one of the men remarked would be good for his sore leg because they would be large and warm.

Of all the tales of crime and justice in the San Juans, none is stranger or more dramatic than the story of the Marlow brothers, George and Charley. Arriving in Ouray County in 1891, the brothers took up a homestead between the towns of Ridgway and Ouray. They subsequently became two of the finest deputies that the sheriff of Ouray ever had. Widely respected by most and feared by others who had reason to be afraid, the Marlows attempted, in the face of incredible odds, to forget the past and somehow pick up the pieces of their shattered lives. Though the narrative terminates in the San Juans, its beginning was played out on the Missouri and Texas frontiers.

In 1885 when the family of Dr. William Marlow moved from Missouri to Texas, there were not just two, but five, brothers. Their names were George, Alfred, Charles, Lewellyn, and Boone. Boone Marlow was named for Daniel Boone. His mother was a direct descendant of this noted frontiersman. The boys led a seminomadic life, changing their abode frequently and living mostly on corn, game, and fish.

Late in August, 1888, the trouble started when two deputy United States marshals arrested four of the Marlow brothers on a charge that they had stolen thirty-three Indian horses in 1885. It later developed that the officers had been unable to solve the crime. Feeling that they had to arrest somebody in order to hold their jobs. they chose four of the Marlows. No shred of evidence supported their action.

Having been absent at the time, George Marlow returned and attempted to secure bail at Graham, Young

County, where his brothers were jailed. The result was that he, too, was thrown into confinement. Their release on bail, one at a time, was secured by their mother. In the face of official loss of face, the authorities turned to prejudice and spread a vicious web of lies throughout the county. The trump card was played when they secured the indictment of Boone for another unsolved crime, the murder of one J. A. Holton, whose body had been found in a gulch.

Sheriff Marion Wallace, who had been friendly to the brothers while they were in jail, was sent to make the arrest. His chief deputy, Tom Collier, accompanied him to the ranch. Collier walked directly to the door, while Wallace detoured around the cabin. Boone greeted the deputy cordially and invited him in. Collier announced his intentions by drawing his gun and firing at the bewildered Boone who dodged and seized a Winchester from the bed. Collier retreated outside as Marlow fired through the door. Running to the opening, Boone saw a man coming around the corner, fired, and struck down Sheriff Wallace who had heard the shots and was coming to investigate. Overwhelmed with sorrow, Boone forced the return of Collier at gunpoint. By this time, Charley Marlow had appeared; and he stopped his brother from killing the deputy.

Wallace lingered on for about a week. The Marlow brothers, all except Boone, surrendered and were soon back in jail. Boone made a hasty escape on horseback and was never again seen alive in Texas because of, or despite, a fifteen-hundred-dollar reward that was offered for him—dead or alive. Following the death of Wallace, Tom Collier became sheriff and a plot for lynching the Marlows was hatched. Chafing under indignities and fearing the worst, the four brothers secured a large knife and literally cut their way out of jail. They returned to their farms and families but were soon recaptured, chained together in a blacksmith shop, and confined behind bars again.

On the night of January 17, the jail was "taken over" by a mob led by the frustrated peace officers. The brothers refused to come out of their cages. One citizen entered Charley's cell and was struck on the head and knocked back through the door and against the wall of the prison. He was swiftly carried to safety by the other mobsters. His identity has never been established; but a coincidental death, two days later, of one of Graham's first citizens gives us a clue. The diagnosis was brain fever. A second mob, led by Marion Wallace, nephew of the former sheriff, also failed to extract the Marlows. A few days later they were to be moved to Weatherford, sixty miles away, for "greater security."

On June 19, the transfer was slated to begin. Three hacks pulled up before the jail. All of the Marlows were placed in the same buggy and the procession left town. The three carriages had not gone two miles before they reached Dry Creek, where the one carrying the prisoners suddenly stopped. A second mob was hidden in the brush. Rifle fire split the evening stillness. Notwithstanding their shackled condition, Charley and Alfred jumped and ran, as well as they could, to the other hack and seized Winchesters from their guards. George and Lewellyn overpowered another guard and secured an additional rifle and a pistol. Surrounded by one hundred armed men, the brothers stood, still chained, back to back. The "Battle of Dry Creek" was under way. In the second charge, Alfred was killed, Lewellyn was down, George was shot through the hand, and Charley was unhurt. Several of the "vigilantes" were killed; and Charley was soon down, shot through the lungs. Following the death of two more of their members at the hands of George and a miraculously recovered Charley, the mob retreated and the battle was over.

The two surviving men freed themselves of their dead

brothers by cutting off the feet, and fled to a farmhouse where friends sheltered them. The fearless Texas mob covered their tracks by saying that Boone Marlow and his gang had attacked the convoy and had killed several of the guards in the battle that followed.

Now the tide of public opinion began to turn. Friends, including the sheriff of Jack County, came prepared to defend the brothers at the farmhouse. Another mob was held off until Federal officers from Dallas arrived and secured the surrender of the Marlows. In 1890 a Dallas court tried them on a charge of horse stealing. Acquittal and the subsequent dropping of all charges against them followed. Meantime, desperados claimed to have killed Boone and collected the longstanding reward. Actually, he was poisoned by the brothers of an Indian sweetheart who had been feeding him. Suit was brought against the mob by the surviving Marlows. Damages were awarded as follows: To Martha Jane Marlow, the mother, $10,000 for the murder of her son Lewellyn. Zenia Marlow, widow of Alfred, received another $10,000. George was to receive still another $10,000 because of his wounds, as was Charles. The actual sums that were ultimately paid were considerably lower.

Having had more than a "bellyful" of Texas justice, the remaining family members moved to Ouray County in 1891 and filed on a homestead under their own names. That same summer old wounds were reopened when two Texas Rangers stepped off the Denver and Rio Grande to the depot platform at Ridgway. Their orders were to arrest George and Charley for the killing of Sheriff Wallace by their brother Boone back in January of 1888. Accordingly, Sheriff Bradley, of Ouray, rode out to the Marlow ranch and advised them to accompany him to Ridgway for a parley. Being their good friend, Bradley agreed to "step aside" in case any trouble developed. The Marlows strenuously opposed any return to Texas. Ridgway citizens rallied to armed support of the brothers and advised the Rangers that they had better send two thousand instead of two if they planned to remove George and Charley from Colorado.

The parley between the Rangers, the Marlows, and Sheriff Bradley was cordial and terminated with an agreement that all concerned should await an appeal to Governor Routt. Upon being informed of all the facts, Routt refused to sign extradition papers as requested by the governor of Texas. The Rangers took their defeat philosophically, shook hands all around, wished Bradley and the Marlows good luck, and stepped back aboard the train, alone.

George and Charley served ably as deputies in Ouray for many years. They were insistent for law enforcement and never abused the power vested in them. On November 15, 1891, C. W. Shores, sheriff of Gunnison City, requested the loan of the Marlows to quell a strike by the coal miners at Crested Butte. They missed the noon train, and Shores sent a special one down to pick them up. The sheriff had befriended them when they were in need and here was an opportunity to repay the favor. The one-car special train carried them, despite delays induced by snow, to Crested Butte. Most of the miners were willing to return to work when protection could be assured by forces of the law. In less than a week, Shores and the Marlows had established absolute control and most of the men who had been on strike were back at their old jobs. Six weeks later the brothers, back at Ouray, received a free carload of coal plus their wages for services rendered at Crested Butte.

In later years, while serving as a deputy under Sheriff Maurice Corbett, George Marlow was asked to intercept two men accused of a dry-goods theft in Telluride. Some four miles outside Montrose, he met a pair that followed the description and took them in. George ordered dinner for them and waited for the train to Telluride. A second telegram ordered him to chain the men to their seats on the night train.

Now, George had some old-fashioned notions about the way prisoners should be treated, arising partly from a series of experiences yet vivid in his mind. To chain a man to a seat was repugnant to his nature. Instead of complying with the request, he took the two men to his home where his wife prepared a good warm supper for all. The three men went to bed on the floor, handcuffed, and slept some. Next morning after breakfast, George met the sheriff of Telluride at Dallas Divide and delivered the prisoners, who were subsequently tried and convicted.

A year later, one of the men, having served his sentence, returned and looked up George who bought him a pair of shoes and gave him a job in the hayfield. Upon leaving he resolved to "change his course," on the basis of the treatment he had received from George as a prisoner.

The years passed and Charley retired, at age sixty-two, with his family to Glendale, California. George and his wife, Lily, lived out the rest of their lives in Ouray and were survived by five children.

Shortly after Jesse Benton arrived in Ouray, he was appointed town marshal. When he was inducted into the office, it marked a turning point in the career of that camp. Lawlessness suddenly gave way to law and order. His former strenuous life with the six-shooter was not immediately relaxed when he took up the reins of government there. Customary encounters with mining-camp life were enacted almost nightly, and he sought to stop them. At that time the camp could not boast of a single frame building. All the stores and houses were built of logs. Out of his own pocket, Benton paid for the lumber and the carpenter work for the first board building erected at Ouray. It afterwards became the courthouse and city hall. The first tenant of the building was Sam Davis, who conducted a "thirst quencher" there. A few months later he moved to another quarter and opened a resort which afterward became the famous Star Saloon. After Davis moved out, it was decided to make the building a combined county courthouse and city hall.

An outlaw known as Wild Hank once resisted arrest by Jesse Benton and stabbed him with a knife during the altercation. He was arrested and kept in jail. Upon his release he swore vengeance on the marshal, declared that he would kill him, and left town. When Hank returned to Ouray to "do Benton in," the latter was then acting proprietor of the Star Saloon. Hank rode up, dismounted from his horse, entered, and demanded a drink. At first Benton did not recognize his customer. Just about the time he recalled who he was, Hank drew a gun and defiantly laid it on the bar. Benton picked it up and returned it to the man saying, "You can have your gun but be careful how you use it." At the same time Benton picked up his own gun from behind the bar with one hand and gave Hank a drink of whiskey with the other. The crowd in the saloon, sensing trouble, began to leave the room. After drinking the whiskey, Hank backed away toward the billiard table where a game was in progress. He interrupted it by throwing the balls around the room. Benton walked from behind his bar, approached Hank, and knocked him down by a blow on the head from his revolver. When Hank left, he was a badly used-up man. As soon as he was able to do so, he left Ouray, never to return.

Once, in Ouray, a colored man killed a chambermaid at the Beaumont Hotel. He was placed in jail, but the results were not the usual ones. A mob took the jail keys away from Sheriff Jesse Benton and set fire to the jail, cremating the victim in his cage.

Sheriff Benton was once seen shooting a man off a mule for putting his boy on the stove. He also killed a man named Lucas in front of the Dixon House Hotel in

Ouray. On another occasion he shot a Chinese laborer for an alleged attack on a white girl.

Juvenile delinquency is by no means a twentieth-century phenomenon. The two stories that follow are sufficient to prove the point. As in most other early mining camps, the Chinese laborers were the persecuted minority of the time. In the early days, children frequently played jokes on them. The story is told of one evening when two boys went to the local Chinese laundry, which was in a building where the Montrose Telephone Office is now located. One of them took a ticktack and made a terrible noise against a windowpane. His companion then dropped a box of broken glass. The old Chinaman suspected celestial intervention and fled into the night. Another time, they put a pail over his stovepipe and then wired the front entrance shut. A railroad tie was braced above the rear door. When he ran out the back, the tie fell on his head. Before the Chinese were driven out of Silverton, the bank employed a Chinaman as janitor for fifteen dollars a month. Word came to the owners that at the bank in Lake City a Chinaman, in the same capacity, was receiving only ten dollars each month. The man in Silverton had his wage reduced accordingly. The Chinese were, in truth, the most abused single nationality group. The history of the entire American West is replete with shameful examples of their mistreatment.

No chronicle of San Juan crime and justice would be complete without at least a superficial telling of the often-repeated and much confused account of poor old Alfred Packer and his monumental feat of gastronomy. (Recent discoveries seem to indicate that Packer himself preferred to spell his first name "Alferd.") Anyone who has ever participated in playing a well-known social game called "gossip," can readily understand how such a variety of versions of the story have come into being.

Undisputed date of the tragedy was the winter of 1873-74, and the site was in the mountains west of Lake

City. Some say the point of origin of the party was Salt Lake City, while others claim Ogden was where it started. Several records have them headed for Breckenridge, while different interpretations have them going to new strikes around Summitville on the slopes above Del Norte. All accounts agree that a group of about twenty men wanted to make a prospecting trip from Utah to Colorado's mines. Their search for a guide terminated in their paying the fine of a petty criminal working on a street construction gang. His qualifications consisted of having driven ore wagons in a number of Colorado camps, and his claim that he could lead them to their goal. Neither assertion was surprising in view of a prospective escape from his circumstances. The man's name was Alfred Packer. Actually he had worked as a jack whacker around the mines in the Georgetown area during 1872-73. Following this, he moved to Bingham Canyon and worked there in the copper mines prior to his arrest.

Packer was born in Allegheny County, Pennsylvania, in 1842. Two decades later he had migrated west, where there is a record of his enlistment with the Sixteenth U.S. Infantry from Minnesota in April of 1862. Total service during the Civil War amounted to only seven months, due to a disability for which he was discharged that December. Migrations to Summit County and then to Utah followed; and now he had been hired to guide a party back to Colorado.

In the fall of 1873, after having lost most of their supplies in an abortive crossing of the Green River, the group arrived at the village of Chief Ouray, government-appointed leader of the Utes, on the Uncompahgre Plateau. Being no stranger to San Juan weather, the chief encouraged them to spend the winter with his people. Had they heeded his advice, there would be no story, and contemporary Hinsdale County folklore would have suffered a severe setback. Following a reasonable period of recuperation, half the group decided to accept the Ute's invitation and lived to play another day. Packer and five others chose to press on. The names of the five are now inscribed in bronze on "Cannibal Plateau." They were Israel Swan, George "California" Noon, Frank Miller, James Humphreys, and Shannon Wilson Bell.

Many weeks later the larger group came through the mountains and inquired for the Packer party, only to find that they had not arrived on the other side. Shortly after search parties had been organized to look for them, Packer appeared at the Los Pinos Indian Agency. He was alone and just a little too fat and healthy for having spent a winter by himself. His story involved a leg injury that had caused the others to abandon him. His first request was, allegedly, for whiskey, not food. Soon he began showing a large roll of money at the saloons in Saguache and some items recognized as personal belongings of the five missing men.

It was Otto Mears, who at that time kept a store in Saguache, who first became suspicious of Packer. The local saloonkeeper, Larry Dolan, was also the town "loudmouth." Since Packer consumed copious quantities of booze at Dolan's "hooch emporium," he also told a wide variety of versions of his story, depending upon the degree of intoxication. The barkeeper faithfully and eagerly reported each tale to the curious populace. In the meantime, all of the others from the original party of twenty had finally arrived either at Los Pinos or Saguache. The canny Mears began to put five and one together.

When an Indian guide found strips of human flesh along the trail, Packer was questioned. Again the story varies at this point, with one version detailing how Packer led his captors up to the place where remains of the five bodies were found. Another account credits J. A. Randolph, an artist for *Harper's Weekly*, with the find. Still another version tells us that Mr. C. P. Foster, while prospecting up the Lake Fork, came upon the camp of the victims of the Packer tragedy. There were towels hanging on the branches of the trees just where they had been left by the murdered men. Their blankets and other camp articles were left lying about on the ground. At any rate, the remains were discovered up on a promontory of land now known as "Cannibal Plateau." The exact spot is just a short distance north of the Slumgullion Pass road, about two miles outside of Lake City.

The surviving men from the original party had lost some of their gold fever and were now more concerned with seeing that Packer got what was coming to him. It was they who had pressed General Charles Adams, the Indian agent, to look into the case. When questioned, Packer first said that Shannon Bell had gone insane and had shot the other four before turning on Packer. "I killed Bell in self-defense," he said. "The bodies were eaten to ward off starvation." Another version of the first confession varies only slightly. In this one Swan died of hunger and was consumed to appease the collective appetites of the remaining five. Several days later Humphrey died and suffered the same post-mortem. Miller and Noon were shot by Bell, who then turned on Packer. In the struggle that followed, Bell lost out to Packer's little hatchet.

General Adams placed Alfred Packer under arrest and made arrangements for him to be confined in the jail at Saguache. A number of versions are available concerning what happened next, but they all add up to the fact that Packer escaped. Nine years later in Wyoming, "Frenchy" Cabazon, one of the original Utah party, heard and recognized the high, thin voice of the cannibal on the other side of a bunkhouse wall. Packer had assumed the name of John Swartze and was promptly arrested for extradition to Hinsdale County.

In the meantime, Lake City had been founded and it was here that the main part of the drama was to be played out. The second confession differed from the first in a number of circumstantial respects but still blamed the killings on Bell and concluded with a fight for survival between the latter and Packer. In general, the second statement was replete with far more of the grisly details than the previous one and Packer had abandoned his trusty hatchet for a less theatrical gun in the death struggle with Bell.

Less than a month had elapsed between his capture and the trial on April 6, 1883. The specific charge involved only the murder of Israel Swan and strangely neglected any mention of the others. Packer pleaded not guilty. Judge Melville B. Gerry, who later served on the bench at Mound City near Cripple Creek, was the presiding Judge. Packer's testimony followed substantially the text of his second confession. The jury failed to believe the party had crossed the necessary ranges in the snow. Neither did they accept his story that game was scarce that winter. What is more, they felt that the murders were intentional with robbery having been his objective since admittedly he was "broke" when they left Utah. Their verdict was "guilty," with death by hanging on May 19 as his penalty.

Larry Dolan, erstwhile saloonkeeper from Saguache and one-time fair-weather friend of Packer while he had money, rushed to the nearest grog shop and poured forth his own vintage version of the trial which, unfortunately, has survived what really happened and is far too widely accepted today. Undoubtedly under the influence of the grape, Dolan recounted a profane, ludicrous, and hilarious distortion of the sober pronouncement of Judge Gerry. In it he had the jurist alluding to the probable canine ancestry of the accused while dragging in partisan politics by accusing Packer of having substantially reduced the already inadequate Democratic population of Hinsdale County.

Packer was kept in the brick jail at Gunnison for three

years while a gallows was being constructed at Lake City, a gallows that would never be used. The Colorado Supreme Court reversed the death sentence, since the legislature in 1870 had amended the criminal code so that death could only be the penalty when a murder had been premeditated. In July of 1886, Packer was arraigned again at Gunnison on charges of manslaughter. He pleaded "not guilty," but the jury felt otherwise; and Judge Harrison sentenced him to forty years, five terms of eight years each.

During his short tenure in the Gunnison jail, a riot broke out among an unruly group of the inmates. The sheriff told them to "Shut up and get back in your cages or I'll turn Packer loose on you." Several unsuccessful attempts to secure parole were attempted over the nearly fifteen years that he spent at Canon City. Ultimately, a *Denver Post* reporter, Polly Pry, became interested in his case. A tremendous campaign was designed and unleashed. Not only did it secure the release of Packer— it sold papers as well. Governor Charles Thomas signed the parole on January 7, 1901. His own resignation, to allow him to run for the United States Senate, came the next day. Some people saw a connection between the two events.

Some new light was recently shed on the Packer case by materials in the files of Fred and Jo Mazzulla of Denver. At the time of Packer's release from confinement, the *Denver Post* was owned and operated by Frederick G. Bonfils and Harry Tammen, two of the most colorful and unpredictable individuals who ever paced across the pages of Western history. Their refusal to support Governor Charles S. Thomas in his bid for higher office until he paroled the San Juan cannibal has often been cited. Increased circulation for their paper seemed like a logical enough motive.

Overlooked by some contemporary researchers is the fact that Bonfils and Tammen also owned the Sells-Floto

Circus during this period. It now appears that the owners were interested in Alfred Packer as a circus attraction and had planned to tour the country, exhibiting him as a sideshow freak. Considering the nature of Packer's only claim to fame, one can only speculate as to what the script for his act might have been.

Governor Thomas got wind of the scheme and began casting about for a way to save his own skin and at the same time thwart the designs of his tormentors. His solution was a superb piece of political chicanery. The parole was signed, and Packer eyed the outside world hungrily for the first time in several years.

But the story does not end here. Since the constitution gives a governor the right of clemency, it also grants him the right to impose any conditions upon the released person that may suit his whim. This was his gimmick. Beneath Thomas's signature on the original document, there appeared a notation in the chief executive's own hand. It stipulated that Packer be paroled with the condition that he not leave the state of Colorado while on parole—making travel with any circus impossible. It was a rare day when anyone got up early enough to get ahead of Bonfils and Tammen, but this appears to have been one of those uncommon instances.

Following his release from prison Packer arrived in Denver where he stayed until spring. Some time was spent at the *Post,* but he generally disliked the city. He once made the statement that he disliked people, too, and some folks wondered how he meant that. Much of his time during the Denver interlude was spent in the Humberg Bar on Fifteenth Street. With the first thaw, he moved to Littleton, which became headquarters for his prospecting trips into the hills.

One of Alfred Packer's contemporaries described him as a very peculiar-looking man, having a large head and almost no forehead, the cranium sloping back from the eyes. He was broad-shouldered and had a waxlike com-

Collection of Fred and Jo Mazzulla

This rare photograph, taken near Idaho Springs during the summer of 1902, shows a reenactment of the Packer case. From left to right are Joe Kokes (holding camera case), Carrie Lutz, Minta Smothers, Clifford Smothers, with hatchet in hand portraying Packer, Peter Lenhart and, at the extreme right, Alfred Packer himself.

plexion, a small goatee, and a very high voice. He had a great love for children. He told stories that made him a great favorite with the local youngsters. Following an illness of about nine months' duration, death came to Alfred Packer at Deer Creek in April of 1907. He maintained his innocence to the end. Burial followed at Littleton's Prince Avenue Cemetery, where his marker may be seen today.

Prior to the Ute cession, a man named Jackson needlessly shot and killed a young Ute and nearly started an Indian uprising. In an effort to preserve peace, the Army Post Commander sent Jackson, with an escort of two men, out of the district for trial. Along the way an ambush by the Utes delivered Jackson into their eager hands. Back at Ouray, the citizens held the army officer responsible and decided to lynch him. Fortunately, news of the plot reached him at a home in town where he was dining with friends. Under cover of darkness he slipped out the back door and fled on foot down the trail along the west side of the Uncompahgre. His host, in a hastily laid plan, lost no time in harnessing a team and driving down the regular road along the east side of the same river. They had agreed to meet at the only crossing, a bridge eight miles below town. When the host reined in his frothing team at the bridge, he was more than a little surprised to find that the somewhat winded and footsore army officer was already there. All this happened a good half century prior to the great Jesse Owens' much publicized race against a horse. On the surface, it would seem that an army career in the San Juans deprived the American Olympic team of that day (if such there was) of a championship contender.

The first part of this story was likely the basis for the similar one so ably told by David Lavender in *Red Mountain*, his superb 1963 novel, laid within the excitement of the San Juan rush.

Not all of those who found themselves on the wrong

side of the law were robbers, cannibals, or murderers by any means; and the story of San Juan crime and justice was not without its Robin Hood. In this case it was Charles Bellows Waggoner who owned and operated the Bank of Telluride. The crash of 1929, with its subsequent closing of banks all over the country, was just a little more than Waggoner could take. On his way home from work on the evening of August 29, he realized that he could not cover the deposits entrusted to him by his neighbors and friends. A crisis with the state bank examiners was imminent, through no fault of his own. Possessed with a deep personal sense of fiscal responsibility to his depositors, he chose a course of action that was to skyrocket him to a position of national prominence, or rather notoriety.

The potential losses to dozens of innocent little people who had managed to save a few dollars at a time in his bank seemed like the betrayal of a trust to "Buck" Waggoner. It appeared to him that Wall Street would be better able to bear the losses than his depositors. In the finest tradition of Don Quixote, this small banker set out to do battle with his own personal windmill, which in this case, actually turned out to be a very real dragon indeed.

His first step involved a train trip to Denver's Seventeenth Street on August 30, where he proceeded to get the lay of the land. Conveniently overlooking the legal consequences of his act in order to achieve the ends of his larger moral crusade, Charles Waggoner utilized an elaborate set of secret banking codes to deceive Wall Street. From Western Union he sent a telegram to the First National Bank of New York instructing them to deposit the sum of $100,000 in the Chase National Bank, to the account of the Bank of Telluride. Of course this was done in the name of the United States National Bank of Denver, but without their knowledge. Five other such deposits were also put in Chase National from as many other banks, all to the account of Waggoner's bank.

On August 31 he appeared in New York at the Central Hanover Bank and paid up all notes owed by the Bank of Telluride. By wiping out all indebtedness, the assets would be left clear to cover deposits when the inevitable day of reckoning arrived. Finally, he deposited the rest of the $500,000 to the account of the Bank of Telluride in a scattered series of banks all over the country to make recovery difficult.

No depositor in Waggoner's bank lost a penny in the crash of 1929, but "Buck" was caught at a Newcastle, Wyoming, hotel with four hundred dollars in his pocket. He went on trial in New York that same year and was sentenced to fifteen years in Atlanta. Because he was a model prisoner, he was paroled in May of 1935. For a time he worked at a private club in Grand Junction. In 1939 he was indicted there as a card dealer but was never prosecuted. He later moved to the West Coast, where he died several years ago. He is still well remembered in San Miguel County and was often called the "Robin Hood of the San Juans." Contemporary accounts do not reveal what he was called in New York.

A number of stories about crime in the San Juans seem to center about Lake City. There the criminal element of the town lived near Henson Creek. This part of the camp was well named "Hell's Acre," according to the Reverend George M. Darley, for the first part of the name was about all that he felt was raised on the acre. The Reverend Darley described how he returned to his shanty one Sabbath night, after having preached a sermon, to find that it had been broken into and a number of his personal possessions stolen. He was surprised that anyone would dare to steal in a new mining camp, for the criminal, if caught, would in all probability receive severe punishment. The only thing he could do was try to recover the stolen goods. He went to Larry

Dolan's saloon and, surprisingly, found a police officer there to help locate the thief. From Dolan's they went through the other gambling halls and then started for "Hell's Acre." In the first large dance hall he was told that a carpetbagger had just left the hall with a coat over his arm and a valise in his hand. As they stepped outside, they noted that the bartender had just shot a man in the neck. The next day the valise and papers were discovered, but the thief was never found.

"Oregon Bill Speck" was an Englishman who wore his hair long and boasted of how tough he was. He settled on a farm in the San Juans and started to work it. He soon had an accident which took him to a doctor in Lake City, where he was laid up for some time. While he was gone, a Frenchman named Derocia jumped his claim. "Oregon Bill" returned to his ranch, shot the Frenchman, and fled to Saguache. The justice of the peace issued a warrant for his arrest and a deputy was sent to Saguache to bring the criminal back. Fearing that he would be lynched, Bill, at first refused to return to the valley. After Sheriff Foster guaranteed his safety, he went back and was exonerated since the settlers had no use for claim jumpers anyway.

On another occasion a young lad from Missouri killed a man named Davis in a cabin just a short distance outside Lake City. Davis had teased him until the boy felt he could endure it no longer. The youth had a small .32-calibre revolver; but Davis, with whom he was living, had teasingly told him not to pull the gun unless he intended to shoot. On the day in question Davis had been prospecting, seeking iron ore with visions of building a steel mill at Gunnison. He goaded the boy into a fight and then hit him on the head with an ax handle. The boy pulled his revolver and shot Davis through the eye, killing him instantly.

The spectacle of a double hanging was always regarded as a potentially festive occasion and a fine example of "togetherness." During the 1880's, two men named Betts and Browning were hanged jointly in Lake City. Their offense consisted of attempting to rob a house, not knowing that the sheriff and city marshal were concealed inside. When they were caught in the act, they shot their way out, killing the sheriff. They made their getaway while the marshal ran into town and organized a posse before starting back up after the outlaws. They were soon caught and jailed, but a mob stormed the cell and took the two out and lynched them. As they were about to be hanged, Betts said, "Come on, Browning, let's perk up. Let's take a good chew before we go." Although not in the Nathan Hale category, the remark nevertheless reflects a certain philosophical whimsy on the part of the man facing death.

On another occasion, this time at Del Norte, after one particular run-in with the law, a local gang was arrested and placed in the lower story of the little courthouse there, which at that time was used as a jail. The upper part of the building served as a court and was also used for church services. On Saturday one member of the gang decided that he would probably be lynched and even went so far as to place his watch in charge of someone to await the coming of the mob. A strong guard was placed around the building. Saturday night wore away but no mob came. While services were being held Sunday evening, guards, armed with rifles, stood outside. The congregation seemed to be a trifle nervous, but the hall was well filled and the services closed on time. Everyone knew that no one would fire into the building while church was in session. Monday night the pastor noticed the mob passing his house and soon heard the inevitable hammers and crowbars being used on the clasp that held the jail door. Almost immediately the shooting began. It was claimed that over one hundred shots were fired. It was not the original intention of the mob to do any shooting. They had planned to take the outlaws out quietly.

When the inmates heard the mob coming, one said to the other, "Let's get up close to the door and the moment the lock is broken, throw the door open and run for our lives. Put your head down and jump right into the crowd. You run to the left and I'll run to the right." This they did, instead of what the mob expected. One man was killed but the other made his escape. It was a moonlight night and they could see where the rifle balls struck the shadows. During the day Tuesday the minister picked up two bullets from his pulpit. They had gone through both the siding and the plaster. Deflected by the ceiling, both slugs had dropped down on the top of the pulpit.

One night after a political meeting in the San Juans, the local judge invited eight or ten visitors from outside the district to sleep on the floor of his cabin. He offered to furnish the blankets. The following morning, the judge arose, prepared breakfast and got ready to wake up his company. The effect of poor politics and worse whiskey had been very bad. One man was still inclined to sleep, although breakfast had been ready for some time. They soon discovered that he was dead. The judge immediately impaneled a coroner's jury and asked them to bring in a verdict as to the cause of their companion's demise. The jury brought in a shameful verdict—"Whiskey!" The judge told the jury, "The young man has a fine mother and sister living back East. How could I write them that this jury brought in a verdict of 'Death by whiskey'?" He patiently told the jury that they must try again. Again they brought in the same verdict. He appealed to them a third time and asked how they would like such a verdict brought in about them if they died. Following this final conference, the verdict was corrected to "heart failure."

Although the "necktie party" was a fairly common means of dispensing justice, the victims were not always of the masculine persuasion. The Cudigan hanging is a well-remembered incident in the history of early-day

Ouray. Mr. and Mrs. Cudigan had adopted a little girl and were rumored to have been very cruel to her. They had forced her to sleep in a straw pile during the winter. Her feet froze and she died of exposure. The Cudigan Ranch was on Dallas Creek, but visits to the town were frequent. While they were staying at the Del Monico Hotel in Ouray, a mob stormed their room and took the Cudigans to a place below town and hanged them both. It was a cold night and, ironically, Mrs. Cudigan is reported to have been barefooted. It was finally becoming unfashionable to die with your boots on. Sheriff Rawls had tried to protect the Cudigans and, in a last-ditch effort, gave a gun to Mrs. Cudigan's brother. The two men tried to hold the mob off at the head of the stairs but were overpowered.

The Cudigan hanging stirred up a statewide protest with armed mobs threatening to converge upon Ouray with ropes. This high degree of feeling was not entirely engendered by the normal revulsion at seeing a woman hanged. Mrs. Cudigan, it seems, was pregnant at the time of the lynching. For some time thereafter, the men in town were careful to wear their pistols wherever they went. Even Father Servant, early-day priest of the district, freely admitted to carrying a gun, "as did all others in Ouray."

Mob action frequently entered the story of San Juan crime and justice. In researching the subject, three separate versions of the following story were found. Since they vary in some details and in regard to the name of the community, we may say that the event occurred in either Ridgway, Ouray, or Silverton. A male offender had been locked up for a reported attack on a young girl. Late that night the inevitable mob formed and appeared at the jail. There the usual pattern ended. One member of the mob had a bright idea and several men were sent to get the town doctor. Having meanwhile been roused from his slumbers, the sheriff was forced to produce his keys and the cell was opened. While two of the town's first citizens held revolvers against his temples, the reluctant physician performed what the mob considered to be appropriate surgery.

Essentially, the story of crime and justice in the San Juan country did not differ particularly from similar chronicles in other established mining districts. The bizarre Packer case is, of course, an exception. No reason exists for believing that crime rates here were materially higher or lower than elsewhere.

Two lonely reminders of this phase of our story still stand as sentinels to law and order in the San Juans. These are the tiny two-celled jails at Animas Forks and Red Mountain Town. Really, when one considers the size of these two communities, it seems remarkable that a "pokey" with only two cells was adequate. Actually, when one compares this to J. Edgar Hoover's most recent report, these two little jails assume the proportions of great monuments to a surprisingly orderly way of life.

～7～

From Here to There—The Story of Transportation

THE DEVELOPMENT OF TRANSPORTATION in the San Juan country is a story of great courage and daring. With the discovery and establishment of mines and their subsequent towns, the whole district found itself in dire need of roads. There were no funds from territorial treasuries for these purposes; and some difficult times elapsed prior to any form of adequate stimulation, resulting in the eventual construction of a series of rough toll roads.

Without a doubt, the earliest method used in moving mining equipment to the high mines and carrying the unrefined ores back down involved the use of packtrains. No story of mountain mining conditions should overlook the role played in this process by the homely and unromantic burro and his close relative, the mule. Either species could walk safely over ledges which brought tremors to the hearts of those who were not mountaineers. The unpredictable emotional propensities that make up the nature and behavior of the mule are extremely well known. In 1830 Warren A. Ferris, a Rocky Mountain fur trapper, speculated that, "Job himself would have yielded to the luxury of reviling had his well-known patience been tried by the management of a drove of packed mules."

Most of the original exploratory work within the San Juan region was done by packing. Both mules and burros were used in this service. When the former were employed, they were strung out in a line and connected by a rope. One man usually rode the lead mule and guided the whole cavalcade. Another man often walked or rode in the rear. When burros (the work donkey was rarely used in the mining regions) were engaged in packing, they were not always tied together but each went loose; and the owner drove them like a flock of sheep, differing from the latter only in that they had learned from the narrowness of the trails to walk in a single file when that was required for safety.

In operating a packtrain, it is essential to remember that one may lead a mule, but not a burro. The burro must always be driven. This characteristic created a unique problem when a train reached a fork in the trail. How does the driver, at the rear, communicate his wishes to the animal in the lead? To get the job done, the operator utilized highly trained dogs. These remarkable animals were taught to bite the lead mule from the proper side, causing him to turn away onto the desired trail. The dogs soon learned to grab and then lie down flat to avoid being kicked in the head. As an example of learning in the "school of hard knocks," this process had few peers. Horses, because of their thinner skin, were less frequently used for packing than the mule or burro.

A mule could carry 250 pounds upgrade and 350 down, while a burro would manage to carry an average of 200 pounds. The mule had to be fed, but the burro could eke out an existence on the scant grass of the mountain slopes. For this reason he was most serviceable to both the pioneer and the prospector. The burro might well be christened "the porter of the hills."

Transportation was a staggering problem. There are records that describe how trains of pack burros carried ore in rawhide sacks, hundreds of tons of rock, over cliffs that look impassable today. Long packtrains of these incredible animals picked their way up all sorts of difficult trails and around the towering peaks, along unbelievably precipitous shelf roads. Supplies of all kinds were carried to the shafts and tunnels on the backs of the tireless and surefooted "Rocky Mountain Canaries." The origin of the nickname comes from the shattering, strident bray which alternately warmed the heart of the lonely prospector or drove him further under the influence of the grape.

In the interests of proper balance, two packs, one on either side, would be placed horizontally along the burro's body. Wearing specially designed pack racks to allow heavy loading, burros have been known to carry as much as seven hundred pounds in a single trip. Since most packers regarded the animals as expendable, it was not uncommon to hear one say, "Load them heavy, the harness will fit another burro."

The San Juan transportation industry began with freighting and packing. It is difficult for us to realize now what a huge proposition this was at the time. In addition to burros, thousands of oxen and horses were also required. Great numbers of heavy wagons of all kinds were needed, along with lighter rigs, stagecoaches, harnesses, and packsaddles. All of these items had to be transferred over rough roads and hazardous trails. Thousands of men made their living, and some of them accumulated small fortunes, in the various lines of the business of transportation. Many ranchmen also made a fair share of money selling hay and feed for the great number of animals during the winter. On first-class stage routes, twenty horses were kept for each coach. Wherever there were people, there were ten times as many head of stock. This made necessary the construction of barns, corrals, blacksmith shops, and livery stables.

The actual mineral deposits and surface mines were frequently a mile or so up the mountainside above the towns or camps. Obviously, road construction was not feasible to such precipitous locations and some more practical means had to be devised. Some camps utilized a mule or horse "express" to carry the miners up to their work, following which the horse would return down the rugged mountain trail to its stable. When stable horses were used to transport the miners to their work, the rider was required to place the reins over the saddle, thus assuring a prompt return to the stable. If this was not done, the horses would stay in the fields and eat.

Sometimes the rigors of San Juan transportation proved too much for human endurance. If the prospectors didn't freeze, starve, or become lost forever among the great peaks, they shot themselves in despair when their pack animals slipped off a shelf trail and fell two thousand feet or more. Others died of fatigue, dreaming to the last of green fields back in Iowa or Ohio. The presence and assistance of some sort of beast of burden was absolutely vital.

Winter transportation in the San Juans on horseback was a trying proposition indeed. One afternoon at Ouray, Father J. J. Gibbons received a telegram from Rico asking his attendance upon a friend, dying from pneumonia. He took the railroad to Ridgway, planning to go by stagecoach to Rico. However, he found this was impossible as the stage had stopped running. If the stage line could not get through, it was certain that a private individual could not make it. Father Gibbons was compelled to return to Ouray, losing more than half a day. Early the next morning he began a second attempt. His plan now was to reach Rico from the south. He knew the journey could not be made in less than two days' time. The priest made an early start on a good trail horse and was soon picking his way over the snow. He was making fair progress when the horse stumbled and fell. Father Gibbons' leg was pinned to the ground beneath the animal. Luckily, the horse was an experienced mountain animal and made no attempt to move after the fall. A struggling horse would almost certainly have meant death in the deep canyon of the Uncompahgre. By means of his hunting knife, Father Gibbons managed to dig his leg out of the hard snow and ice into which it had been pressed by the weight of the horse. After freeing himself, he was able to help the animal to its feet.

The trip in crossing from Telluride to Ouray by way of Marshall Basin was a perilous one, particularly during the winter. The trail through the snow was so narrow that when a person met a pack train with ore coming down the trail, he had to turn his horse loose because it was impossible to get past the descending animals on horseback. The rest of the distance had to be made on foot. The town of Telluride is at an altitude of 8,400 feet, but Virginius Pass, through which it was necessary to go, was at 13,400 feet. On both sides of the pass for quite a distance, traveling before the snow was gone was dangerous. Before getting to the pass, for three quarters of a mile the possibility of starting a snowslide made every step a dangerous one. On the farther side the greatest danger was from slipping on the ice and being dashed to pieces over the precipices.

The developing story of transportation in the San Juans is, in many ways, the story of Otto Mears. Often referred to as the "Pathfinder of the San Juans," sometimes as "The Little Giant," or by equally appropriate sobriquets, Otto Mears' life began without ostentation in the Russia of 1841. Born of a union between a British father and a Russian-Jewish mother, Mears knew little of what would pass today for a normal childhood. Both parents died while he was quite young and the youth was subsequently passed about among a succession of uncles, both in Russia and, ultimately, in England and America. It was a decision to try his own wings that resulted in his emigration to this country and that ultimately led to his being stranded in the streets of San Francisco in 1851 with only a few cents in his pockets. This happened when he was only eleven years of age.

By today's standards, this chapter in the Mears' story

would constitute great material for a "throat clutcher" on the soap-opera circuit, with appropriately doleful pipe-organ music bleating in the background. The only difference is that this really happened.

The rise of Otto Mears from rags to riches constitutes a superb example of the stereotyped nineteenth-century American success story. In the finest Horatio Alger tradition, young Otto worked his way up through a succession of occupations that included selling newspapers, working on a farm, tinsmithing, and delivering groceries. Never afraid of hard work and, undoubtedly, endowed with a tremendous amount of drive and initiative Mears perpetually attempted, and frequently accomplished, tasks that others had labeled "impossible."

He had done some early pioneering in California, living for a time in the Sierra Nevada gold fields after being abandoned by the last in a long series of "uncles." A Civil War enlistment brought him out of California for the first time with the state's First Volunteer Regiment. Otto Mears took out naturalization papers in San Francisco. When Abraham Lincoln ran for President, Mears boasted that he had voted for him. Following the Civil War, Mears was paid a pension of fifty dollars per month for his services. After his release from the service, Mears took up residence in New Mexico and entered the cattle business as a government meat contractor for a brief time. The following year he emerged upon the Colorado scene, opened a general store, went into partnership with Major Lafayette Head, and constructed the first flour mill in the San Luis Valley. A highly profitable sawmill was also built and operated by the two men. Mears extended his horizons once more by raising his own wheat to supplement the short supply being raised by other farmers in the vicinity. A drop in prices caused him to look elsewhere for a market. A new mill on Chalk Creek in the Arkansas Valley seemed to offer good prospects. Only one obstacle stood between the man and his plan—there was no road, only a trail across nine-thousand-foot Poncha Pass.

The influence of geography was a profound one indeed upon the career of Otto Mears. For wagon traffic, the trail across the pass was a monument to inadequacy. However, overwhelming odds had never bothered him before. With the conquest of this latest obstacle, Mears, with a shovel and an ax, carved out an entire new life for himself and countless others.

While the road was under construction, ex-Governor William Gilpin chanced to pass by. The former official encouraged Mears to take out a charter on the road and to construct it with no more than a gradual 4 percent grade, in order that railroads might eventually make use of it. The route across Poncha was only the first of many that were to be built over and into the formidable Rockies. In order to keep his head above water financially, Mears employed the familiar toll-road motif, as authorized in his charter. A tollgate was installed across the road and those who wanted to use it paid for the privilege.

The Mears road over Poncha Pass connected with California Gulch, where it in turn met another road going straight through to Denver by way of South Park. Mears' next road was a thoroughfare that ran from Saguache to Lake City. His third enterprise was one that ran from Lake City across the divide to Silverton. The first fifty miles of road originally built by Otto Mears eventually became about four hundred and fifty miles built throughout the mountains of the San Juan country at a cost of about $325,000.

In 1873, for a time, Mears operated a freighting business out of Saguache with three teams or yokes of oxen. Optimistic news of the San Juan bonanza filtered into the San Luis Valley with increasing frequency. Never one to pass up a profitable opportunity, he visualized construction of a wagon road that would extend from

Saguache, across the great peaks and eventually down Cunningham Gulch to Howardsville, a few miles northeast of Silverton on the banks of the Animas River. One source dates the event two years earlier and says that in 1871 when the first San Juan silver excitement began, Otto Mears, Enos Hotchkiss, and other Saguache citizens organized a company to build a wagon road from that city to Howardsville over Cochetopa Pass to the Cebolla Valley and from there over to the Lake Fork of the Gunnison River to the present site of Lake City. They did build to Lake City, but the Howardsville end was constructed later.

Howardsville at that time was the center of an excellent mining district. The Veta Madre was two and a half miles up Cunningham Gulch. It had a splendid six-foot vein which yielded $120 to the ton. The Pride of the West was half a mile above it and had one of the largest and best developed of lodes, reported to have been forty feet wide. On the opposite side of Cunningham Gulch were the Mountaineer, Highland Mary, and others. The Stony Pass road came down Hamilton Creek to Stony Creek, down this to Cunningham Creek, and then followed it to the Animas River in Baker's Park. An early report described it this way:

The trail is steep and difficult but not dangerous. It has mostly earth, dense willows, and cobblestones in the creek bottom with mostly earth and no grass of any kind until Baker's Park is reached. The valley of Cunningham Gulch is never more than four hundred feet wide and has small growth of anything but willows.

In June of 1874 a prospector named John Davie records having crossed Stony Pass and then traveled down Cunningham Gulch. He left his wagon at a park above Wagon Wheel Gap and packed his materials on burros for the descent.

Since the nature of the San Juans frequently precluded

construction of gentle grades, and since steep inclines require less time to build anyway, the lofty passes contributed materially to an incredibly high mortality rate among beasts of burden. Mules or horses that died in harness from exhaustion were often disengaged and kicked unceremoniously over the side. Far too many of these early thoroughfares were liberally endowed with decaying carcasses along the steeper grades. These circumstances gave rise to the early Colorado saying which implied that a blind man could find his way to Red Mountain Town—or whatever the community in question happened to be. The stench must have been a formidable olfactory experience indeed.

A few operators were more tenderhearted, and not all beasts of burden that died in harness were kicked over the side. Several freighters who operated in the camps around Ouray buried their horses at an animal graveyard across from the American Nettie Mill at the north side of Ouray. An average of one to two of these beautiful, eighteen hundred pound draft horses died pulling the steep grades each day and were interred in the little plot far below. A fine picnic ground now has been bladed out, over the top of the old burial plot. Some old-timers are notably reluctant to partake of their "tea and biscuits" at the spot even today.

Many of the more fortunate people owned their own horses, which might be ridden in the conventional manner or harnessed to a light buggy as a means of affording comfortable travel between widely separated points. One of these was Father J. J. Gibbons who had two missions in addition to Ouray—one at Ironton and another at Ridgway. A small church was eventually erected at each town. For the purpose of attending these missions, he kept a pair of horses, weighing perhaps eight hundred pounds each, and they were fast steppers. Leaving Ouray on Sunday morning at about 6:00 A.M., he would drive up to Ironton, a distance of nine miles. There was, and still is, an elevation of two thousand feet to be overcome in this ascent. On the return down to Ouray, he reputedly never let any grass grow under the horses' feet. Many a time he descended the stony road along the narrow wall of granite with the outside wheel only twenty inches from the edge. Now and then some visitor to Ouray would ask to accompany him and view the magnificent scenery along the way. Usually, after one experience, his curiosity would be more than gratified. The pace was too rapid and too thrilling even for the wildest sensation lover. He once took a young man to Ironton and having been delayed beyond his usual time, he let the ponies fly over the road on the way back. His companion clutched the seat of the buckboard and held on. He screamed and said, "Father, I must have heard something crack." Father Gibbons inquired if the wheels were on and the boy said, "Yes." "Well, then," said the priest, "there is no danger," and he cracked the whip again. The ponies, being light and willing, moved down the mountain at a tearing pace, fortunately without injury to themselves or their passengers.

The broncho was regarded as by far the best and fastest saddle horse in the San Juans. The broncho as such was not actually a separate species, but is described as a small wild horse, a member of the Mustang family. Not too heavy to climb to the highest places, the animal was light enough to move down steep inclines with ease and security. Nearly as surefooted as a mule, but without its slow gait, the broncho could pick its way with skill over a narrow stony pass along a mountain ridge which was scarcely a foot wide. At such places, the broader-footed horse would destroy himself and his rider. The broncho might fall without injury to himself, and once down, was usually able to get on his feet again, turn around on a trail, or dig himself out of the snow. The staying powers of the broncho were of first quality here, since a large horse cannot stand fatigue, hunger, hardship, or abuse as well.

It was said time and again in the San Juans that a man
could outrun a horse carrying a rider down a steep
mountain. This claim was once put to a test on the steep
and narrow trail which lies between the Marshall Basin
and Telluride. The endurance, speed, and certainty of
the broncho in keeping its feet in places where it was
impossible for a man on foot to go down these almost perpendicular cutoffs, proved to the satisfaction of all that
the broncho was capable of accomplishing leaps down
precipices and over craggy points, where even Rocky
Mountain sheep would not dare to go. Thousands of
dollars are said to have changed hands on this event.
Many people came to see the novel contest of four miles
down the mountain between horse and man.

Wagon freighting in the San Juans was a rocky proposition at best. It was sometimes necessary to construct
roads over the tops of trails that had been used by migratory Indian travelers since early times. By this means,
wheeled vehicles came permanently to the Colorado scene,
following trails that were little more than many pairs of
successive ruts.

When machinery for the first mill in the San Juans was
hauled in over Stony Pass by wagon, it was found that
yokes of six to ten oxen could pull only five hundred
pounds on each successive trip to the summit. Then the
load was snubbed down, as the miners said, by tying the
wagon wheels so they could not turn, and easing the
vehicles down by ropes wound around their rear axles.
For better control, the other ends would be wrapped
around rocks. As the loads reached timberline and below,
the ropes were cinched around the larger trees and the
wagons could be lowered gently down the slopes. Even in
July, snowdrifts often blocked the summit of Stony.

Some of the richest mines were discovered in some of
the most inaccessible country. Wherever there was a

mine there was a good chance for a town to take root and, therefore, a road of sorts was built up the steep and narrow canyons. At times, every kind of burden-bearing animal was pressed into service to bring supplies and trade goods to the miners and to take the valuable ores back down.

Ore wagons of that day were simply modifications of the earlier freight or supply wagons. Constructed with heavy-duty axles and heavier timbering in the beds, they were used extensively to transport the unrefined, raw silver and gold from the high and remote mines down to the more conveniently located smelters at Silverton or other refining centers. Some drivers are known to have used oxen, but the horse was by far the predominantly preferred animal. However, not a few wagon operators were known to have chosen that most surefooted of all animals, the mule. These supply wagons often operated on a regular schedule.

Most ore wagons used in the San Juans were of the Studebaker five-inch type. The size designation came from the measurement of the hub. Specifications for this country always called for the wheels to be equipped with double steel tires. In addition to the more conventional way of driving these wagons, some San Juan operators employed a "jerk line." Instead of sitting on a seat, the driver actually rode the wheel horse immediately in front of the wagon, holding a jerk line connected to the bridles of the lead team.

The Concord coach, fashioned in faraway New Hampshire, and others of its contemporary competitors, provided the optimum in comfort and speed for their day. Usually drawn by two or three spans or pairs of mules or horses, the coaches were capable of speeds that ranged between four and five miles an hour. San Juan staging, however, often necessitated the addition of another span of animals and the miles traveled in any specified length of time had to be revised downward on many of the runs.

On some of the crude mountain roads, grades were so steep that the drivers found it necessary to drag big logs to act as brakes on the trip down; and travel was truly hair-raising.

Employing a peculiar suspension system, the Concord coach was admirably suited to the hazardous, sloping grades that typified the problems of San Juan transportation. Long leather straps, sometimes three to four inches thick, were stretched out horizontally from the front to the rear of the frame. Since no springs were employed, the straps afforded a poor substitute for any sort of cushioning in the suspension system. Such a ride was notoriously hard. The principal virtue of the straps was that they allowed the coach to swing from side to side, sometimes causing "seasickness," but always finding its own center of gravity, pendulum-like, on sloping mountain roads. Compared to their contemporaries among vehicles, they were nearly impossible to tip over in normal use. Persons who rode on top frequently became "seasick," as they called it, due to the undulating motions of the coach body. At times the real and imagined hazards or annoyances attendant upon stagecoach travel seemed to offset its more obvious advantages.

The miners, either on horseback or afoot, frequently crossed and recrossed the Sneffels Range on their way from Ouray to Telluride. They preferred such methods of travel because they were cheaper than paying seven dollars to ride in the cold on one of Wood's large stages, listening to the monotonous humming of the stage driver who had plied his whip for forty years over Western hills and plains. Wrapped in blankets and generally seated alone atop a high seat on a cold day, anyone might well fall into the habit of humming. The old gentleman could have thought that his soft humming helped the horses, but it became so much a matter of course with him that the moment the wheels began to revolve, the

Collection of Claude Miner
A typical stagecoach, pictured on a section of Otto Mears' original toll road south of Ouray.

tiresome refrain was struck up and held with a dreary reiteration from station to station.

From Dallas to Telluride, a distance of some fifty miles, three stagecoach stations provided the necessary relays. Their new stages were among the best equipped in the West. The horses likewise were in good condition, well-fed and groomed. Being strong animals, they whirled their coach over the road at a rattling gait. With the approach of the stage, the attendant had fresh horses promptly at hand and ready to put into the traces. Seldom over three minutes were ever occupied in the change. Until they were replaced by narrow-gauge railroads, the stages extended their lines to serve all but the most remote communities.

The Pennsylvania-spawned Conestogas, or covered wagons, long regarded as the regulation outfit in earlier migrations, played only a minor role in the San Juan story. Perusal of old photographs shows only a limited number of Conestogas in the San Juans. Possibly their cumbersome size and extended length may have been determining factors.

When his road reached the site of present-day Lake City, the versatile Otto Mears added two more occupational feathers to his cap—town developer and newspaper publisher. His *Silver World,* printed in a tent he had erected near the shores of Lake San Cristobal, brought a rush to the Lake Fork of the Gunnison and resulted in the expansion of Lake City. Another source credits publication of the *Silver World,* not to Mears, but to Harry Woods and Clark Peyton. The year 1875, however, is agreed upon by both sources. Materials for the paper were hauled in from Saguache. Publication began with only three paid subscriptions.

In 1875, Mears negotiated a contract with the government to haul the mail to Ouray. At that period, the town was prospering; but it had no way of receiving mail, since it was eighty miles from the nearest point with no road in between. Otto Mears and Senator Jeffrey approached the Post Office Department in Washington and informed them that a mail system was vital for Ouray. The official said it was impossible to get anything into the town since there was so much snow.

In 1876 Mears was at last given the contract for carrying mail to Ouray, an experience that led to more extensive road building later on. He was informed by the Postmaster General's office that a heavy fine would be imposed on him for failure to deliver. To make sure of prompt service, he had the mail carried on a toboggan drawn by dogs, with a man alongside on Norwegian snowshoes. Delivery was to begin in the middle of the winter. The erstwhile "Pathfinder" built a series of relay stations some twenty miles apart and marked the trail with tall willow stakes. Mears' dogsled wrote another chapter in the story of San Juan transportation and was, for a time, Ouray's only contact with the outside world.

The loads grew huge as the citizens resorted to using this facility as a freight service. Mears had a weekly deadline to meet with the mail; and once, during a spring thaw, he personally hiked seventy-five miles through waist-deep slush to make his delivery. Not a single trip was missed until the snow became soft in the spring. Only a few people were in Ouray at that time. These individuals got their tobacco, coffee, sugar, and other supplies by mail, along with ladies' hats and dry goods. Occasionally, these things got mashed in the transportation process, because the mail carrier would sometimes sit on the toboggan. The citizens of Ouray complained to the Post Office Department. Washington decided that mail henceforth would be carried on snowshoes and that toboggans should not be used to bring in ladies' hats and other general supplies. In March of 1876 the snow got so bad that neither dogs nor shoes could be used and the carriers quit their jobs. Mears also had mail contracts in other portions of the San Juan country.

The so-called snowshoes used in the San Juans were actually broad skis, sometimes called Norwegian shoes. They were boards ten or twelve feet long, about four inches wide, and with their front ends turned up. A strap was placed in the middle for the foot. With a long pole carried across the chest with one end touching the snow, the shoes were slid forward alternately. Snowshoeing was not so bad with good snow, but it was fearful work when the snow was soft and stuck to the bottom of the shoes.

In 1879 the snow was eight feet deep on the Continental Divide the last of December; and the mail to Lake City was carried on sleds from November 25 to April 8, a period of almost four and a half months.

Additional toll roads were completed, providing access from the remote and isolated San Juan mining camps to the outside world. Following expulsion of the Utes, military troop movements over the Mears system of roads amassed a toll bill in excess of $100,000. In all, Mears built fifteen separate passes over the Rockies, including nearly five hundred miles of roads. He actually hacked out much of it with his own hands, as he drove a right-of-way up some of the steepest grades in North America. The one to Leadville paid back more than its own cost of construction in the first three months of operation. In 1878 he built a road across Marshall Pass to capitalize on the rush to Gunnison. After operating it profitably for a year and a half, he sold it to the Denver and Rio Grande Railroad for $40,000. His roads soon spiraled into nearly every town in the San Juans. By today's standards they would certainly be regarded as self-financed monuments to individual fiscal responsibility.

It had been said that although Mears had no training in engineering, he had a natural gift for building roads.

Collection of Robert L. Brown
The vacant main street at Eureka as it looked in August of 1964.

Collection of Fred and Jo Mazzulla
Eureka, still in the log-cabin phase, looking north toward Animas Forks. Absence of a cut along the slope dates this view as prior to construction of the Mears toll road.

Going to the top of a mountain range, he determined where he could best lay out his road. Otto built his railroads, as well as his highways, not from a swivel chair in a city office, but by actually being present on the scene of construction from the beginning until the job was finished. Although he employed capable engineers, Mears really bossed the jobs himself. Between 1867 and 1886 he constructed about twelve wagon roads in the Southwestern mountains.

In regard to the manner in which he received a franchise to construct a mountain toll road, Otto Mears once said:

All that was necessary to obtain this right to construct and operate a road was to acquire a charter from the county for five dollars, which gave me a franchise for twenty years. I didn't have to file a location map; a simple statement of the terminal towns being all that was required. Concerning toll charges, I had a lot of trouble. They were rated as to what the road had cost me, and also what I could get. From toll stations to cross over the mountains I charged two dollars for a single rig and for four horses it was four dollars. The highest toll was from Ouray to Silverton, a distance of twenty-six miles, for which I charged five dollars for a single span team with a fee of one dollar extra on each additional head of stock. From Ouray down the Uncompahgre Valley on the road which I bought, one dollar was charged for a single span team. The toll from the valley to Telluride was two dollars for a two-mule team.

During 1875, he also constructed a shelf road up the Animas Valley from Silverton to Mineral Point. It was profitable as a toll road; and he later constructed a narrow-gauge railroad, the Silverton Northern, over its right-of-way as far as Animas Forks. It extended over about fifteen miles. The commissioners of La Plata County appropriated one hundred and fifty dollars toward costs of the road between Silverton and Howardsville. An additional one hundred and fifty dollars was

Collection of Fred and Jo Mazzulla
Here is a section of the original Otto Mears toll road between Eureka and Animas Forks. The Silverton Northern Railroad was eventually constructed over this same general terrain. View is looking south.

Collection of Fred and Jo Mazzulla
An early but undated view showing a loaded burro packtrain at Silverton, ready to carry supplies to the surrounding mines.

put up for the grade between Howardsville and Eureka, along with a three-hundred-dollar appropriation for the steep incline that climbed into the mountains between Eureka and Animas Forks. Otto Mears personally arrived in Silverton on the fourteenth of July, 1875, to begin work on these roads.

The wagon road following the Animas Valley opened up a market for ores having a base of copper and iron. In its issue of September 23, 1882, the *Animas Forks Pioneer* carried the following advertisement for the Pioneer Stage Line which used this same road.

We have put on one of the finest buckboards ever on a road, between Animas Forks and Silverton, and are prepared to carry passengers safely and put them there on time. We drive a four-horse team with careful driver, and all passengers by this line will receive the best of attention.

Connections made with the Rocky Mountain Express, running from Animas Forks to Lake City, which makes prompt connection at the latter point for stages for Gunnison; at Silverton with the Denver & Rio Grande Railroad.

Almost always passable as far as Eureka, the road today can often be driven as far as the Forks. However, a Jeep or horse will be needed if you want to see the few remaining structures at Mineral Point.

Mears once said that he personally built all the way from Animas Forks to Lake City, a distance of about twenty-five miles. On August 10, 1877, a party arrived in Silverton from Lake City by stagecoach, being the first to make the trip by way of the Henson Creek Toll Road. The delegation of nine men was formally received at Johnson's Saloon by F. M. Snowden and was given the freedom of the city in celebration of being the first group that had crossed over Engineer Pass.

In 1877 the Lake Fork and Ouray Toll Road was built from a point on the Saguache-Lake City Road, near the

Courtesy Library, State Historical Society of Colorado
Animas Forks in the late 1880's. The Gold Prince Mill is visible at the extreme left.

Collection of Robert L. Brown
Roughly eighty years separate this picture from the one at the left. Notice that the Gold Prince foundations were still visible in July of 1960.

mouth of Indian Creek, through the Uncompahgre Indian Agency and the Uncompahgre Valley to Ouray. The length of this road was close to one hundred miles. The Mears tollgate was half a mile below Ouray.

In 1880 Mears constructed a twenty-seven-mile road from Dallas Divide to Telluride. By 1890 this was largely occupied by the Rio Grande Southern Railroad. During 1881, he hacked out an additional six miles of road from Vance Junction, six miles below Telluride, to Ames. That same year he built the ledge trail from Ouray up to Sneffels. He offered to sell it after there was trouble about the toll charge and finally the county of Ouray purchased it. He once said that he had it about a year before trading it to them in exchange for county bonds. There was some difficulty about the bonds being legal, and a trial followed. They were ultimately declared to have been legal.

Probably the best known of all the Mears thoroughfares was the monumental Million Dollar Highway—the present U.S. 550, which crosses Red Mountain between Silverton and Ouray. This incredible cliff-hanger, now paved, widened, and safe, is a fitting tribute to Otto Mears' ingenuity, stubbornness, and superb engineering skill.

The rich discovery at the Yankee Girl Mine on the sixteenth of August, 1882, made necessary a trail from Ouray up to Red Mountain. In association with Fred Walsen and others, Mears built twelve miles of road, about half of which was cut through the solid rock walls of Uncompahgre Canyon. During 1882 and 1883, this road was extended by twelve more miles from Red Mountain down to Silverton. This Ouray-Silverton road through the canyon and over Red Mountain Pass was perhaps Mears' most spectacular accomplishment and the one for which he is most noted. For many years it served as the road for the famous Circle Route Stage.

The Million Dollar Highway was originally located on

Collection of Claude Miner
A very early photograph of Red Mountain Town, looking north.
The Miner's Delight was a saloon.

Collection of Claude Miner
An enlarged copy of a business card for real estate and mining
properties at Red Mountain.

. R. CLARK.   F. H. MINER

Real Estate and Mining Agency,

CLARK & MINER.

Correspondence Solicited.   Information Furnished.

COMMISSIONS LOW.

RED MOUNTAIN, OURAY COUNTY, COLORADO.

a somewhat lower grade than the one it presently occupies. A matched pair of pictures, shown elsewhere in the book, illustrates this difference, at the point where it climbed up out of Ouray. Nearby, it originally crossed the Uncompahgre on a small bridge close to Box Canyon before it started the ascent up an extremely steep grade that was responsible for many accidents, particularly during the winter. In later years, the state relocated several sections, including some where the cut was a mere fifteen feet above the river, until it assumed today's familiar contours.

Particular difficulties were encountered at some places along the proposed grade. One of the worst was a section located about a half mile above Bear Creek Falls where a single fifty-foot section was blasted out at the startling cost of one thousand dollars per foot. Nearby, at the falls, was the familiar tollgate, long a landmark for those who used the road. At this point, Mears had a delicately balanced log, several feet long, to block the way until the fee had been collected.

During 1883 the nine miles of road between Silverton and Eureka were constructed over the previous rougher grade that had been completed in the early seventies. Late in 1896, four more miles of this road between Eureka and Animas Forks were also rebuilt. This connected with his older road from Animas Forks to Lake City, about twenty-five miles distant.

Packing and freighting with mules and oxen eventually proved inadequate for the growing activity and prosperity of the mining camps. There was a period of thirty to forty years when animal and railroad transportation overlapped in the mountainous San Juan country. Packing to and from the mines was almost eliminated by the innovation of the aerial tram and the motorized truck.

Although most accounts identify Otto Mears most frequently with his toll roads, many people feel that his crowning achievement was his narrow-gauge railroad

Courtesy Library, State Historical Society of Colorado   *Photo by S. G. White*
Guston, as it was photographed in 1891 by S. G. White, of Ouray. Otto Mears' Silverton tracks and engine Number 100 are shown in the foreground.

Collection of Robert L. Brown
Guston today. Note the same rock formations on either side of the cut. About half of the Yankee Girl shaft house still stands.

empire. A total of four lines was ultimately completed, and three of them used Silverton as their starting point. First to be built was the Silverton Railroad in 1888. Sometimes called the Rainbow Route, it followed the same general terrain as the Million Dollar Highway. Tortuously, it wound its way northward up the valley of Mineral Creek through Chattanooga before attempting a series of switchbacks to its early terminus at Red Mountain Town, elevation 11,235 feet.

The line was eventually extended farther down the northern slope with Ouray, only twenty-six miles from Silverton, as its objective. It actually reached only as far as Ironton, eight miles short of its goal. Steep canyons and hairpin turns precluded the possibility of any connection with Ouray from the south. The Silverton extended for a distance of sixteen miles, including the several switchbacks, between Silverton and Red Mountain and down by the way of Sheridan Pass to Ironton. The line was built with a 5 percent grade in places and had an average rise of two hundred and sixty-two feet per mile. It reached Red Mountain in September of 1889 and came into Ironton during November of that same year.

Total construction costs amounted to $725,000. At that time this was considered a tremendous sum for one man to raise. From the end of the line, Mears threw out switches or branches to all of the great mines of Red Mountain. Among these were auxiliary tracks that ran to the Vanderbilt, Yankee Girl, Guston, Silver Bell, and the Joker. Construction of this railroad made possible the shipment of low-grade ores from the Red Mountain district to smelters in Silverton or Durango. Passenger fare on the Red Mountain Railway was twenty cents for each mile with no reductions allowed on a round-trip ticket. Its abandoned grades are still visible from several vantage points along today's highway.

During the peak years, the railroad carried upwards

of twenty thousand tons of rich ore from the National Belle at Red Mountain, the Yankee Girl at Guston, and other rich mines that lined the tracks. Armed guards were sometimes hired to ride the cars down to the smelters at Durango. In winter the miners laid off work during heavy snows in order to shovel the tracks so that train service would not be interrupted.

In 1888 at the expiration of Mears' term as state representative, the General Assembly authorized the erection of a Colorado State Capitol Building. Mears was appointed as one of the commissioners to supervise its construction. This began a twenty-nine-year term of service which was made continuous by a succession of reappointments. Mears' political influence has been the subject of considerable speculation. One source said that he personally named and made sure of the election of Governor McIntyre. One day after his election, the governor got on the streetcar in Denver. When the conductor came to collect his fare the governor found that he had not a cent in his pocket. "I can't pay. I have no money with me." "Pay or get off," said the conductor. "But I am the governor," replied the official. "I can't help that," answered the conductor. "If you were Otto Mears himself, you would have to pay or get off."

Although many things have been written about Otto Mears, little was recorded about his wife. Mears was married in 1870 to Miss Mary Kampfshulte near Granite, Colorado, where she had come with her brother from Germany because of their health. He first met her on one of his trips to California Gulch, where he traded in cattle and produce. Living in the San Luis Valley, Mrs. Mears led a typical pioneer existence. She took her baby daughter and drove a pair of horses all the way from Saguache to the Uncompahgre Valley on one occasion. She was described as having been "A helpful and charitable person to all of her neighbors in need."

The Mears' home stood on the site of the present Saguache County Courthouse. Mr. and Mrs. Mears had two daughters: Laura, born in Saguache, who married Marshall Smith, and Cora, also born in Saguache, who married James Robertson Pitcher. The Mears family lived in Denver and Washington over a period of several years and finally went to live in Silverton in 1907. They bought a brick house and remodeled it, adding a conservatory and electric heat at a cost of five thousand dollars. When Mears was building roads, his wife often accompanied him, driving a frisky team of black horses. She once drove straight down a mountainside with one of the children tied to the seat beside her and logs tied onto the back of the buggy to prevent it from hitting the horses.

Since the combination of deep canyons and heavy snowfalls frequently combined to retard the advance of civilization, railroad transportation from October through May became an uncertain business at best. During the winter of 1883-84, the San Juan country was covered by a normal snowfall until the end of January. At that time, the snow began to fall heavily and the railroad track into Silverton was blocked from February 4 until April 17, a period of seventy-three days. It had snowed for twenty days without letup. February 3 was the last day the train got into Silverton until the next April. The whole country was deeply covered and slides were runnning frequently.

At Chattanooga the drifts were twelve feet high. It became so deep that people could no longer shovel a trail. They finally dug a tunnel under the snow to connect their houses and barns, in order to take care of the stock. The situation became desperate in March for the people of Silverton, Howardsville, and Chattanooga. The mines had closed and nearly all the men were in the towns. There were about fifteen hundred people in Silverton alone that winter. All fresh food was gone and there was practically nothing left but flour. Starvation seemed to be in sight for people and animals alike. There were

Collection of Randy and Morine Baisch
This Byers photograph looks east across the Ophir Loop. In the
meadow at top center was the town of Ophir. Ophir Pass crossed
the background peaks over the lowest saddle.

Collection of Robert L. Brown
Only the mountains still look the same at the site of the Ophir Loop

three carloads of food down the Animas Canyon at Needleton Station. The telegraph wire was down, but several workmen made the trip on snowshoes and repaired the line. Altogether, about twelve trips for supplies were made to Needleton, going down one day and back the next, until April. During this time, mail was taken all the way to Santa Fe and then packed on horses from Fort Wingate to Durango, or was carried from Ouray to Silverton on snowshoes. When the spring thaw came and the railroads were ready to begin hauling the ore, floodwaters came down and washed out their tracks.

The budding city of Durango, by virtue of the advantages of its location, soon became a great smelting center. All railroads and highways of every sort from the mines of La Plata, San Juan, Ouray, Telluride, and Rico led down the hill to Durango. Otto Mears' Rainbow Route from Ironton to Silverton commanded transportation of the products of Ouray and San Juan counties.

Detractors of the Silverton Railroad described it as "Eighteen miles of iron leading from nowhere to nowhere." Nevertheless, it profitably operated two trains every day at a cost to the passengers of twenty cents per mile. The cars were almost always packed.

The next Mears railroad was built in 1890-91. Still feeling a strong compulsion to extend railway facilities into Ouray, Mears built the Rio Grande Southern. It involved a distance of one hundred and sixty-two miles, extending between Ridgway and Durango around to the west of the range and thence north by way of Dolores, Rico, Lizard Head, Ophir, and Telluride. From that side, access to Ouray was easy.

In connected with the Denver and Rio Grande at both ends. Mr. Mears established the town of Ridgway as a terminus for his railroad. During the panic of 1893, he lost control of this line and much of his fortune as well.

In 1889 he began construction on the Silverton Northern. He first built five miles of track up to Howardsville,

Collection of Robert L. Brown

Our Jeep sitting on top of Cinnamon Pass, 13,009 feet above sea
level.

Collection of Robert L. Brown

View looking to the south up Swamp Canyon with 13,767-foot, U.S.
Grant Peak at the left and an unnamed 13,400-foot summit at the
right.

where the great mines of Arastra and Cunningham Gulches could be served. It provided front-porch service for many of the most productive San Juan mines located along its right-of-way. One reason that has been advanced for construction of this road was the fact that Mears had speculated financially in a number of these rich properties along the Animas.

In 1894 he added an additional four miles, extending the line into Eureka. In 1903 he built another four miles on up the steep valley to Animas Forks over a 7 percent grade. During construction of the line up the Animas Canyon, Otto Mears once tried his hand at bossing a crew of Navajo laborers. Not being able to talk to them, he made signs with his hands. It was quite a show. The angrier Mears got, the faster he waved his hands and arms around. It was very funny to the Indians and they made the same motions back at him. He gave up trying to boss the job and finally left for his home. In four months, the four miles of track from Eureka to Animas Forks was completed.

One of the early engineers once said that a car of coal and one empty car was all that one engine could pull from Eureka up to the Forks. They often, however, handled more than three loads on the way down after making sure that their brakes were functioning. As they began the steep ride down the canyon, a brakeman rode the cars and clubbed each as soon as they got rolling. If the rails were wet or rusty, he would let them down on sand, holding to a slower speed. It was always a relief when they were stopped safely at Eureka.

Mears had also dreamed of extending the tracks beyond Animas Forks, across Cinnamon Pass to Lake City. Anyone familiar with the approaches to Cinnamon at 13,009 feet will understand at once the frustrations he must have felt. Rising sheer behind Animas Forks, the mountains presented a formidable barrier to anything other than burro trains and wagons. Nevertheless, when he planned to extend his railroad beyond the Forks over the pass toward Lake City, the surveyors went to work. They found that the snow was so deep in many places their stakes could not be driven, so the turning points were cut in the crusted snow with a hatchet. It took only a week, since they went just to the top of the pass and there the project was abandoned.

The Silverton Northern continued to operate well into the twentieth century. In 1906 Mears signed a contract for hauling ore on a year-round basis from Animas Forks to the smelters in Silverton. The other parties to the agreement were the operators of the great Gold Prince Mill, a tremendous structure that stretched out across several layers or steps at the edge of the canyon on the southeastern side of the town. Today, only its crumbling foundations remain and weeds cover the spur line built to its entrance. A unique series of snowsheds were projected, and a few were actually built in the high country between Eureka and the Forks. The idea was to afford all-weather protection, even during severe storms so that year-round railroad service could be maintained. In this deep canyon, where history records some of the most dramatic of snowslides, the initial sheds were destroyed; any further extension of the system was forgotten, and the contract was not renewed. Old records tell of snow-packs that approached a depth of twenty-five feet at Animas Forks, not too surprising when one considers its 11,200-foot elevation.

Located on Bonita Mountain at the head of Cement Creek was the bustling community of Gladstone, seven and a half miles up the valley from Silverton. It became the terminus, in July of 1899, of Mears' last railroad venture. Originally planned by Cyrus W. Davis as an ore carrier for his valuable Gold King properties, the Silverton, Gladstone, and Northerly came into being.

The Gold King holdings were happily named for a realm of gold worthy of a crown. The Gold King lode was first discovered in 1887 by Olaf Nelson, a miner employed at the Sampson. This property was then being developed on the vein. Several hundred feet from the entrance, a stronger vein crossed at an acute angle. When this vein was encountered, the superintendent of the Sampson followed the deflection, believing it to be the original vein. Nelson took a different view of the situation. After severing his connection with the Sampson, he proceeded to locate the Gold King at a point where he was convinced it would strike the extension of the cross vein. Nelson had no capital to develop the property but managed to sink a shaft to a depth of fifty feet and to run a fifty-foot drift, from which he shipped several cars of rich ore before he died in 1890.

By 1893 W. Z. Kinney, who at that time was managing the Harrison Mine, had induced Cyrus W. Davis, of Waterville, Maine, and Henry M. Soule of Boston to purchase the Gold King claim for fifteen thousand dollars. At that time, only the fifty-foot shaft had been developed. This was the nucleus of the later magnificent Gold King property, which was enlarged into a gigantic proposition through the energy and sound mining judgment of Mr. Kinney. Davis, a prominent capitalist of Maine, had been a candidate for governor of that state on the Democratic ticket in 1904 and 1906. Since Maine has only rarely looked with favor upon the office-seeking propensities of those persons who choose to run as Democrats, one can only speculate upon the audacity and colossal optimism of the man. He was defeated after two remarkable campaigns. Later, he and Soule became interested in the Harrison Mine. It was at this time that Kinney was engaged by them as superintendent of their property. After two years of work, they gave up all efforts to develop it and instructed Kinney to try to find something that promised greater success. He finally selected the Gold King. Upon his advice, the property was purchased in 1894.

Collection of Mrs. Bertha Neal
Chief mainstay of Gladstone's economic life was the huge Gold King Mill. Tracks of Silverton, Gladstone and Northerly are in the foreground.

Collection of Robert L. Brown
The abandoned site of the Gold King in 1962

A crosscut tunnel was started during 1896 and at a depth of four hundred and seventy-eight feet the great ore body was tapped, from which the Gold King ultimately became a paying mine. The ground above the tunnel level was stoped out nearly to the surface and produced splendid results. The original Sampson Mine, after fine production records, was finally purchased by the Gold King. The Sampson still holds the record for a single shipment of gold. It showed an assay value of $180,000 to the ton.

There are three principal veins in the Gold King group —the Gold King, or Sampson; the Davis; and an unnamed flat or blanket vein. All of these were developed through the same system of working throughout six levels, forming a veritable labyrinth of golden avenues of immense wealth. The Gold King Mill at Gladstone was one of the finest in the country. It had a daily capacity of about four hundred tons and turned out fifty to sixty tons of concentrates carrying good values in gold, silver, and copper. Forty men were regularly employed there. The mill was four hundred and sixty feet long and the total floor space was about twenty-five thousand square feet. The mill and equipment cost $350,000. The original mill had twenty stamps. It was later increased to forty and then to eighty. At Gladstone the buildings of the Gold King Company alone made a veritable town, and everything was fairly humming with life and energy.

The Gold King Consolidated Mines Company was a State of Maine corporation, organized in July, 1900, with a capitalization of six million dollars to absorb the interests of the Gold King Mining and Milling Company, the American Mining and Tunnel Company, the Anglo Saxon Mining and Milling Company, and the Rocky Mountain Coal Company. The Silverton, Gladstone, and Northerly Railroad, although a separate corporation, was owned by the same people and was built to effect railway con-

Collection of Mrs. Bertha Neal
Gladstone in the late eighties showing the Bowman General Store
at extreme left. Large structure up the street was the assay office,
while the dance hall was beyond it.

Collection of Robert L. Brown
Gladstone's main street now, covered with pipes for the projected
American Tunnel. Entrance to Poughkeepsie Gulch is straight up
the valley.

nections between Silverton and the Consolidated companies at Gladstone. The company also owned about
forty claims of coal land at Durango.

The Mogul Mining Company at Gladstone was a peculiar one in many ways. One of these peculiarities was
its shrinking from publicity. A group of capitalists from
Ohio quietly gathered up a group of claims in Ross Basin,
which had been located and partially developed by Colonel
F. M. Snowden, Silverton's first citizen and probably its
oldest mine promoter. They added to their claims by
purchase and location until the group, known as The
Mogul Holdings, embraced a total of fifteen properties.
For six years the work of development progressed. Not a
dollar's worth of stock was ever sold, the owners being
satisfied with their holdings and sanguine as to what they
would have when the ore bodies were opened up and developed. All the knowledge that the public ever gained
at that time had been from rumors.

Mr. and Mrs. Grebbles kept a large rooming house at
Gladstone. When Mrs. Bertha Neal was sent by the
county to teach at their one-room school, she boarded
with the Grebbles family for three years. Most of the
other structures in town were the small four-room
houses, owned by the company. In the evening, people
went from house to house playing such card games as
Five Hundred, Euchre, and High Five.

In 1899 Mears purchased the Silverton, Gladstone, and
Northerly and added it to his railroad empire. During
the early times, two trains each day ran up the tracks
along Cement Creek to Gladstone. But as the economic
sun began to wane in the San Juan skies, service declined
to three times a week. All operations were terminated in
1915. During the summer of 1962, only three of Gladstone's original buildings were still standing. These are
known to be original, since they can be positively identified by comparison with early photographs of the town.
C. A. Bowman, founder of Denver's Bowman Biscuit

Collection of Mrs. Bertha Neal
The principal street of Gladstone about 1889, with the Gold King Mill at the right.

Collection of Robert L. Brown
The former location of Gladstone and the Gold King. Very little of the town remains at present.

Company, had a livery stable and operated a commissary at the Gold King properties in Gladstone.

In 1917 Mears moved to Pasadena, California, where he lived until his death at the age of ninety in 1931. There are three versions of what happened next. One story has his remains being interred at Pasadena. The second version involves his request that he be cremated and the ashes scattered over the San Juans he knew and loved so well. In a manner of speaking, we could say that he is still there—if the second story is true. The third version says that Mears died in Pasadena, and a memorial service was held at Silverton during August of that year. It was conducted in the Episcopal Church with Bishop Ingley officiating. At a later time, the ashes of both Mr. and Mrs. Mears, according to their wishes expressed some years before, were scattered on Engineer Mountain above Animas Forks. And so, fittingly, their remains entered into the soil of the land where they had lived and loved and labored.

Among the many unusual innovations originated by Otto Mears was his unique approach to the issuance of passes to ride on his various railroad enterprises. Most such passes used elsewhere were of cardboard or paper. Those given to important personages by Mears were of silver and gold, although he issued some made from buckskin in 1888. Some were shaped like watch fobs, while those issued in 1892 were embellished with a delicate gold and silver filigree. Each kind was good only for the one year, except the filigrees which were lifetime passes. The Rasmus Hanson pass, pictured elsewhere in this book, is of the gold-fob type and carries the 1890 date. It is set with a diamond in one side, and a ruby in the other, and reposes in the collection of Fred and Jo Mazzulla, of Denver, who now have the largest collection of Mears' passes extant.

The number of these passes issued is a subject of considerable debate among railroad fans. The system by which they were numbered is likewise a mystery, leading one to believe that there probably was no system at all. An invoice shown to the author during research may shed some light on the cost of the passes. The manufacturer was S. Spitz, manufacturer of Mexican filigree jewelry in Santa Fe. The date was June 18, 1892. There were 527 silver filigree passes made at a cost of $4.00 each, and three gold filigrees were billed at $46.00 or $15.33 1/3 each. These items now command a premium price from collectors, when they can be found.

In a manner of speaking, Otto Mears erected his own monuments in the highways and railroads he constructed. Among the landmarks by which a grateful state remembered this unusual man were Mears Junction, an extinct town called Otto near Poncha Pass, and a mountain named Mears Peak in the Telluride country. The contributions and influence of this diminutive immigrant will long be remembered in southwestern Colorado. The many high points of his long and useful life were inextricably tied up with the story of transportation in the San Juan country.

✺ 8 ✺

From Lake City to Silverton

THE FOUNDING OF LAKE CITY was partially the result of accidental civic jealously between this latter town and Saguache. In 1874 the businessmen of Saguache sought to capture the expanding trade of the San Juan camps which had thus far allowed Del Norte to profit handsomely. As a first step, they formed a company and employed the noted road builders, Enos Hotchkiss and Otto Mears, to knock out a toll road from Saguache to the Animas Valley. By the end of August, 1875, they had completed a generous portion of the projected 130 miles, and Hotchkiss found himself in the picturesque and attractive valley formed by the Lake Fork of the Gunnison River. Following the river into the mountains, his experienced eye detected the presence of several pieces of valuable float rock. Tracing out the vein, he staked a claim. When the lode was opened, it proved to be a very rich one and the news of its discovery started a rush to the valley. Ore from the mine was conveyed by mules to Del Norte, then shipped to Pueblo and New York for refinement.

The town that grew up was named Lake City, allegedly because of the multiplicity of beautiful lakes in the vicinity, thus displaying a sparkling burst of originality.

The Crooke Smelter was built at Lake City in August of 1875 or 1876—the accounts vary. Thereafter, the ore did not need to be shipped out of the district. The smel-

Collection of Fred and Jo Mazzulla
Lake City in 1871, as photographed by the noted pioneer lensman,
William H. Jackson.

Collection of Robert L. Brown
Lake City now. Note how a lush growth of trees nearly obscures
the town.

ter was built about a mile up the Lake Fork, and a small
suburb grew up around it. There was a fifteen-stamp
mill with crushers, steel-faced pulverizer rollers and
twelve Kron concentrators. Later, chlorination works
and a few other smelters were built. For power, coal and
coke were hauled over from Crested Butte by wagon.

Lake City was situated on the Saguache and San Juan
Toll Road, built from the San Luis Valley to the forks of
the Animas River. It was also the terminus of the Antelope Springs and Lake City Toll Road, thus giving it two
good outlets to the east and one wagon road to the mines
beyond the range. Barlow and Sanderson's overland line
of stagecoaches made triweekly trips from Canon City to
Lake City, carrying mail and passengers so that, for a
time, Lake City was the primary distributing point for the
San Juan mines. It had five general stores, two bakeries,
two blacksmith shops, two sawmills, three restaurants,
one livery stable, a millinery store, one shoe shop, a
weekly newspaper—the *Silver World*—two meat markets, and five saloons. Hotels and banks were also
founded, along with the inevitable billiard rooms and
dance halls. Lake City also had a good public school.
Several lawyers awaited the usual troubles that attended
mining camps; but there was not a single physician, a
fact that was regarded as a sufficient comment upon the
healthfulness of the place.

In 1876 there were no church buildings in Lake City.
The Reverend George M. Darley became the first minister. He would preach wherever he could find a place
and a group of miners. Darley was well liked and seemed
to understand the people. The oldest Presbyterian church
on the western slope is still standing at Lake City.

A. E. Reynolds, who developed the Revenue properties
at Sneffels, once threatened to make grass grow in the
streets of Lake City. Being one of the chief operators,
Reynolds closed down all of his equipment in a pique

when the county refused to help him build a road to a mining property near Rose's Cabin.

Lake City was, and is, nestled in a broad amphitheatre created by the adjacent mountains, with wide, tree-shaded streets that stretched far up both the Lake Fork and Henson Creek. In 1875 the taxable property in Hinsdale County was assessed at $18,349.50. Their brick school alone cost $30,000, and a $20,000 waterworks was completed in 1890 to refine water taken from the Lake Fork about a mile above town. The Pitkin Guard was organized and made its headquarters in a new Armory Hall. The Guard proved to be an effective force in quelling a number of Indian threats in southwestern Colorado.

True to the typical pattern of life in early mining camps, a disastrous fire destroyed the largest part of Lake City's business district in November of 1879. Since the nearby mines continued to spew forth their riches, the town rebuilt with brick and many of the present masonry structures of Lake City date from that time.

The population of Lake City grew to a peak of 2,500 in 1877 before declining, partly due to a poor decision that raised costs by shipping crude ores out of the district again. Later discoveries across the range were closer to transportation routes and dominated the market.

Lake City was the only town of consequence in Hinsdale County, the other settlements being small camps located along the stage roads up Cinnamon or Engineer passes. Sometimes these were merely clusters of cabins around a single mine, but several grew up to become incorporated as towns in their own right. Hinsdale County had its share of these small settlements.

About six miles up Henson Creek, on the approach to Engineer Pass, was the town called Henson. It was, in many ways, hardly deserving of the "town" classification and to so call it involves begging the term almost to the point of incredulity. Its sole economic base was the Ute-

Ulay Mine and Mill, which had the capacity to reduce sixty tons of ore daily.

A little beyond Henson, on the same stream, was Capitol City, another small mining camp built around the Lee Mining and Smelting Company in Capitol Park. Originally named Galena City, the town grew into a fair-sized community. Galena City was laid out at the junction of the north and south forks of Henson Creek. The site was surrounded by a number of rich mines which carried names like the Ocean Wave, Big Casino, J. J. Crooke, and Joaquin. The lodes carried a high percent of galena ore. George Green erected a smelting works there which consisted of two large furnaces. One was a blast type and the other was reverberatory, capable of working fifty tons of ore per day.

With the town's expansion there occurred an inflation in the dreams and ambitions of a resident named George S. Lee. As owner of the town's only sawmill and smelter, Lee assumed the role of first citizen and soon began to entertain fanciful notions about Galena City, rather than Denver, as Colorado's logical capital. He chose to name it Capitol City, using the incorrect spelling which denotes the capitol edifice in Washington, a structure rather than a city.

Although the name change was accomplished, the Lee dream, of course, was never realized. However, such small obstacles failed to deter George Lee, who had bricks hauled up from Pueblo at a cost of a dollar each, and built a handsome two-story home which has since become known as the "Governor's Mansion." It had a ballroom, orchestra pit, fine guest rooms, and most of the improvements of the day. The decline of the state's silver fortunes spelled the end of the Lee dream and the "City" along with it.

Today, the great house is a mere roofless shell, its outer wings are gone, and the willows grow high in its

Collection of Robert L. Brown
Remains of upper end of Capitol City, located west of the mansion
in Capitol Park.

Collection of Robert L. Brown
The "Governor's Mansion," George Lee's dream, at Capitol City

front yard. Farther up the road are a few other assorted buildings that remain from the earlier day.

An even smaller outpost of civilization was constructed in 1874 by Corydon Rose at a point some distance beyond Capitol City. Called Rose's Cabin, the settlement consisted of the cabin itself, which was a combination stagecoach stop, bar, and office, a stable for livestock, and a hotel across the street for overnight guest accommodations.

Elevation of the cabin, which became a landmark, was 10,850 feet. Just below it were the buildings of the Bonanza Mines. Often the traveler would see long lines of pack mules along the road up Henson Creek, on their way across the transmontane route to Silverton, Rico, and Ouray. Rose's Cabin, with its large stable, was a logical rest stop before crossing the range.

Of the three original structures, only the sixty-mule capacity stable still stands today. Beside it, the original cabin is down and fast approaching the status of a rubble pile. Across the street, one may see the concrete foundation and a part of the old hotel fireplace. Part way up the meadow is Corydon Rose's old safe, a huge one by any comparison.

A familiar figure to the tired traveler, Rose personally met the stagecoaches in most instances and took a great interest in the passengers' comfort. There was some mining done nearby and Rose's Cabin functioned as the community center for these outlying districts.

Not far above the cabin is timberline, where the old trail quickly becomes a rough, narrow, Jeep road. It winds its way across mountains over Engineer Pass to expose the fortunate traveler, then or now, to some of the wildest and most spectacular mountain scenery to be found anywhere. From the higher summits, the view is still magnificent. Below are acres of vast, billowy, land seas, covered with dense woods and sculptured by deep ravines. Here and there are exquisite emerald dells,

Collection of Robert L. Brown
Corydon Rose's Cabin in 1961. The old stable, out of the picture, still stands.

ROSE'S OLD CABIN.

Collection of Fred and Jo Mazzulla
An etching made from an 1890 photograph of Rose's Cabin. The original is in the Colorado State Historical Society collection.

swept by immense shadows of all shades from bright green to solid black. Beyond is a crescent of mountains, some of which are bald and barren while others display broad fields or deep furrows of snow.

To the west, the massive Uncompahgre Range dominates the skyline. The sharp-domed pinnacle is Mount Sneffels. Directly south, or to its left, is Potosi Peak, a flat-topped giant with a tremendous sliver of vertical rock standing on its southern slope. In the same group is the descriptively named Teakettle Peak. A quarter turn to the north brings an equally spectacular range into view. Dominating this section is the truncated Uncompahgre Peak, highest of all the San Juans. Close by, the pointed summits of Matterhorn and Wetterhorn pierce the intensely blue sky. Two other descriptively named mountains may be seen in this group. The twin upthrust ears of Wild Horse Peak, with its rounded summits— stand out in marked contrast to the sharply contoured formation called Cockscomb. From the top, this great panorama more closely approximates a calendar picture of the Swiss Alps than the usual gradual contours of the Rockies that we have come to expect. Here, indeed, is the "Switzerland of America."

Charles A. Mendenhall, as a boy of sixteen years of age, carried the mail over Engineer Pass from Rose's Cabin to Animas Forks. He had endured almost every kind of experience with snowslides that it was possible to have without being buried by one. On the Henson Creek Road, in the short space of the fifteen miles between Lake City and Rose's Cabin, there are twenty-three known snowslide areas which regularly run and cross the road.

In January of 1881 the Frank Hough Mine on Engineer Mountain was started, and late that same year they shipped sixty tons of high-grade copper-silver ore which had an average value of $125 to the ton. The Frank Hough Mine was located well above timberline on American Flats above Ouray. In the early days many people made the trip up on foot, but in later years only a few have attempted it. American Flats was regarded at that time as the largest above-timberline area in the United States. Around the mine there grew up a collection of buildings that eventually became known as Engineer City. With an altitude that ranges between twelve thousand and thirteen thousand feet, this was one of the highest communities in the civilized world. Needless to say, the "City" was always deserted in winter.

The Lake road to Cinnamon Pass may be approached by another trail that leads out of Lake City in the same direction as the one up Henson Creek, except that it follows the next valley. Lake San Cristobal was created when a mud slide came down into the valley during prehistoric times and formed a natural dam across the Lake Fork of the Gunnison.

The lodes along the Lake Fork were admirably located for economical working. The shafts, in most cases, were cut near the base of the mountain, where good wagon roads could be cheaply built. The Lake Fork mines were also strategically situated near the valley, cutting the mountains at right angles so that tunnels could be driven in on them. In this way expensive shafts and crosscut tunnels were unnecessary. On the west side of the stream and two miles from Lake City was the Gold Coin Lode, worked by one of the Rand steam drills. On the opposite side of the river from the Hotchkiss were the Belle of the West and the Belle of the East, both on the same vein.

Wager Gulch leaves the Cinnamon Pass approach a few miles beyond the lake, and its narrow rocky trail winds off into the high country to the south and eventually reaches the old town of Carson. The road was never a good one and today the bridge is washed out, willows have grown across it, and there are bogs and rock outcroppings along its right-of-way. The actual length of the road to Carson is only four miles. Its condition is largely responsible for the well preserved state of the town.

There were really two Carsons. The town at the head of Wager Gulch was started in 1896 when a gold strike was uncovered following the silver crash of 1893. The older original Carson, which was a silver camp, is another two miles up the trail, perched on the top of the divide above timberline. Accounts vary concerning its founder. One account gives him the name of J. E. Carson, while others call him "Chris." The Bonanza King Mine was staked out in 1881, and its huge yellow dump can still be seen surrounded by the remaining cabins that were the town. Several of these have badly buckled roofs, probably due to the crushing weight of heavy winter snows at this altitude. The complete roof, all in one unit, was moved intact off the supporting walls of one cabin. Carson was one of the highest, if not the highest, of the San Juan towns. Its mines were rich but geography doomed it to oblivion. Except for its location, Carson would have become a big town. Severe winters precluded the term of its occupancy to a "summers only" basis.

Access was always the problem. Considerable time elapsed between the founding of the town and completion of the difficult wagon road that came up Wager Gulch. Another road, hardly more than a path, wound up along Lost Trail Creek from the Creede side. Access is still a problem today. The road to the lower town, the later gold camp, may be driven in a Jeep from mid-June until the first snows render its impassable. Today's visitor must return by the same road.

A few miles beyond the mouth of Wager Gulch was the town of Sherman, currently so overgrown with willows that many who search there are unable to locate it. Like so many other San Juan towns, Sherman, too, was doomed to oblivion by its own geography. In this case snow was not the sole offender, since Sherman was at a

Collection of Fred and Jo Mazzulla *Photo by H. H. Buckwalter*
H. H. Buckwalter took this picture of Sherman in 1898. Second cabin from right is still there. The Black Wonder Mill is visible in the background.

Collection of Robert L. Brown
Sherman and Shadow Mountain in 1961

relatively low altitude. The problem was that the town was constructed at the point where Cottonwood Creek flows into the Lake Fork of the Gunnison River. This town was surrounded on three sides by high mountains, and the spring runoff, an almost annual flood, quite regularly inundated the town. Except for the riches that poured forth from the vitals of the Black Wonder Mine, it is doubtful that people would have returned year after year to rebuild after the waters had subsided. Down in the town itself stood the huge sloping-roofed structure that was the Black Wonder Mill, almost the sole economic base of the community.

Following the crash of 1893, mortician of many ailing mining camps, little encouragement was needed to induce the population to evacuate and Sherman has been a ghost town ever since. The road up Cottonwood Creek, from its point of departure off the Cinnamon Pass road, was the town's main street. Walking up the trail for a mile or so, one is impressed not only with the phenomenal willow growth but also with the abundance of smooth medium-sized stones, the unmistakable hallmark of floods. Here and there among the undergrowth are a number of well-washed roofless cabins that were once a part of Sherman's main street.

Above Sherman the road becomes a steeper ledge trail for several miles, until it enters a high narrow valley that was called Burrows Park. Here was the site of another small camp, founded in 1874, that stretched out for some distance along the road. A number of yellowing dumps indicate the sites of the several mines that provided an excuse for the town's existence.

Burrows Park had some very fine looking lodes. Ores were shipped from the Napoleon III assaying as high as $3,600. The Del Norte had a vein four to six feet wide with a large percentage of copper and iron pyrites. Two cabins adjacent to a U.S. Forest Service sign mark the location for present-day purposes. Burrows Park became

Collection of Robert L. Brown
Periodic floods have erased all traces of the Black Wonder

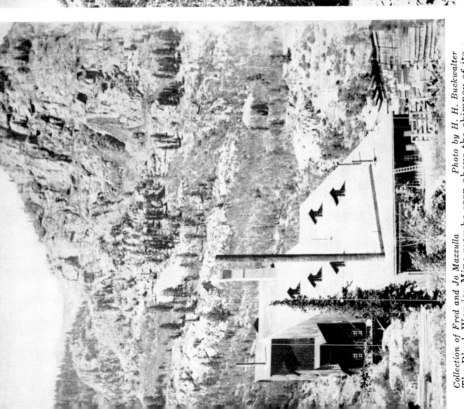

Collection of Fred and Jo Mazzulla   Photo by H. H. Buckwalter
The Black Wonder Mine may be seen above the chimney of its
mill at Sherman. H. H. Buckwalter photograph.

the nucleus of a number of small camps in the vicinity, notably Tellurium and Argentum.

The Park District, so called, was situated here on the headwaters of the Lake Fork of the Gunnison about twenty-two miles west from Lake City. The old town of Tellurium grew up as the center of its early activities. The residents of Tellurium often boasted that they were not dependent on Lake City for their supplies and would deal with them only when the merchants of that place traded fairly. When the Antelope Springs Toll Road was completed, it intersected with the Lake Fork road three miles above Lake City. The citizens of the Park District then became even more independent.

Some accounts say that as Burrows Park grew, it encompassed both Tellurium and Argentum. In any event, their exact locations remain nebulous.

A short distance beyond the park was the community of Whitecross, named for a formation of white quartz shaped like the letter "X" that may be seen above the town to your left as you go up the pass. All of the town's roofless buildings are on the right side of the road. There was once a hotel and a small population lived here until winter snows set in. Many men were employed at the huge Tobasco Mill, located on the hillside a short distance above the town.

The Tobasco Mine and Mill were financed by the Tobasco Meat Sauce Company. A crooked assayer was once employed there, and during his tenure false reports of the value of the ores were given. Such reports were profitable for him, but costly to the stockholders. Except for the cabins around the Tobasco, Whitecross was the last outpost of civilization before crossing 13,009-foot Cinnamon Pass.

A short distance to the northwest was the little known and infrequently mentioned Denver Pass, altitude 12,536 feet. It crossed the range in between Cinnamon and Engineer passes and ran somewhat parallel with them, in-

Collection of Robert L. Brown
Two of the remaining cabins at Burrows Park. View is looking west along the road to Cinnamon Pass.

Collection of Robert L. Brown
Ruins of the Tobasco Mill above Whitecross on the eastern slope of Cinnamon Pass.

tersecting with the road down below on the western side for access to Ouray.

Nearby was another trail that topped the range north of Engineer Pass at 12,250 feet. This was the less popular Yvonne Pass which went around Engineer Mountain to the left, between it and Dolly Varden Mountain. Neither it nor Denver Pass should be attempted by anyone other than hikers.

There are stories about another town named Sterling that once existed above timberline, near the top. No traces of it remain, however, and it probably was so crippled by its elevation that it failed to advance beyond the status of a tent city.

During 1874, far down the valley in Baker's Park, the town of Silverton was born to become the center of a humming network of camps like Middleton, Howardsville, and Animas Forks. The Greene Smelter was erected there in 1874 when Silverton became the county seat. Later there would be others built at this desirable spot, including the prominent Tom Walsh Smelter near the mouth of Cement Creek. Silverton was laid out and incorporated by Dempsey Reese, Thomas Blair, William Mulholland, and F. M. Snowden who, incidentally, built the first cabin in the town.

Silverton's first hotel was opened that same year by Isaac Grant. The first school in Silverton was held on the lower floor of the Foreman House, on the east side of Reese Street between Fourteenth and Fifteenth. The teacher was Mr. William Munroe who was also the first county surveyor. Later, a log school building was erected in the block where the present school now stands. This was replaced two or three years later by a two-story, four-room frame building on the same ground, which, after many years, gave way to the substantial brick edifice now in use.

It was no unusual sight to see from one hundred to one hundred and fifty animals out for grazing on the slopes

of the surrounding hills. During the summer, sleeping
quarters for the human element were usually all taken
by sundown of each day. For several years Silverton
was the end of the mail route in winter, except such mail
and supplies as were packed over the hill by men on skis.

At the time of F. V. Hayden's visit to the San Juans in
August and September of 1874, he reported that comparatively little mining development had been done. A
greater portion of the miners' time and energy was devoted to prospecting, and few of them had developed their
lodes to any extent.

During the Hayden Survey, the town of Silverton was
reported to have contained about a dozen houses, situated
near the center of the level area on the south side of Cement Creek at the point where it flows into the Animas
from the west. The isolation of Baker's Park can best
be realized by a description of the passes leading out of
it. The great canyon below it was such that travel
through it at that time was a matter of great difficulty.
Only a few miners passed up from the plains on the
south into Baker's Park by that route. Most persons
from the south traveled over the slopes of Sultan Mountain on the southeast side. At the divide this trail had
an elevation of 10,460 feet. This route was the roughest
and most dangerous of any leading into the park and
even in the best summer weather it was considered unsafe for pack or riding animals. Another crossing was
the one on the southwest side of Sultan which had an
elevation of 11,570 feet and though not as dangerous as
the preceding one, it was very disagreeable with many
bogs, much fallen timber, and numerous rock slides along
the way. Bear Creek Pass led from the head of Bear
Creek to the start of the San Miguel. On the west side
of the mountains its elevation was 12,600 feet. On the
east a long stretch of fallen timber, in a bog through
which the trail passed, made travel very difficult. On the
west there was a great rock slide over which the trail

led. Two passes were cut over to the head of the Uncompahgre River, but since Box Canyon bars all egress they require no description here. Another pass goes out from the head of the Animas River at an elevation of 12,540 feet. Still another extends from Cunningham Gulch to the Rio Grande over an elevation something above 12,000 feet, the present Stony Pass Jeep road.

About this time Howardsville was likewise a busy place, boasting of no less than four saloons and the first brewery in the county. It was operated by Charlie Fisher, who later built and operated the brewery at the lower end of Silverton. While it was still a part of La Plata County, in the early days, Howardsville was the county seat and chief center of population.

The town was named for Lieutenant Howard, a member of the Baker expedition. It also was the location of the first post office, the first assay office, and the first public blacksmith shop. It remained the county seat until the designation was moved, without authorization, to Silverton in 1875. Despite the inclemencies of the weather, Henry Gill and Captain G. S. Flagler opened a general store and a saloon at Howardsville on January 1, 1875.

Howardsville was a happy place as described by Mrs. Bertha Neal, a very gracious lady who once taught school there. Saturday night dances were held in the boardinghouse. The waltz and schottish were the favorite rhythms of the time. Tables were pushed back against the walls as a fiddler, who came up from Silverton, began to play. Because of the shortage of women, so common a lament in pioneer societies, no girl was supposed to dance twice with the same man. Since that great American institution, the baby-sitter, had not yet appeared, small infants were parked in the back room where they are said to have slept through the whole thing. Dances were sometimes held in the schoolhouse, since the desks there were never fastened down and could be moved to provide a clear floor. More often than not the desks were put outside.

Late refreshments were served and finally, in the wee hours, the fiddler would be returned to Silverton via a moonlight sleigh ride over snow-encrusted roads.

Incidentally, a teacher at Howardsville was expected to instruct a total of twenty-six classes each day with all grades, first through ninth, in the same room at the same time. This was the town that became, for a time, the terminus of the newly constructed pass from Saguache.

Most San Juan banks charged for their services. One day Emil B. Fischer came into the Silverton Bank to buy a small draft. A teller made it out, said there would be no charge, and handed it to Fischer. The customer was so nonplussed by this generosity that he actually dropped dead on the spot. This story sounds very much like one of the myriad fantastic tales that someone has heard from "Gran'pa," who had got it straight from some alleged eyewitness; and, as historians and researchers know only too well, "Gran'pa" in his old age was often a confirmed liar.

In the spring Mrs. W. H. Nichols, one of Silverton's earliest settlers, gave birth to the first boy baby to be born in the San Juans. The first girl was born near the summit of the range, at the head of Stony Gulch, under a fir tree in a snowbank. The date was June 5, 1876, and the mother was Mrs. George Webb. Civilization was on the way. The town of Silverton presented the "snow-line baby" with a city lot.

The first mine worked to any extent was the previously mentioned Little Giant, the gold mine located in Arastra Gulch, three miles above Baker's Park. The gold was washed out by various other methods until the Little Giant was discovered. The lode was a gold-bearing vein situated on the northeast side of Arastra Gulch with a course of about forty degrees. This lode had an eight-inch pay vein of quartz. Twenty-seven tons of this ore produced $150 per ton, or over $4,000 in gold. A mill was built one thousand feet below the mine and the ore was brought there with a wire tramway. It was an amalgamating installation, consisting of a 115-horsepower engine, Dodge crusher, and ball pulverizer.

During that summer and fall many more prospectors and miners entered the park. As additional rich strikes were made, the region came in for a great deal of attention from the outside world. Investments by Eastern capitalists suddenly became more common.

Below Silverton on Sultan Mountain were the Empire and Jennie Parker, operated by Melville and Summerville. Traveling up the canyon of the Animas River, the original road followed the right bank. A short distance above Silverton was the North Star Mill, where John J. Crooke used the old Augustin process, roasting silver ore with salt and leaching the resulting chloride with hot water, finally precipitating the silver on copper. Further up the hill was the Stoiber residence, "Waldheim," a thirty-room house with all modern appointments, built by the former owners of the Silver Lake Mine.

Edward G. Stoiber did more for the development of mining around Silverton than almost any other man, and he did it under the most adverse conditions. His mine was above timberline, thousands of feet above the town, and accessible for years only by the steep, mile-long trail which could only be traveled by mules. They dragged up the lumber and machinery that built the first concentrating mill at that high altitude. He had to fight a severe winter climate with deep snow, which interfered with transportation of the ore from the mine. There was labor trouble, too, and sometimes a snowslide would tear away a flume and close him down for weeks. Due to the impossibility of shipping his product in winter, there were only two paydays in the year—the Fourth of July and Christmas. His men would come down from the mountain with an accumulation of paychecks and indulge

Collection of Mrs. Bertha Neal
Howardsville about 1895. Hematite Gulch is shown above and to the right of the town.

Collection of Robert L. Brown
Howardsville now. Note pyramid-roofed school at lower right in both pictures.

in a Bacchanalia which lasted for a week or two until their money was gone.

With a gross production of over eleven million dollars from approximately seventeen and a half miles of underground workings, the Silver Lake Mine held a unique place among the great producers of the San Juans. At one time it was the most extensively developed property in the Silverton Quadrangle. There were about two hundred claims in the group, covering an area of about fifteen hundred acres. The nucleus was in Arastra Basin, but there were strong branches extending down Blair Gulch and along the crest of Kendall Mountain. The average altitude of the mines was around 12,300 feet. Prior to 1902, the principal holdings of the company were comprised of the Silver Lake and New York City groups, subsidiary to which were numerous branches which were also held by the company. Shortly after the turn of the century the Silver Lake Mines became a subsidiary of the American Smelters Securities Company, which in turn was held by the American Smelting and Refining Company.

The lodes of Silver Lake Basin were large and prominent and were discovered and located at an early stage in the mining development of this region. Nearly all of them carried more or less high-grade ore in connection with large bodies of low-grade, and some of them made a notable production of the better deposits while being worked exclusively along those lines. It was not until the erection of the Silver Lake Mill, about 1890, that they were worked on a scale necessary for the profitable and permanent extraction of low-grade ore. Most of these veins were largely lead, carrying some silver and gold and smaller amounts of copper and zinc. All of the veins of this group were developed by numerous crosscuts and adit levels. A four-and-a-half-mile-long tramway connected the mines and the mill on the Animas River with the Silverton Northern Railway.

Mr. Stoiber finally sold his Silver Lake Mine to the Guggenheims for $1,300,000. Strange as it may seem, the new purchasers never profited, although competent engineers were employed. They finally gave up operating on a large scale.

Just beyond, in Arastra Basin, one can see the Silver Lake Mill and the tramway which extends in swinging lines to the old mine beside the lake at 12,250 feet above sea level. Often these great aerial ropes would employ as many as forty buckets or cars, each carrying about six hundred pounds. Placed at intervals of six hundred feet, they traveled at a speed of six feet per second. Two miles of steel ropes were often used in these systems, their total weight being over thirty tons. Spanning the intermountain spaces like great spider webs, the aerial trams were very important features of mining in the San Juan region.

The first cost of a tramway depends upon the contour of the country traversed, and the distance from the manufacturer who supplies the material. In the high altitudes of the San Juans, say at ten thousand feet or over, the cost of material for an installation having a capacity of two hundred tons per day of ten hours was about $2.10 per foot of tramline. The cost of freight, plus erection, would be about $1.15 more, so the total cost per foot would be $3.25. A tramway one mile long having the capacity mentioned, would involve an expenditure of about twenty thousand dollars. Actual expenditure for trams in this district has ranged between $2.50 and $8.00 per foot; as a rule, the cheap one proved to be the most expensive in the long run because of the greater cost of maintenance and repairs.

The Camp Bird Tramway was 8,550 feet long, with an angle station. The fall, in the length mentioned, was 1,840 feet and the cost all told was $55,094. The spacing of the supporting towers in a tramway is, of course, governed by the contour of the ground. In this regard, the double ropeway systems with their independent flexed cables for bucket tracks, permit a comparatively more direct path and more uniform movement of buckets because the cable can be stretched to a high tension, lessening deflection in the swing of the cable. In the case of a single ropeway that both carries and propels the bucket, high tension leads to overstraining the wire rope. It is avoided by use of a greater dip in the cable and the employment of a larger number of supports—a decidedly expensive drawback in a rugged mountain country.

The Old Hundred Mining Company, a corporation organized under the laws of the state of Maine, owned thirty well-located claims on the southwestern slope of Galena Mountain. Some of the holdings of the company had been worked in earlier times with very satisfactory returns. Until the advent of the Old Hundred Company, however, their extensiveness was practically unknown. There were seven very large and strong veins showing almost the entire distance covered by the locations, which extended over one mile in length. The veins were strong, being from ten to twenty feet in width where they were prepared for stoping. They were exceedingly well mineralized, showing values for the entire distance in gold, silver, lead, and copper. The gold values varied from a small showing to bonanza values which recurred with regularity.

The properties of the Old Hundred were located on a long extension from the base of the mountain to its summit and were connected vertically with a tramway system, each level being a complete mine within itself. To overcome the great height as well as the rugged exterior of the mountain was the reason the property was developed by levels. These began nearly a thousand feet above the mill and extended almost to the top. The two veins, the Old Niegold and the Vita Madre, paralleled each other; and the latter outcropped about eight hundred feet below the summit on the western line of the

Old Hundred property. A modern power plant was located just below the mill on the right-of-way of the Silverton Northern Railway. It contained boilers capable of developing seven hundred horsepower. In this way a bare mountain was made into a complete mine in which there were eighteen thousand feet of underground workings.

All the way up and down the Animas River for twenty miles there were splendid mill sites and many chances to take out ditches or races for running mills. No other power would ever be required since the river has a tremendous fall, probably not less than sixty feet to the mile, perhaps a hundred. It is about fifty feet wide opposite Cunningham Gulch and from three to four feet deep.

Major Cunningham, for whom the gulch was named, headed a party of capitalists from Chicago who investigated the San Juans. There was a Missouri mule in the party who carried nothing but a whopping load of twenty-dollar gold pieces. The boys all liked Major Cunningham. He was described as being "A fat, jolly good fellow who could play the guitar and sing the 'Spanish Cavalier' on horseback going uphill or down." Howardsville was then the headquarters for almost everything. It had a blacksmith shop, one little store that carried almost everything in stock, mostly old rye, and this was held ready to accommodate the boys should any of them make the sale of a claim.

During 1874, the town of Eureka was formally laid out and streets were platted. Its location was at the mouth of Eureka Gulch, at the same spot where the Baker party had panned and sluiced the gravels of the Animas for gold. Now it was silver. The town of Eureka had between twenty and fifty houses. Its altitude was about nine thousand feet. Near it were many very rich and well-developed mines. The Eureka district took in all the territory on the east side of the mountains that divide the waters of the Animas from those of the Gunnison and the Uncompahgre. It extended two miles above the town of Eureka where it joined the Animas district. The Eureka district had a great many locations, none of which was worked to any extent at this time except the Silver Wing, Sunnyside, Lucky, and Emma Dean.

George Howard was the original locator of the Sunnyside Mine. Howard finally combined finances with R. J. McMutt. Their Sunnyside Extension Mining and Milling Company was noted as being one of the largest operations in the county. It was not famous for silver alone, but for gold as well. The Sunnyside Extension was originally discovered by Rasmus Hanson in 1882. It became one of the best developed and most productive of a group of seven claims in the immediate vicinity, all owned by the Sunnyside Company. This group was composed mostly of Denver capitalists and the principal offices were in the Ernest and Cranmer Block. The Sunnyside Company was formally incorporated in 1892 with a capital stock of $400,000 represented by four hundred thousand shares at a par value of one dollar per share.

The character of the ore produced in the Sunnyside Extension was 70 percent free milling gold, 20 percent silver, and 10 percent lead, so that to all intents and purposes it was a gold property. This mine had been successfully worked for the previous ten years and the average value of the ore taken since the date of its discovery was twenty dollars to the ton. During a four-month period in 1892, $35,000 in gold and $15,000 in silver were produced. The total production since the time the mine was first operated until 1893 was $215,000 in gold and $122,687.42 in silver.

Between Eureka and Animas Forks were both the Silver Wing and the Tom Moore mines. In the late eighties Sam Martin secured an option on the original Tom Moore property and began to study its problems. The first winter was devoted to blocking out the immense ore re-

Collection of Fred and Jo Mazzulla   *Photo by Joseph Collier*
A Joseph Collier photograph of Eureka, taken about 1885. The rocky lower slopes of Crown Mountain are at the left.

Collection of Robert L. Brown
Eureka in July, 1961. Note that trees have failed to gain a foothold on the talus slope, a constant peril to the town.

serves which the Tom Moore vein contained. For fourteen years Martin had labored and planned to get together the one thousand or so acres that eventually became the exclusive holdings of the Tom Moore Gold Mining Company. It covered almost two miles on the famous Toltec vein which crossed the Moore vein at an
obtuse angle.

Among the first things he did was to open the smelting
streak along the fault made by the promontory vein. It
was heavy lead, carrying gold, silver, and some copper,
which averaged nearly thirty-five dollars to the ton. It
extended up the mountainside and through the big basin
which the erosion of the vein had made to the crest of
the range which forms the dividing line between Eureka
and Treasure mountains. There were numerous open
cuts and short tunnels used for discovery and assessment along the main deposit.

West of the Silver Queen property, in the neighborhood of the Gold Prince and Sunnyside, was the Argosy
group, generally regarded as the west end of the Tom
Moore holdings. Developments on the Gold Prince, Sunnyside, and Sunnyside Extension demonstrated the richness of the great mineralized ledge. This huge fissure
was one of the most notable in Colorado. It was known to
run as far as the Tomboy group of mines in the Marshall
Basin on the west, on the east through the Barstow and
Gold Lion group to the Yankee Girl-Guston properties at
Red Mountain; then on to the Gold King, Sunnyside, Gold
Prince, and into the Tom Moore and through it to the
Golden Fleece at Lake City and on to the northeast where
it finally disappears. On it are located some of the great-
est mines, for output and dividends, ever discovered in
Colorado.

Farther up the canyon, Animas Forks and Mineral
Point grew up and were added to the list of towns. The
community of Animas Forks was situated at the junction of the two branches of the Animas River. Here were

Collection of Fred and Jo Mazzulla
Eureka, looking southwest, as photographed by an unknown lensman about 1890.

Collection of Robert L. Brown
Eureka in the summer of 1961 from the same angle as the 1890
picture.

the smelting and refining works of the Dakota and San Juan Mining Company and the San Juan Smelting Company. The former was said to have had the best approved waterpower in the county. Their works were completed and an experimental run was made in the late fall of 1876.

Also at Animas Forks was the Gold Prince Mill which was partially owned by a steel company. As a consequence, it became one of the few that employed steel rafters. More than four hundred cars of structural steel were used in its foundations and floors. The structure was as nearly fireproof as it was possible to make it.

In order to treat the ores from the Gold Prince properties, this largest of all concentrating mills in the state was constructed at the Forks. No structure in the entire San Juan region was so imposing as the great Gold Prince. It loomed up against the landscape as huge as a small mountain. The steady pounding of the hundred stamps made a din and rumble like distant thunder as it kept up its ceaseless work of pounding out the silver and gold. The mill had a daily capacity of five hundred tons. The total cost of this installation was a half-million dollars.

The mill building proper had outside dimensions of 336 by 184 feet. The walls of the upper and lower terminal were constructed of heavy one-inch-thick boards and covered with building tar paper, which in turn was sheathed with No. 22 corrugated steel siding. The Gold Prince Company, like the Gold King, was capitalized at three million dollars with a state of Maine charter. Both Davis and Soule also had financial fingers in the Gold Prince properties.

The owners used money from the mill to develop their mine. This was quite a common practice in the San Juans and elsewhere. In such country, a mill was almost a sure money-maker and, therefore, a ready source of speculative capital for drilling exploratory holes on promising lodes.

An early-day publicity man, who obviously missed his calling since there was no Madison Avenue at that time, wrote the following account of the Gold Prince Mines: "Into insignificance sinks the boasted riches of the caves of Alladin when compared with the vast wealth now blocked out in the Gold Prince Mine at the head of Mastodon Gulch, two miles from the town of Animas Forks." It was connected with the Gold Prince Mill by a Bleichard tramway, 12,600 feet in length and erected at a cost of $75,000. The tram could carry a capacity of fifty tons every hour. The speed of its ropes was three hundred and fifty feet per minute and over fifty thousand feet of steel cable was utilized in its construction. The Gold Prince group was on the great Mastodon Vein which was 75 to 150 feet in width and was known as the Sunnyside Extension group previous to being acquired from Rasmus Hanson, the pioneer miner, by the Gold Prince Mines Company in 1903. It was undoubtedly on the same vein system as the Gold King, described earlier, with the Sunnyside group intervening.

At the Gold Prince Mine a splendid boardinghouse was built to accommodate 150 men. It was a model facility in all its appointments. Its supplies and those for the mine were transported from Animas Forks by way of the tram. Due to the scarcity of timber and the expense of supplying a mine of such immense proportions, no timber was used in stoping its shafts except for ore chutes and mill holes. Each stope was started as a blind drift with strong blocks of ground left standing for support. The Neptune Mining Company property was an extension of the Gold Prince Mining Company's lodes and was also located on what was commonly known as the Sunnyside or Mastodon Vein.

Rasmus Hanson was another empire builder of the San Juans. His life was a part of the history of the mines around Animas Forks, Eureka, and Picayune Gulch. He was born in Denmark in March of 1847. His parents were farmers and landowners. He attended college in Salby, Denmark, after which he obtained the right to study agriculture in that country. He landed in Quebec, Canada, at the age of twenty-one and went to Chicago where he remained for a short time. Eventually he migrated westward to Cheyenne. Hanson followed the mining booms into Nevada and ultimately to Denver and Central City in 1870. He later extended his mining operations into Clear Creek and Park counties and built the first house on the north spur of Lincoln Mountain.

In 1876 he migrated to the San Juans. For nearly ten years he prospected and took mining contracts throughout the district contiguous to Eureka and Animas Forks and gradually acquired a number of valuable properties. In 1886 he was elected mayor of Animas Forks, which was then a scene of considerable activity. For a time he was also connected with the Sunnyside Mine at the head of Mastodon Gulch as superintendent. In 1892 he completed the purchase of the mine and later sold it at a handsome profit to the Sunnyside Extension Mining and Milling Company in which he became a large stockholder while still retaining the management.

Hanson's star of good fortune rose high in the San Juan skies. In 1890 he received that great status symbol to end all nineteenth century status symbols—a gold filigree pass for the Silverton Railroad Company, from Otto Mears himself.

His new-found wealth also brought him a host of well-known and influential friends. During a nostalgic trip to his European homeland, he attempted to sell one of his mining properties for a quarter of a million dollars. Despite the often touted interest of British capital toward Colorado mining properties, Hanson found no takers until his close friend, the Prince of Wales, interceded in his

Collection of Fred and Jo Mazzulla

Animas Forks in the 1890's. The Gold Prince Mill is shown at left center and the school is at lower left. A large amount of restoration was done on the original photograph by the late Herndon Davis.

Collection of Robert L. Brown

The principal street of Animas Forks in August of 1962. The two-story house with bay window is the disputed Walsh house.

behalf. The Prince threw a huge party in Hanson's honor, and the mine was sold as a result.

Upon returning to Colorado, Hanson divided his time between his profitable Sunnyside Extension properties and the Brown Palace Hotel in Denver. Rasmus' interest in the Denver hostelry was prompted in no small measure by Miss Laura Leesburg, proprietress of the cigar concession in the hotel lobby. On March 29, 1904, they were united in marriage at the Denver home of General Fred Walsen.

Inevitably, a honeymoon in Europe came to pass; and the couple literally spent a fortune, until a letter arrived from Silverton. The unwelcome missive was sent by genial Guy L. V. Emerson, Rasmus Hanson's banker. The gist of his message was, "Whoa! The money is all gone!"

A return to Denver made it appear for a while that it would be back to the cigar stand for Laura. Rasmus, on the other hand, seemed nonplussed by this latest turn of events. His solution to the problem was typical of the man. "Honey," he said, "let's go find another mine." Incredible as it may seem, he did just that and had regained his fortunes by the next year, 1905.

The couple's time was divided between Denver and the San Juans; but, apparently, they never returned to the watering places of Europe for another financial unburdening. Hanson prospered in most of his ventures, until his death on September 28, 1909. Following her husband's demise, Laura showed uncommonly good sense by marrying banker Emerson, a remarkable man in his own right. Laura died at Silverton in 1921.

Guy Emerson, now in his nineties, lives in Denver. As of this writing, he is president of the Denver Mining Club, having successfully spanned the years between frontier life and automation. In addition to his duties as banker in Silverton, his long and impressive career has included such other occupations as attorney, Indian

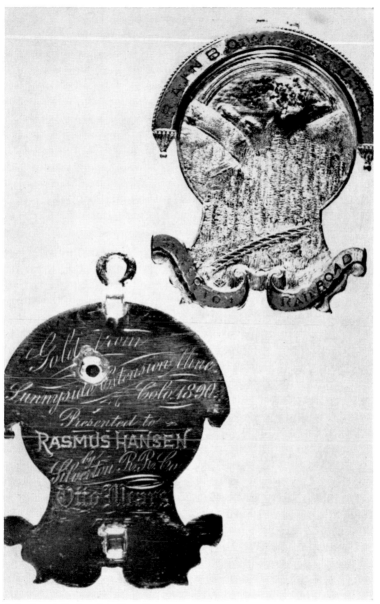

Collection of Fred and Jo Mazzulla
Two photographs showing the front and the inside inscription of the
Mears fob pass given to Rasmus Hanson. Note incorrect spelling
of Hanson's name by the engraver.

agent, miner, cowboy, and gunfighter. In 1908 he was elected secretary of the Colorado Bankers' Association, and in 1910 he became its president.

An early prospector named John Davie recorded an unusual funeral at Animas Forks. It seems one of the miners in the Davie party had died and the others had a meeting at their campfire in the town to make arrangements to bury him. At that time no minister, preacher, or undertaker was available in the county. One of the boys said, "Gentlemen, we must dig that grave. Who will do it?" Everyone volunteered. They dug the grave and had another meeting at which it was inquired, "How shall we fix the grave?" Someone suggested, "Let's line it with split logs." This was done the following day after first covering the bottom of the hole with grass. One of the men suggested giving him a Christian burial and said, "Some of you fellows will be able to conduct the services." There were no volunteers and he asked each individual until Davie told him he had belonged to a church back in Scotland. All agreed that Davie should conduct the services. He was not twenty-one at the time and told them he had never preached in his life but went through with it anyway. That night he tried to remember some verses of scripture he could use for the service. They gave the man a funeral the next day, and all the boys said that Davie did just fine. When the Silver Wing Mill was built Davie told the manager about the grave and asked him not to disturb it. It was not molested.

Animas Forks was once called La Plata City. Since names were often used more than once, this earlier designation should not be confused with the La Plata City west of Durango. In this earlier period the Forks had about twenty cabins, one general store, and a post office.

During the years in which Tom Walsh is rumored to have lived in Animas Forks, he at various times is said to have held leases on both the Early Bird and the Ben

Collection of Fred and Jo Mazzulla
An autographed picture of Rasmus Hanson

Butler mines. The leases are not questioned, only his residence in the town. All this was prior to his owner- ship of the Camp Bird.

The Mineral Mountain Mining Company dry concen- trator was completed at Animas Forks in 1879 by E. G. Greenleaf and C. H. McIntyre. It was used to dress ores from the Boston, Red Cloud, and other lodes. The Ani- mas District mines were situated along the Animas River and its tributaries. Their lodes, with a few exceptions, occupied positions ranging from eleven thousand to twelve thousand feet above the sea. The veins nearly all took the usual course, northeast and southwest. The greater part of the ore was galena, impregnated with gray copper. The veins were often large and well defined.

Above Animas Forks one may start the ascent of Cin- namon Pass. This divide separates the watershed of the Animas from that of the Lake Fork of the Gunnison River. On the divide was the Isolde Mine. Beyond the pass, on the other side, are the towns of Whitecross, Bur- rows Park, Sherman, and the others mentioned earlier in this chapter.

At no time in history has the road over Cinnamon been considered satisfactory. In the 1920's Claude Miner of Golden drove the first Model T Ford over the pass and described how ropes were used to keep it from tipping over. Before reaching Burrows Park, the oil plug was knocked out on the high rocks and a wagon from Lake City had to meet them there and take them the rest of the way.

Four miles north of Animas Forks, at an altitude of twelve thousand feet, was Mineral City or Mineral Point, a town of some twenty houses and one supply store. Here also was located the concentrating works of the Decatur and San Juan Company. These mines were once regarded as the most extensively opened in the dis- trict and had names like Aspen, Susquehanna, McGregor, Pelican, Philadelphia, Porcupine, and the far-famed Maid

Collection of Fred and Jo Mazzulla
The only photograph of Mineral Point that I have ever seen

Collection of Robert L. Brown
The town of Summit, at the crest of Red Mountain Pass

of the Mist, a particularly rich property. Nearby was the ambitious Mineral Point or Bonanza Tunnel. It was driven for the purpose of intersecting at great depths the lodes mentioned above, as well as any blind lodes. In 1876 it had already cut one vein of great size, which was supposed to be the Norris.

The history of Mineral City and the mines in its vicinity dates from the autumn of 1873 when Captain A. W. Burrows and the Hon. C. H. McIntyre visited the section. Both men were attracted by reports of rich quartz leads. They spent several months there, locating a number of mines, building several cabins, and taking out a large quantity of promising specimens.

Mineral Point is difficult to find today since most of its buildings are gone. The remains of a few sun-bleached cabins still stand in the meadow. On the hill is a rubble pile that was once the San Juan Chief Mill. Across the tundra, another mile or so, are some much better preserved structures along the road from Ouray up to Engineer Pass. These were probably not connected with Mineral Point. One source names them as part of the Benack Mine.

Still another San Juan town grew up nearby, along the perimeter of Engineer Mountain. It took the name of Park City and was located about twelve miles below Mineral City (or Mineral Point) at the head of the Uncompahgre Valley. A further direction in the old records said that it was about six miles from the border of the Ute reservation. Since no trace of Park City remains today, it is highly unlikely that its development ever passed the tent stage. Quite apart from the fact that hindsight is always superior to foresight, the founders were afflicted with typical civic pride and loudly boasted that Park City would shortly become a formidable rival of Lake City.

These small camps along the roads between Silverton and Lake City were reasonably typical of the literally

dozens of tiny settlements, some of which became towns
that grew up around the richer diggings in the seventies.
Many survived for a decade or two but most lasted only a
few years at best. Their lives could usually be paralleled
with the rising or declining fortunes of whatever nearby
mines happened to justify their existence at the time.

9

The Red Mountain Camps

A VERITABLE RAINBOW of gold and silver promise hung brilliantly over Red Mountain. Those were the halcyon days when the Yankee Girl, Guston, National Belle, Genessee, Silver Bell, and other mines in the heart of the district were making the world gasp at the richness of their output. More than twenty-five million dollars was added to the imperishable wealth of the world in a remarkably short time. Today most of the mines of this district, once a whirlpool of mining activity, have been abandoned to the gods of idleness and decay.

A few hundred yards south of Ouray are the entrances to several canyons of incomparable beauty, having perhaps some of the grandest and most picturesque scenery in Colorado. Immediately to the west is the winding road up Canyon Creek to Sneffels and Camp Bird. A short distance from its mouth is the start of scenic, narrow Box Canyon. Almost directly east, one may take the spiraling road up to the Amphitheatre, a high sheltered meadow now occupied by a Forest Service campground.

Here also, the canyon to Red Mountain opens, cutting a mighty seam through the granite formation. Far down below in the unexplored depths, two streams dash along and eventually mingle their waters in the suburbs of the city. This combined river is called the Uncompahgre. As you swing around the turn on your way south, to the right the bubbling stream rises from the rocks. Springs of hot water gush forth not two hundred yards from the swift current. To the left, far away up the heights, tall rocks like the minarets of a Moslem temple stand out in relief against the rough, serrated points and wooded plateaus that were strewn around when the earth was in the course of eruption.

Heading south out of Ouray today, the traveler follows U.S. 550, the fabled Million Dollar Highway. Winding sharply up out of the Ouray Amphitheatre, the road gains altitude quickly. A short drive south of the town will take you to an intersection where a rocky trail starts its incredible spiral upward to the east. During the mining period, this obstacle course was an extremely important thoroughfare since it provided access from Ouray to both Engineer and Poughkeepsie passes. Engineer Pass carried freight and stagecoach traffic over the divide to Lake City by way of American Flats, Rose's Cabin, and Capitol City. It was reached by taking the left fork of the trail toward Mineral Point.

A right fork from this same trail went off to the southeast and eventually provided a similar connection with Silverton. Pougkeepsie Gulch slopes northward from the high range of mountains which divides the waters of the Animas from those of the Uncompahgre River. Poughkeepsie Pass is over 12,600 feet above the sea and nearby Hurricane Peak is another thousand feet higher. In going from Silverton to Ouray by this route, one ascended 3,200 feet in a distance of thirteen miles and then dropped nearly 5,000 feet in the next seven miles. Poughkeepsie Basin is circled by a barren, rocky range. Since the entire section is well above timberline, provisions such as tools, firewood, lumber, powder, and everything else that was needed had to be carried to the mines on the backs of pack animals. The materials for the many shaft houses and cabins were taken up over the Cement Creek wagon road by packtrains or by teams. There was little or no timber or any other form of vegetation up among those barren wilds. Beef was obtained by driving the cattle up to the mines and slaughtering them there.

Snow rarely disappears from the northern slopes of Poughkeepsie Gulch, and when winter set in there was no further ingress except by the use of snowshoes. The town of Poughkeepsie was accessible from Silverton by way of the trail up Cement Creek for a distance of twelve miles. From Howardsville, by way of Eureka Gulch, there was also a good trail over the total distance of nine miles. A wagon road was constructed from Animas Forks and reached within a half mile of the camp. It terminated on the crest of a ridge overlooking the settlement in the valley below. From Mineral Point, the distance was only two miles and from Ouray it was seven miles. The nearest market for their ore was at Animas Forks.

The best of these roads was the one constructed up from Silverton in 1879, following the old trail up Cement Creek to Poughkeepsie Pass. From this route two other trails led off to the mines. On the summit of the pass were the Adelpheh and the Alpha. On the mountain nearby were the Tribune and Columbia lodes, owned by the Gladstone Company. Each of these properties produced about thirty-five tons of ore each averaging one hundred ounces of precious metal. Among other notable lodes around Pougkeepsie Gulch were the Alaska, Red Roger, Saxon, Pittsburg, Bonanza, Gypsie King, and Alabama. The Red Roger and Saxon were owned by H. A. W. Tabor, of Leadville, whose mining empire has rarely been thought of as extending beyond Lake County. Mr. J. F. Tabor superintended operations at the mines. The purchase price was said to have been $55,000. During the time that he spent in the San Juans, while establishing residence in La Plata County in order to divorce his wife Augusta, Tabor also had a stage line and mail contract between Rockwood and Rico. His black-

Collection of Mrs. Bertha Neal
Gladstone on Cement Creek about the year 1890. The town is at the base of the tramline cut.

Collection of Robert L. Brown
The valley of Cement Creek, looking toward the site of Gladstone as it appears today.

smith shop was at Rockwood. He regularly employed two men there. Tabor lost money because his overhead was too heavy; and although he paid high wages, he did not always get good service from some of his men.

Traveling more directly south from Ouray, U.S. 550 climbs steeply up Uncompahgre Canyon for several miles and then levels out in a magnificent park. The marble-ized color combinations of yellow, brown, orange, and red occur here in flamboyant mixtures, due to the presence of iron oxide and other compounds. Above Ironton Park the Red Mountain Peaks, formerly named the Scarlet Peaks, loom up to complete a panorama of unusual beauty.

Here, near the south end, was the town of Ironton, founded in 1883. Probably its most distinguishing characteristic was its mile-long main street, so frequently photographed by early-day lensmen. Ironton Park was the end of the line for Mears' Silverton Railroad, but at least the residents had one-way rail service. In order to gain the necessary altitude, on the return trip south from Ironton, the train covered a total of six miles of climbing, curving track to accomplish travel over an actual distance of three miles. Passengers who wished to continue on to Ouray took the four-horse stage, which also carried express and the mail down Uncompahgre Canyon.

The earliest discoveries here were made in September of 1879 but were not developed until 1882-83 because of the difficulty encountered in trying to build roads into such an inaccessible place, plus the seeming impossibility of moving in supplies and taking out ore. A further deterrent was the severity of their winters. During these long cold spells that were the rule rather than the exception at Ironton, the miners developed the morbid but realistic practice of "counting the smokes" each morning from the remote claims on the mountains surrounding the town. Failure to see wisps of smoke emanating from the chimneys at dawn was indicative of trouble and called

Courtesy U.S. Geological Survey　　　　　　　　*Photo by W. Cross*
Ironton, after the turn of the century. The photographer was W. Cross.

Collection of Robert L. Brown
Ironton in 1963 during a rainy day in August. A few of the original buildings are visible.

for an investigation. It usually meant that someone "hadn't made it" through the most recent prolonged snowstorm or through a particularly cold night. Failure to keep an adequate wood supply on hand for very extended cold spells caused death by freezing to not a few of the inexperienced who courted Dame Fortune in the San Juans. Very few chose to winter at Ironton.

In addition to the larger mining properties around Ironton Park, there were also several smaller operations located up Gray Copper and Corkscrew gulches. Originally, Ironton was regarded as the center of the Red Mountain district which extended south for about five miles and would have included the small settlements of Guston and Red Mountain Town. Surrounding Ironton were the principal mines, bearing such picturesque names as Silver Bell, Saratoga, Candice, and the Genessee-Vanderbilt.

Quite apart from its historical importance, production of the great mines, and the peculiarities associated with living here, life in Ironton had its lighter moments too. A sense of humor was by no means lacking. Two Ironton residents named Jake and Jim (last names withheld to avoid embarrassment to descendants) feuded long and hard over conflicting mining claims. Jim, in an attempt to settle the matter once and for all, put half a box of blasting power under Jake's cabin during the night and set it off. Not only did it disintegrate the structure, but the force blew the sleeping prospector out through the roof. Fortunately for Jake, the blast came from below, caught under his mattress and propelled it, with him still on it, for an unscheduled night flight through the skies above Ironton Park. The only casualty was a broken leg, suffered at the time Jake and his "magic carpet" mattress returned to earth some distance away. A slight stretching of the imagination could result in Jake's being classified as America's first astronaut.

As the fortunes of Ironton began to wane, the task of

Collection of Fred and Jo Mazzulla
Main Street at Ironton showing loaded packtrains and an ore wagon
drawn by double span of horses.

Collection of Robert L. Brown
The long, dusty street of Ironton, in the park of the same name.
The slope of Brown Mountain is at the right.

closing out the town's post office was assigned to the late Claude Miner, of Golden. As an aftermath to this event, during the prohibition years some people attempted to convince Mr. Miner that the abandoned and empty post office would be a superb location for an illegal still. Since the offer was not seriously considered, the story may safely be told. Many abandoned mining camps have been subverted into serving a wide variety of purposes during their sunset years and one cannot help but wonder what effect the water of Ironton, laden as it is with iron oxide and deadly acids that forced the closing of nearby mines, would have had on local brewing recipes.

At the present time the paved highway, U.S. 550, by-passes Ironton and climbs up out of the park to the west of the site. The long street is still there but only a few houses at the south end remain of the original town.

A short distance south of Ironton, approaching the top of Red Mountain Pass, is a large contemporary mill surrounded by a vast expense of gray tailings. Acoss the valley to the east is the shaft house of the Yankee Girl Mine. Around it, there grew an assortment of fine-looking frame houses that passed for the town of Guston.

During the summer of 1881, John Robinson and three companions made the initial discovery at this point which resulted in development of the Guston Mine. Another of those deer-hunting stories is said to have resulted in discovery of the nearby Yankee Girl. The same John Robinson allegedly picked up a rock while hunting in Red Mountain Park during August of 1882. While he was prospecting for its source, an enormous body of valuable ore was opened up. Although the shaft was only twenty feet deep, he was able to sell it at once for $125,000 in cash. Strangely enough, the Yankee Girl and Guston were only about three hundred yards apart. In order to preclude any chance "discoveries" by others, the own-

Collection of Fred and Jo Mazzulla   *Photo by M. Brunfield*

Guston town and the Guston mine, as photographed by M. Brunfield, of Ouray, in the winter of 1895.

Collection of Robert L. Brown

Shaft house of the abandoned Yankee Girl workings at the former location of Guston in 1962.

ers staked the Robinson and Orphan Boy claims on land adjacent to the Yankee Girl. Both proved to be almost equally valuable.

When the Treasure Tunnel was bored, it cut across several faults, releasing quantities of high-pressure water into the workings. Its force was so great that powder for blasting was literally blown out of its holes. As a solution, charges were put in place inside of gas pipes and inserted into the desired area. Needless to say, underground water was the greatest single problem here and eventually contributed to the termination of operations. A second problem was the high acid content of the water inside nearly all of the Red Mountain mines. As a precaution, bronze-lined pumps were imported from Belgium at a cost of thirty thousand dollars each. Conventional pumps could not withstand the erosive action of the acids. A shovel, accidentally left in the water overnight, would be largely eaten away by the following morning. The water, heavily charged with sulfuric and other acids, quickly destroyed most pumps, bolts, rails, and nearly any other metal with which it came into contact. It ate them away and perforated pipes like honeycombs. The acid waters came from the great bodies of iron and copper ores extending down to a depth of several hundred feet. Below a certain level, however, the acids of the water changed and a deep tunnel which would drain the mines under this flow became the only solution of the difficult dilemma.

To this end, as well as for general economy in mining and opening the immense ore reserves of the Red Mountain District, George Crawford projected the Joker Tunnel. It started at a point near the junction of Red Mountain Creek and Commodore Gulch, over three thousand feet from the Yankee Girl shaft which by this time had been sunk to a depth of nearly 950 feet. Work was begun on July 9, 1904. A lateral from the tunnel tapped the Yankee Girl shaft between the sixth and seventh levels and another intersected with the Guston at its sixth level.

By so doing, both shafts were unwatered for the greater portion of their old workings. The Joker Tunnel not only overcame the water problem but also made available immense reserves of both high- and medium-grade ore which were now opened in the old workings. It also resulted in the discovery of two heretofore unknown ore veins on the Yankee Girl. There were originally twelve levels on the Yankee Girl and fourteen on the Guston. All of the workings on the Robinson mines were conveniently drained through the Guston.

After the turn of the century George Crawford, who since the first discoveries of ore on Red Mountain in 1882 had been more closely identified with the great mining projects of the camp than any other man, consolidated several of the claims and tried to place them on a substantial working basis. The Crawford interests included the Red Mountain Mining and Smelting Company, the Blue Bell Mining Company, and the Gold Lions Mining Company. Over the long haul the Yankee Girl produced more than eight million dollars, which was only a drop in the bucket compared to the ore reserves it still contains. The Guston produced about seven million and several additional millions were produced by other properties nearby. Incidentally, steam was the only available source of power for mining at this time.

Mining by tunnel was nearly the only practical method. The up-on-endness of the country must be seen to be appreciated. Baker's Park, which contains the town of Silverton, is the largest and probably the only flat area in the county. The park is less than a mile wide and little more than a mile in length. The north end of the town is two hundred feet higher than the south end. This should give the reader some idea of what the rest of the country is like. In a country which nature had set all on edge, there was no use in sinking a shaft vertically when the same or better results might be obtained by driving a tunnel horizontally.

In the San Juans when a man located his vein of mineral he started it on the level. When he struck ore he got some little steel rails for a track and with an ore car, pushed out the product horizontally. When water was encountered, he used it to run his machinery. It did not take a mining expert in hip boots and corduroy suit to determine the economy of this method of mining. Where most of the scenery is tilted at an angle of forty-five or more degrees, the tunnel scheme was the whole solution of the problem. Few mines in the San Juans could have been operated successfully or at a profit if the ore had to be hoisted and the shafts and drifts kept clear of water by pumping.

The problem of water for the operation of large wet-crushing mills was always a serious one in the San Juan country. In the southern portion, water was abundant and, for the most part, the mills were situated along the lower courses of those streams which afforded from one to two thousand miner's inches of water even in the dry seasons. For the great veins, however, situated in the valleys and canyons tributary to the upper Animas and the head of the Uncompahgre, huge stamp mills utilized all the surface flow available in their motors and for grinding and concentrating purposes.

In 1888 the Guston was purchased by an English syndicate and was formed into a stock company. The management of the Guston property was dedicated to carrying out a systematic plan of deep development before any shipments began. Some new ore was discovered at a depth of two hundred feet and total output of the mine for the year 1890, as reported by the United States Mint, was $1,173,051. The mine was regarded as a constant producer. New ground was explored and added to the property whenever possible.

The White Cloud was an extension of the Guston vein. It was also operated by an English company. The nearby Colorado Boy uncovered good ores that showed assay values of sixty to four hundred ounces of silver to the ton. Due to the lack of roads, the minerals were packed out on muleback over Red Mountain Pass to Silverton for refinement. The first wagon road was not started until the fall of 1883.

The Yankee Girl was once claimed to contain the richest ores of any property in America. It was a large producer for many years, and its output in the 1890's was rated in excess of six million dollars. The Yankee Girl and Guston mines were worked until 1896; but the low price of silver, coupled with the increase in costs as the work became deeper, the extensive trouble in handling the corrosive waters of the mine, and the low grade of the ore ultimately taken from the lower portions, caused both these mines to close down. Here at Guston one could attend the only church in the entire Red Mountain district, an edifice which utilized a mine whistle instead of the traditional bell. The townsite was a particularly steep one with streets laid out in stratified layers, one above the other. Frequently, the front yard of one house would be on the same level as the rooftop of the next.

Otto Mears' Rainbow Route, the Silverton Railroad, passed right through Guston and there are some fine old photographs that show the tiny engines perched precariously on their narrow tracks, clinging dangerously to the steep hillside. The old grades are still visible but the rails were torn out long ago. Evergreen trees now grow between the old rotting ties; the houses are gone and a heap of rubble marks the original site of the little church as the townsite gradually returns to its natural state.

Less than a mile south of Guston was the location of the great National Belle Mine, perched on the side of a round knob of evergreen-crested earth above a beautiful, sheltered meadow. This location became the last resting place of the highly migratory community called Red Mountain Town. Prior to 1883, Red Mountain was Indian territory. After that time the country was settled and mines of tremendous value were added to the wealth of the county. The town was built at an altitude of 11,200 feet above sea level and enjoyed a special reputation as a health resort. After its incorporation as a town in 1883, only four deaths were recorded by natural means during the next decade.

From June until November, the snow was out of the way and Red Mountain was annually visited by large numbers of tourists, travelers, and investors from all sections of the country. Across the narrow valley that held the town, opposite the National Belle, stood a smaller and less well known mine named the Swamp Angel, so called for the soft and mushy nature of the soil at Red Mountain. Since this condition still exists, caution should be observed by those contemporaries who visit the old site. Red Mountain started life on the Silverton side of the pass under the name of Congress, Congress Town, or Old Congress Town. The location was up the hill from Chattanooga on the railroad tracks. It was later known as Red Mountain or Red Mountain City as its location moved up the hill. The final leap, to the high meadow beside the National Belle, has been ascribed to a variety of reasons. The most amusing version, and probably the most improbable, says that when the town saloon proprietor decided to move his stock up closer to the top of the pass, the whole thirsty population just naturally followed along. Equally unlikely was the early census tabulation showing a population of ten thousand at Red Mountain, a geographical impossibility. Even the combined populations from all the previous locations would hardly have reached such a total.

Lying about two miles south and west of Red Mountain was the center of a wonderful mineral area owned by the Bullion King Mining Company in Porphyry Basin. The group comprised eighteen claims, compactly located, and each one showing strong mineral indications. The

Collection of Fred and Jo Mazzulla   *Photo by George Stephan*
Red Mountain City, or Town, as photographed by George Stephan in 1889. Buildings at left were burned in the 1892 fire.

Collection of Robert L. Brown
Only a few scattered remains still mark the last resting place of Red Mountain.

overall development of the property consisted of about two thousand feet in tunnels, drifts, upraises, and shafts. The most important work was a drift of about five hundred feet on the Bullion King vein, which subsequently disclosed minerals throughout the entire length.

At first the mines at the head of Canyon Creek were worked vigorously. Red Mountain and Ironton were very active from 1882 to 1893. The fall in the price of silver and apparent exhaustion of the richer portions of the ore body caused the mines to collapse. The site may be seen today by leaving U.S. 550 shortly before you cross the top of Red Mountain Pass. A poor dirt road, about a half mile below the crest on the Ouray side, leads east for a short distance to the town. The streets, a few houses, the mine, the railroad grade, and a quaint little jail are still there.

It is difficult indeed for today's visitor in the San Juan country to envision a time when a total of five communities existed within the short expanse of the few miles that separate Ouray and Red Mountain. The scenery is part of the most spectacular in the state and is the primary attraction at present. For the student of history, however, the points of interest are somewhat more obscure and require a bit more effort before anticipated goals can be achieved. Yet for those who would rediscover and can appreciate visiting the landmarks of a bygone era, the possibilities are limitless.

Courtesy Library, State Historical Society of Colorado
Red Mountain Town on the day following the fire of August 12,
1892. Note erection of tents to shelter the homeless.

Collection of Robert L. Brown
The dump of the National Belle at right and a few houses are all
that remained at Red Mountain in 1962. The Million Dollar Highway is just beyond the trees.

∽ 10 ∽

South of Red Mountain

IN THE EARLY DAYS an active rivalry existed between Ouray and Silverton, with each community struggling to obtain as much of the trade and commerce from nearby districts as possible. As a consequence, Chattanooga was able to grow and thrive on the basis of the commercial services it provided. There were only a few promising mineral deposits there, certainly not enough to justify its existence as a mining town.

Near the foot of Red Mountain Pass, on the south or Silverton side, was and still is the location of the Chattanooga. Some early prospecting was done here and a few paying locations were found and worked for a time. An early newspaper account tells us that:

Joel B. Warner, manager of the Silver Ledge Mine at Chattanooga, San Juan County, reports the opening of a new body of ore which in size and value is superior to anything yet opened in the mine, yielding values which will permit the shipping of the crude ore direct to the smelters. The ore body was found at the fifth level in a cross-cut and shows that there is fifteen feet of ore that will yield paying amounts for the entire width of the vein. The Silver Ledge is rapidly becoming one of the leading enterprises of the San Juan country. It was opened originally by a Denver Company upon the recommendation of Mr. Warner and showed large bodies of low grade ore. The mine is equipped with a first class mill and the concentrates are of a uniformly high grade. A large amount of contract work is now in progress in

Collection of Robert L. Brown
Site of the Ouray-Red Mountain Stage stop now

Courtesy Library, State Historical Society of Colorado
Stagecoach stop of the Ouray-Red Mountain Stage. Taken from half of a stereo pair made by the San Juan Studio in 1888.

the way of upraises to connect the different working levels. By the end of the present season the mine will be in a condition to make an output that will put it in first place among San Juan County producers.

Ore deposits notwithstanding, the chief contribution of Chattanooga was not mining. Instead, its people kept the home fires burning by selling supplies and equipment to the surrounding towns. Blessed with a strategic location, the community thrived as an outfitting center. Fresh horses and mules were usually available, and arriving or departing packtrains were a common sight.

U.S. 550 now passes Chattanooga's front door. A few cabins and a fine ranch currently occupy the townsite. Up the hill a short distance, just below the highway, one may see the crumbling remains of a huge shaft house, and the nearby grade of the Rainbow Route, two unmistakable reminders of a colorful past.

Between Chattanooga and Silverton was a tiny camp known only as Burro Bridge. Its approximate location was just west of the present highway, at the point where the Jeep road over Ophir Pass leaves U.S. 550 and crosses the creek. Only the bridge is there now, and doubtless it is not the original one.

Admirably situated in the center of level, two-thousand-acre, treeless, Baker's Park, was Silverton, the seat of San Juan County. Hardly prolific as an agricultural area in view of its 9,400-foot elevation, some of the hardiest vegestables were nevertheless produced. Its prominence in the San Juan story was due to its strategic geographical location and to the richness of its mines, fortunately located in the high mountains that surround the park on all sides. Although there were settlers here at various times during the earlier period, the first town plat was not filed until September 9, 1874. Actual incorporation, however, did not occur until November 15, 1876.

Collection of Fred and Jo Mazzulla   *Photo by Joseph Collier*
Chattanooga, as photographed by Joseph Collier about 1885, before the Silverton Railroad reached the town.

Collection of Robert L. Brown
Chattanooga in late October, 1962. View is looking south toward Silverton.

Originally, the major part of the business section was confined to a single, mile-long thoroughfare running east and west through the center of the settlement. This was Blair Street, lined with shops, saloons, hotels, saloons, stores, and saloons, to name just a few of the varied and less indelicate enterprises that flourished there. One block north, running parallel with Blair, was Greer Street, now the principal thoroughfare.

More and more people who had come to the district began acting as though they meant to stay. Families arrived in increasing numbers to build, and others began prettying up their homes and started hauling pianos and various gimcracks across the soaring multicolored San Juans. Wives exchanged information with other wives about the important discoveries they had made in the art of high-altitude cooking, what to do about mountain fever, and how to have babies safely in a blizzard.

The Animas Canyon Toll Road Company constructed a grade from Silverton down the river to Animas Park, a distance of about forty miles, to the new town of Animas City which was located in September of 1876. From this point the Animas Town Site Company built one additional road which extended down into New Mexico for a distance of about eighty miles.

Barely to the south there occurred another community that is more often than not associated with the San Juan story. It became noted as a smelting center, but in the beginning Durango was an accidental city. Animas City, three miles north of it, was the most important town of the region while Parrott City was the seat of La Plata County.

Animas City opposed an appropriation for the railroad, so its track was then projected through Durango. Almost in a night the town sprang into existence as the leading center of business south of the San Juans. Houses could not be built fast enough to accommodate the incoming rush of trade and of desperadoes who flocked wher-

Collection of Mrs. Bertha Neal
Looking northwest across Greer Street in Silverton in the 1880's

Collection of Robert L. Brown
Some of the original buildings appear to be still there

ever there were good pickings. Tents arose like magic to cover saloons, dance and gambling resorts, and to provide sleeping quarters. Dugouts were made, log cabins were hastily constructed, and every stage from the east, north, and south came in gorged with passengers. Stage robbery became so common that it excited no special notice since the money taken from passengers was often spent in Durango.

The founding of Parrott City is sometimes regarded with detachment in terms of its geographical relation to the overall San Juan picture. Located some distance to the south, and slightly west of the more prominent centers of the rush, Parrott City was built on the La Plata River in the mountains, a short distance to the west of present-day Durango and north of Hesperus. There is almost no trace of Parrott City remaining today. The last few cabins were torn down many years ago and the Parrott Ranch, near Mayday, now covers the site.

During the summer of 1873, Captain John Moss led a party of ten prospectors from California to the San Juan Mountains. The entire distance had been covered on horseback, with pack animals carrying their equipment. The Californians came in by way of Arizona and Utah and brought very complete camping and mining outfits with them. After crossing the San Juan River, Captain Moss gave the name "Montezuma" to the wide valley by which they had entered the La Plata country (a name it still retains). Why he chose the name of the last Aztec emperor of Mexico, long dead and not even remotely connected with the migration, remains a mystery. They took up claims on some nearby placer grounds and also located a few ranches while searching for gold.

They set up camp at the entrance to La Plata Canyon and immediately started to look for riches. It seems paradoxical that they should seek gold in the midst of an area already becoming famous for its production of silver. What seems even more peculiar is their selection

PARROTT CITY, County Seat of LaPlata County, Colo., June, 1881.

Collection of Fred and Jo Mazzulla
An etching of Parrott City in 1881 showed artistic license in regard to the size of the background peaks.

Collection of Robert L. Brown
This empty meadow was the locale of the once busy community of Parrott City.

of a canyon whose name, La Plata, means "silver" in Spanish.

Since food supplies were diminishing, the party determined to seek an Indian camp. The superstitious might, at this point, say that the hand of fate intervened, for while hunting or while cleaning his gun (the accounts vary), Richard Giles accidentally shot himself in the neck—an event that resulted in a change of plans for the California party. While one group, led by Moss, started toward New Mexico for supplies, the other erected a shelter for the comfort of the wounded man. Moss's party returned days later and finding Giles much improved, decided to move their camp to a spot beside the Mancos River. Their location there likely became the first permanent ranch in La Plata County.

While awaiting the recovery of his wounded comrade, Captain Moss made a treaty with the Utes which allowed the Californians to mine and farm thirty-six square miles of territory surrounding their camp. The Utes generally were very hostile toward prospectors and settlers; but Moss apparently had little difficulty coming to an agreement with Chief Ignatio, under which he was given control of land along the river to use as he pleased. Moss was not among those eager and premature San Juan prospectors who defied the Indians. He had deliberately sought out Ignatio and learned that the chief was not averse to the terms of a treaty then under consideration. Under the terms of this treaty, the Utes would receive a quantity of wool blankets and one hundred ponies, sheep, and other gifts. Near the center of this newly acquired territory, the miners planted the seeds of their town and called it California Bar. This strip also became known as the California Mining District.

As a result of the treaty with the Utes, a number of families now crossed the range from Baker's Park to establish farms in the lower valley. During the summer

of 1873, several other pioneers, who now recognized the
desirability of an agricultural region in close proximity
to the mining camps, came down from Silverton to locate ranches for themselves and their families across the
range in the valley of the lower Animas River. Fresh
produce, they reasoned, would command a handsome
price in remote and nonagricultural mining camps.

Later in 1873, a party from Arizona also prospected
up La Plata Canyon and reached La Plata Bar in November. Good placer gold prospects were indicated, and preparations were made for full-scale gulch mining. A heavy
snow in December, however, put a stop to their operations until May of the following season. It was later
determined that the La Plata Bar would be a disappointment. The gold definitely was and is still there. Splendid
returns were obtained from prospecting the surface, but
the formation was such that bedrock could not be
reached; hence, the impossibility of a successful, long-
term operation.

Nevertheless, Moss had satisfied himself that the La
Plata country was undoubtedly rich in both placer and
lode gold. Armed with a copy of his Indian treaty plus
some samples of gold quartz and much free gold, he returned to San Francisco on horseback. There he showed
the fruits of his labor to Parrott and Company, a family-
owned and highly respected banking firm of that city.
The partners approved of what they saw and granted
Moss carte blanche to draw on them for all necessary
funds. Moss, being somewhat overawed at the generosity
of Tiburcio Parrott, patriarch of the clan, returned and
changed the name of their little camp. California Bar
now became Parrott City in honor of the elder member
of the family.

John Thomas Moss was one of the most enigmatic and
controversial personalities ever to enter the San Juan
story. He was born at Utica, New York, March 4, 1839,
and was baptized and brought up a member of the Epis-

copal faith. In the spring of 1854 his father moved to
Iowa and bought a claim in Delaware County, where he
built a log cabin for his family in anticipation of their
following him west that September. Here they lived
for more than a year and a half, until the spring of 1856,
when they moved to Mitchell County. During the fall
of the next year, young Moss went west for the first time.
His destination was California. The following twenty-
two and a half years, or until his death in April of 1880,
were spent in that section of the country.

During subsequent years Moss often boasted that there
were few locations west of Iowa where he had not
traveled. He once served as a pony express rider, as a
scout, and later as an Indian interpreter. He was also
entrusted with several important missions for the Federal government. Moss was reported to have been one
of the first white men to explore many of the obscure
sections of the Southwest and was almost certainly the
first Anglo-Saxon discoverer of the ruins of the prehistoric Pueblo people near the present site of Mesa Verde
National Park. Being very highly regarded by the Indians, he was given the tribal name of Narraguanep,
which means "live forever." Moss served during a short
period as a guide for the Hayden expedition, although
he is rarely credited with this service. On another occasion he worked as an Indian agent in the San Juans for
a short time.

Although Moss lacked the advantages of a formal education, he, nevertheless, gave his contemporaries the impression of being a well-educated man. According to
those who knew him, he was most generous and open-
handed with his personal possessions. This characteristic, if true, probably accounts largely for his popularity
with the Indians. They, in turn, would do anything he
asked of them and Moss always reciprocated most freely.
Moreover, he could talk to them in their own tongue;
and he was said to have been able to understand the

language of most of the tribes in the Southwest. He was
once observed sitting on the ground talking simultaneously with a Spaniard, a Frenchman, and an Indian.

Moss had traveled about in the mountains of northern
Arizona and southern Utah for at least a dozen years
prior to his arrival in Colorado. Much of his time was
spent with the Indians. He was a nomad by nature,
drifting from tribe to tribe. Reportedly, he betrayed the
Indians' confidence only once and had more influence in
their councils than almost any other contemporary white
man.

He was once rumored to have been the legendary white
man who led the Paiute Indians at Mountain Meadows,
where they allegedly assisted a group of Mormons in the
massacre of about 120 emigrants of the Fancher party.
Characteristically, instead of refuting the rumor, Moss
bragged about his intimate friendship with John D. Lee,
who became the chief scapegoat. Moss related details of
the crime that damned him in public opinion. These details had actually been gathered several years later from
the Indians themselves. That there was a white leader
among the Indians was a fact amply testified to by witnesses at Lee's trial.

According to his daughter, Moss was not the kind of
man to participate in such an atrocity. He would have
more likely tried to prevent it. In truth, the Mountain
Meadows massacre occurred in September of 1857; and
John Moss did not even reach that country until 1860
or 1861. Here again, the narrative becomes confusing
with one contemporary account relating that at the time
of the Mountain Meadows massacre John Moss had been
seen frequently in the company of John D. Lee. Moss was
then living with the Paiutes, about twenty-five miles
from the scene of the massacre.

Realistically, Moss could not possibly have taken part
in the massacre. In September of 1857 he would have
been only eighteen years old and either on the way or

freshly arrived from Iowa. It seems extremely unlikely that he could have gained the trust of the Paiutes this early in the game, let alone having lived with them or having been their leader.

Lee was not tried until 1877, when he was convicted and ultimately shot by his own people in March of that same year. During the two decades between the massacre and Lee's execution, Moss could have known him and could have gained enough details to confound and shock his contemporaries. Direct participation, however, was almost assuredly out of the question.

Among the other exploits for which Moss claimed credit was the first exploration of the Grand Canyon of the Colorado. Unfortunately, the details of his reported achievement appear to have been lost to the world and, so far as is known, they appeared in print only in connection with the promise of a later, fuller story which never appeared.

In 1864 John Moss was appointed agent for the Mojave Indians of Arizona. At that time, Moss allegedly performed a feat that gave him a deserved national reputation. He had made plenty of money and was anxious to spend it. He believed that if the Indians knew the real strength of the white population of our country along the Atlantic coast, as compared with their own numbers, they would "despair of keeping us out of the West and would submit to the inevitable invasion and thus save much bloodshed." He conceived the bold plan of taking an Indian chief named Aratopa, or Ahrata, on a trip down the Atlantic seaboard to show him proof of the size of the white man's population centers. Moss also planned to take him to Washington to visit the "Great White Father," who happened at that time to be none other than Abraham Lincoln. Moss was to pay all expenses and see to it that the chief was returned to his own people after "three moons."

He was as good as his word in most respects, and better in some. He took the chief not only to see the President, but also to see the beehives of population in the Eastern states—and in a manner that caused them to be viewed in multiplied form. The Indian had never seen more than a few white men together at a time, and his knowledge of an Eastern civilization was very limited.

Moss and his companion went from lower California to San Francisco in a steamer. East of the Rockies, they boarded what proved to be the chief's first train. Aratopa was terrified. When the speed got down to thirty or forty miles per hour, the old man tried to throw himself out the window. During the remainder of the first day of their journey, it took two men to prevent him from breaking his neck. He finally got used to railroad travel, however, and actually said that he liked it toward the last. The more he saw of city life, the more his amazement grew. Moss and his friend lived at one of the best New York hotels for a week, faring sumptuously.

During the night run south from Jersey City, Moss repeatedly made the chief get up and look out the window at the gaslights—the object being to make the Indian think that he was still riding through New York City. They arrived in Philadelphia before daybreak and remained there until night. When the journey to Baltimore was resumed, Moss still practiced his deception by waking the chief at every town to convince him that they were still riding under the New York gaslights. The game was continually played on the unsuspecting and bewildered Indian until the trip ended in Washington.

When they returned to the wilds of the West, Aratopa's people could not understand the long absence. The chief had three wives and many children, all mourning him as dead. Upon his arrival he wore a cocked hat with a black ostrich plume gracefully falling over his shoulder. He was attired in a full major general's uniform, including the yellow sash. At his belt was a curved Japanese sword with a long handle. On his breast were ribbons and orders, and there were epaulettes on his shoulders. However, there were no shoes to match.

Aratopa feared to relate his experiences since he knew that his people would think he was lying, or worse yet, that he had been bribed to deceive them. He finally consented to tell his story. On a certain day the whole tribe assembled to hear it. When he described the journey by rail and told of riding two whole nights under the gaslights of a city, the untraveled Indians denounced his narrative as a monstrous "stiff." They nearly mobbed the old man. A council was called. It was decided to banish Aratopa from the tribe and he was accordingly stripped of his Eastern-made clothes and abandoned on an uninhabited island of the Colorado River, from which he was afterward rescued by his old friend Moss.

Moss was once identified with the great Colorado diamond swindle, which attracted widespread attention about this time in many parts of Europe as well as in the United States. He appears to have been employed as a boomer in behalf of this fraudulent enterprise. Apparently Moss had arrived in Denver where he was heard telling the story that an ordinary, industrious man might pick up from $500 to $5,000 worth of diamonds daily. He mentioned two men who had realized $30,000 from the gems that came from only two days of washing. Moss said that he had been with another man, Stanton (first name unknown), when he picked up a gem which one of the Tiffany experts later valued at $250,000.

Moss does not appear to have lost caste on the Pacific Coast because of his connection with the swindle. Soon after the exposure of this disgraceful affair, he was sent back to the San Juan country by Tiburcio Parrott.

John Moss was married at least twice. The first union, in California, proved to be a tragedy to him and might be one possible reason for the reckless behavior he pursued in the years following. In 1875 he was said to have been married in Denver to a beautiful Southern girl from

Courtesy Library, State Historical Society of Colorado
John Moss, without his pioneer garb, sat for this portrait in San
Francisco.

one of the aristocratic families in New Orleans. This was alleged to have been his greatest happiness. Here again the narrative breaks down in confusion. His daughter mentions only two marriages. Nevertheless, there is also a record that he married Miss Alida Olsen at Parrott City on October 20, 1876, only a year after the Denver service. Alida was once described as being the "most prepossessing" woman in the camp. She was the postmistress at Parrott City when Moss married her. There were only three or four other women there at the time. She had originally come to the La Plata country with her parents.

Years went by and Moss ultimately became quite firmly entrenched in Parrott City. As the months passed, word of the La Plata strike inevitably found its way to the outside world; and a small rush migrated up the canyon to the new community, which may be properly dated from the summer of 1874. In June the first of several lodes was uncovered. Named the Mother Comstock, after the justly famous Nevada lode, it was hoped that the property would produce to the joyful tune of its well-known namesake.

The need of contact with the outside world prompted the location of a post office at Parrott City in 1875. At a constitutional convention later that year, the town was designated as the seat of La Plata County, and John Moss was made a member of the initial Board of Commissioners. The first sawmill was hauled in piece by piece all the way from Pueblo by oxcarts, and the first logs were sawed in May of 1876. This may be regarded as the beginning of the lumber business in La Plata County, still a highly profitable enterprise in the area today. E. H. Cooper brought in the first commercial stock of groceries and inaugurated the initial enterprise of that kind at Parrott City. Healthy growth of the town continued unabated as more and more people migrated into the district.

Moss was truly in his element at last. Parrott City was surveyed and subdivided on a large enough scale to allow for its development into a potentially great metropolis. The first home to be erected was a fine one. It served both as the office of the Parrott Enterprises and also as the personal establishment of Captain John Moss. With the first wagonload of furniture, the largest barrel of whiskey available also arrived. It was set up in the office, tapped, a faucet set in, and several tin dippers were hung along the wall near it. Every visitor was invited to take a dipper and put it under the faucet and fill it to the limit of its capacity. There was no restriction on the number of times each day a visitor might call and none as to the size of his drink. At the Parrott City office there was always a barrel on tap and another on the way.

In 1874 William H. Jackson, the noted pioneer photographer, came to the San Juans for the purpose of photographing its "grand and marvelous scenery." With him was Mr. Ernest Ingersoll, well-known writer of the day. These two men were visitors at Parrott City, where they were entertained by Captain Moss. He put them up at his house and introduced them to the miners, ranchers, and to the barrel. "I will be glad to show you around," said Moss, "and I will show you something else no white man has ever laid eyes on, except myself." It developed that he meant the ruins of the cliff and cave dwellers previously known only to Moss and the Indians. He told Jackson that while visiting in one of the Moqui pueblos, he had learned of the legend of the Cliff Dwellers. The date of Moss's first discovery of the cliff structures was probably 1869; certainly it was no later than 1873.

The personal letters of Jackson recall vividly his visit to the San Juans and his acquaintance with Moss. The photographic division of the U.S. Geological Survey of 1874 was outfitted as a separate unit. They left Denver on July 21, 1874, and made their way to the San Juan region. Jackson recalled that:

Our intinerary had been talked over and changed many times before our plans took definite shape. We had planned to photograph some of the reputed wonderful mountain scenery. I am very certain that there was no intention of our going south of Baker's Park into the San Juan Basin until we met Tom Cooper and his outfit near the head of the Rio Grande on the way into that country. Having worked over most of the territory assigned to us we finally reached the Rio Grande on our way into the heart of the San Juans by way of Cunningham Pass. On the twenty-seventh of August we camped early in the day at Jennisons' Ranch since it was too late to cross the pass that day. We also wanted to do some photographing in the neighborhood. While we were unpacking, a burro train came along and went into camp nearby. As they passed us, there was much hilarity over the very comical appearance of one of the party who was astride a very small burro with another one of the party following with a club, with which he was belaboring the little "jack" to keep him up with the rest of the train.

On our return to camp from our photographing day, this same man came over to visit us. A mutual recognition followed our meeting as I remembered him as a fellow townsman in Omaha, when I was in business there a few years previously. With all of us grouped around a rousing big fire after supper, we talked long into the night. The man's name was Tom Cooper. He explained that he was one of a small party of miners working some placers over in the La Plata country. He had been out of supplies and was now on his return to camp. Since he appeared to be well acquainted with this part of the country, we "pumped" him for all the information that he could impart. As he was a naturally loquacious individual, he had a great deal to say, and, understanding in a general way the object of our expedition he urged us by all means to come over to the La Plata and he would undertake to show us something worthwhile.

It was generally known that many old ruins were scattered all over the southwest from the Rio Grande to the Colorado, but Cooper maintained that around the Mesa Verde, only a short distance from their camp, were cliff dwellings and other ruins more remarkable than any yet discovered. We decided to follow Cooper over to his camp as soon as we could outfit for the trip. It was from Cooper that we first heard of John Moss who he described as the high muck-a-muck or hi-yas-ti-yee of the La Plata region. He recounted how Moss, through his personal influence with the Indians, had secured immunity from trouble not only for his own operations, but also for others traveling through the country.

Soon after leaving Animas Park, we overtook and passed Cooper's outfit. A few miles farther we were very much surprised to see Moss himself, coming from behind at a jog trot, with the evident purpose of overtaking us. Riding along together until we reached the camp, cordial relations were established very soon. Moss promised us his cooperation and possibly his company in our further operations. At this time he appeared to be about thirty-five years of age, of slender wiry figure, rather good-looking, with long hair falling over his shoulders. He was as careless in his dress as any prospector or miner. Quiet and reserved in speech and manner generally, he warmed up to good-natured cordiality on closer acquaintance. We found out later that he could be a very agreeable camp companion. The Moss camp was located on the La Plata River where it emerged from Babcock Mountain and it was in truth a camp only, with a few small tents and some brush wickiups affording all the protection that they had provided for themselves up to this time. Their mining operations consisted of a ditch line, partially completed, running out onto a bench of the land extending down the river some two or three miles. (This would have been the flume of the Parrott City Company, conceived and operated by Moss.) It was supposed to contain enough free gold to pay for working it. I believe afterwards this was found unprofitable and the work was abandoned.

Both Ingersoll and myself were donated generous shares on the bar, but it didn't mean anything to us in dividends. They were a jolly lot of old-timers, mostly from California and the Southwest generally. Their operations were financed by San Francisco gamblers and engineered by Moss and their representatives. Just at this time, however, they were all very much worked up over an election that was about to come off. A new county, or township perhaps, had been formed from the newly acquired territory and officers were to be elected.

After the polls closed that night, Moss and Ingersoll and I made a rapid ride over to Merrit's Ranch on the Mancos where we all put up for the night. Merrit was one of Moss'[s] outfit who had taken up a claim on the Mancos, built a log house, and was experimenting in gardening. Just now he was bewailing the loss of some of his vegetables by an early frost. His heartier crops, however, had turned out very well.

With this ranch as a base of operations, John Moss showed William H. Jackson a variety of cliff dwellings that are now justly famous as Mesa Verde National Park. The Jackson and Moss party started out from Merrit's Ranch on a bracing September morning. Moss, of course, acted as their guide.

Cooper came with us, not that he was of much help, but because of his former friendship; and in that he was the means of bringing us to the acquaintance of John Moss. He was an easy-going chap, somewhat indolent and content to follow along with the packs—very loquacious and full of wonderful stories concerning himself—supplying most of the amusement in the banter around the campfire after the day's work was over. Ingersoll and myself, with the two packers, represented the survey. We had three pack mules carrying the photographic outfit. Steve and Bob, with their packs, kept roaming all over, investigating every indication of possible ruins that came to our notice. When photographing was decided upon, one mule would be dropped out and unpacked, tents set up, and the views made while the others jogged along until we overtook them again.

Our first discovery was of a cliff house that came up to our expectation. This was made late in the evening on the first day out from Merrit's Ranch. We had finished our evening meal of bacon, fresh baked bread, and coffee and were standing around the sagebrush fire enjoying its warmth. Looking up at the walls of the canyon that towered above us some eight hundred or one thousand feet, we began bantering Steve, who was a big heavy fellow, about the possibility of having to help carry the boxes to the top to photograph some ruins up there. With no thought that there were any in sight at the time, Steve

asked Moss to point out the particular ruin that he had
in view. The Captain indicated the highest part of the
wall at random. "Yes," said Steve, "I can see it." And
sure enough, upon closer observation there was something that looked like a house sandwiched between the
strata of the sandstone very nearly at the top. Forgetting
our fatigue, all hands started out at once to investigate.
The first part of the climb was easy enough, but the upper portion was a perpendicular wall of some two hundred feet, and, half way up, the cave-like shelf on which
was a little house. Before we had reached the foot of this
last cliff, only Ingersoll and I remained. The others had
seen all they cared to, realizing that they would have to
do it all over in the morning. From this height we
had a glorious view over the surrounding canyon walls,
while far below our campfire glimmered in the deepening
shadows like a far-away little red star.

On the party's return trip, they spent three days getting back to the La Plata camp. It was a busy time with
a good deal of photographing and some digging about
the ruins. When they came out on the broad, open divide between the Dolores and San Juan rivers, they went
off on a wrong trail that led them into Lost Canyon. The
following day, however, the party returned to their
original route. They stayed long enough on the Mancos
to make some negatives of the ranch house and then
started back to the La Plata camp at top speed, getting
there just in time for dinner before dark.

The miners had all moved down from the upper camp
and were just starting a new one for the winter, the
ditch having been brought down to this point. On the
sixteenth of September, 1874, the Jackson party
started back for Baker's Park again, after a very cordial
leave-taking all around. Upon their return to Animas
Park, they found it almost deserted because of an Indian scare. The farms had also been abandoned.

In 1877 the most pressing need at Parrott City was
first of all a better system of communication with the
outside world. A second desire was for a military post,

a military road, and a settlement of the Indian troubles. An appropriation was sought for the construction of a wagon road and mail route from Fort Garland, via Pagosa Springs, to Parrott City.

An early-day account, typically optimistic, described the La Plata settlement as follows:

Parrott City is sixty miles from Silverton. It is a lively mining camp that is growing rapidly. Thus far, it has suffered from difficulty of access, there being no wagon road connecting it with other towns and districts in the San Juans. Goods and supplies have to be packed in on burros. Notwithstanding its comparative isolation from its neighbors, especially during the winter season when the intervening range is almost impassable, the day is fast approaching when it will take rank with its sister towns of the San Juans. The gold placer mines in and around it are said to cover an area of ten miles long and from one to two miles wide along the La Plata River and are extremely rich. The quartz mines are equally rich in gold and silver and the veins are quite distinct and well defined.

The Moss company was eventually compelled to abandon the riverbanks and take to the mountainsides. Going farther up, they located the previously mentioned quartz lode which they called the Mother Comstock in honor of the great mine in Nevada. This property was also abandoned later.

Population growth continued until enough had arrived to result in the election of John Moss to the state legislature in the general elections held in the fall of 1876. This was the first general assembly convened in the state after its admission into the Union. Arriving in the capital, he made several speeches in the House of Representatives.

At this time even the military rank of Moss was open to question. On February 15, 1877, the *Rocky Mountain News* reported that:

Among the Democrats sent to the lower house in the

Colorado legislature was Colonel John Moss of La Plata County. The Colonel is convivial, not to say bibulous in habit and distinguished his entrance in politics by making himself hail-fellow-well-met with all the men about town. His worst sin was drinking. He kept a big supply on hand at all times and was under its influence much of the time. While in the legislature at Denver, Charlie Leichsenring's saloon held more attraction for him than the assembly.

Becoming disgusted with the lawmaking process, Moss took "French Leave" for San Francisco, abandoning his constituents to look out for their own interests. It goes without saying that John Moss did not make a brilliant record as a legislator. Because of the fact that he remained there only a half day in one account and less than two days in another, he was given the names of the "Great Absentee," and "The Missing Member."

The *News* article further speculated that:

As a Representative, Moss was entitled to pay of four dollars a day. Since he removed himself to California, it is expected that the watchdog of the treasury, honorable Alva Adams, of Rio Grande County, will probably see to it that Moss is not allowed to draw any pay that does not properly belong to him.

A later letter from Parrott City to the Pueblo *Chieftain* recited a long list of grievances which that part of the state had been forced to endure, most of which could be traced to their sending a Democrat to represent them at the legislature. In view of Moss's continued absence from the Chambers, the correspondent called upon the house to declare the seat vacant and order a new election, promising that politics will be ignored and that a good man would be sent to Denver.

Moss personally did not want the position and once said that there was not enough money in it. For another thing, the weather was nice and he had the wanderlust again. Frankly, it appears that he just wanted to be free to go where he pleased. For some reason, best known to himself, he chose never to return to the town he had founded. There is a rumor that Moss and his wife, who accompanied him when he left Colorado, had another child born to them after arriving in California.

In September of 1879, three years after his much-publicized removal from Colorado, the name of John Moss mysteriously turned up along with those of William C. Chapin and John Reed in an association organized to build a toll road from May's Ranch on the Dolores River to the mouth of Bear Creek in La Plata County. The affairs of the company were to be controlled by a board of three trustees. At the same time the incorporators filed for permission to build a road from the lower reaches of Lost Canyon to intersect with the main road at Grouse's Gulch. The capital stock of this company was twenty thousand dollars and its term of existence was to have been twenty years. The eventual fate of the enterprise is unknown.

The first of these two roads was called the Dolores Valley Toll Road. It was to have been a wagon road and its articles of incorporation were dated September 4, 1879. The second enterprise was named the Lost Canyon and Dolores Toll Road Company. Reception Numbers 2093 and 2094 were assigned by the state in the names of the two companies respectively. In both instances Parrott City was listed as being their headquarters. Curiously, less than a month earlier, the same three men, in conjunction with John S. Putnam, had filed still another set of articles of incorporation on August 15. The Mancos and Dolores Toll Road Company was to have built a road from the Lee Ranch on the Mancos River to Silver Creek on the Dolores River. It also listed its headquarters as Parrott City.

According to records in the State Archives, three additional toll roads seem to have been involved with Parrott City. Earliest of all was the Parrott City, Animas Valley, and Tierra Amarilla Wagon Road Company of 1877. Its route from Parrott City followed the river for six miles to Lightning Creek, then over and across the Animas River to the Florida River, then southwest to the San Juan River, and finally terminating at Tierra Amarilla, New Mexico. During 1878, the Parrott and Animas City Toll Road Company was planned by J. H. Shaw, J. W. Dobbins, and Washington Finley. Its purpose was simply to connect the two cities mentioned in the title. Last of all came the Durango, Fort Lewis, and Parrott City Toll Road Company, chartered on November 17, 1881. Otto Mears, A. P. Camp, and Charles Munn were listed as incorporators. Since the state merely issued charters and did not follow up to see what became of such enterprises, it is now nearly impossible to find out what, if anything, was ever done with these roads. It is quite possible that many were never built at all.

The efforts of the original Californians to establish themselves continued for several more years, until some time after John Moss's departure. As a matter of fact, some of them remained in the country permanently. Moss died in San Francisco in April of 1880 at the age of forty-one years. One reputed cause of his death was a combination of mountain fever and pneumonia, contracted while he was prospecting in the mountains. A more remote cause was a gunshot wound through his left lung, which had been received years before when he jumped between a brother Mason and an infuriated Indian.

Moss's life was indeed stranger than fiction. Whatever his failings, he was, nevertheless, often described as being filled with human kindness. It would be interesting to know if Moss ever reflected upon that peculiar turn of fate, the accidental shooting of Richard Giles, that had originally detained his party in the San Juans, altered their plans and changed his future life and the subsequent history of La Plata County.

With or without John Moss, life at Parrott City went

on with a "business as usual" attitude. At its peak, there were about fifty houses at Parrott City. The *La Plata Mines*, a weekly newspaper, also flourished there. The largest producing mines were the Mayday, Idaho, Jumbo, Lucky 4, Lucky Moon, Comstock, Gold King, Neglected, Inca, Muldoon, Bessie G., Little Mona, and Red Arrow. Chief among the minerals produced were gold and silver tellurides with some copper and galena.

About a quarter mile beyond Parrott City is an old cemetery containing the graves of twenty-one old-timers who reportedly died "with their boots on." Only one other landmark still remains at the site. The last of the original buildings, the Barbee Hotel, was struck by lightning and burned to the ground on July 7, 1963. Only its charred foundations and the remains of its fireplace can be seen today. Beyond these two relics, Parrott City is merely a name that appears on old maps.

Several miles north of Parrott was La Plata City. Chronologically and historically, the two settlements seem to have paralleled each other. Like Parrott, La Plata City began with the development of gold placers. During 1875, lodes were discovered that made the earlier stream deposits pale into insignificance by comparison. Among the best producers were the Lady Eleanor, La Plata, and Snowstorm. The accompanying pictures reveal that the settlement was never a large one. One source gives a population of two hundred people who had moved in by 1882. In 1889, there were five hundred residents. A daily stagecoach plied its way north from Hesperus through Parrott City to La Plata City and returned the following day.

At present, the winding dirt road is passable all the way in from Hesperus. It follows the creek bed in most instances. Beyond Parrott City, the canyon narrows and the road becomes rougher. All along the way are well-placed markers indicating the access roads into some of the more notable mines. Most of La Plata City's orig-

Collection of Fred and Jo Mazzulla
An undated photo of La Plata City, taken when the community was
obviously past its peak.

Collection of Robert L. Brown
The nearly vacant site of La Plata City in August of 1963

inal buildings are gone. The old school still sits above the road at the southern edge of town and now serves as a summer home for an artist from California.

The road continues on and is usually passable for another few miles beyond the city, as far as the Gold King properties. Following the old trail into the mountains for this short distance past La Plata City will take you to a fork in the road where a sign discourages travel beyond that point in conventional vehicles. A turn to the right will enable today's traveler to follow Lewis Creek back into the high country, traversing Lewis Mountain. Beyond that point is old Eagle Pass, a trail more suited to hikers than to any sort of vehicles.

Returning to the sign where the trails divided, take the one to the left and follow it up into Cumberland Basin. The road winds its way up to a high, timberline meadow where the old town of Cumberland was located. Only two buildings and a few scattered piles of rubble occupy the site at this time. Local opinion seems divided as to whether Cumberland was ever a town or not. In any event, the name came from the rich mine and a good-sized settlement grew up at the location to house those who toiled there, since commuting would have been quite impractical. Even today, the ride to Cumberland from La Plata City by Jeep consumes about two hours.

In 1885 a five-stamp mill and an arastra were constructed at Cumberland to extract free gold, although the Cumberland Mine itself produced only ruby silver. Beyond the town, the road continued on to the north and crossed Kennebec Pass at an elevation of 11,500 feet. Like Eagle Pass, this one should not be attempted by means other than foot travel.

The La Plata camps represent the most southerly extension of the terrain associated with the San Juan excitement. By following the narrow trail that winds gradually upward toward the snowy La Plata Peaks, one may relive vicariously a portion of one of the most exciting migrations in our history.

Courtesy Library, State Historical Society of Colorado
An unknown photographer made this picture of La Plata City in 1894.

Collection of Robert L. Brown
A dense timber growth prevented duplication of the exact angle from which the older picture was made. Very little remained of La Plata City in 1963.

⤳ 11 ⤳

Ouray and Its Western Environs

OURAY IS ON THE PACIFIC SLOPE of the range and is considered to be the center of the northwestern portion of the San Juan region. In 1874 prospectors were at work in the headwaters of the Uncompahgre River and in Poughkeepsie Gulch, well within the present boundaries of Ouray County. They were also digging up the terrain just over the present county line in what is now San Juan County. During 1875 the Grand View Claim was located, just below the town, and by 1879 it was patented. Early in 1881 work was being done at both the Belle of Ouray and Union Mines on Bear Creek, three miles from present-day Ouray. Ouray County contains some of the most rugged and perpendicular mountains to be found anywhere. Its inaccessibility had, of course, retarded its rapid growth.

The city of Ouray itself was started in July or August of 1875 by A. W. Begole and Jack Eckles but was not incorporated until the next year. Two other men who had come to hunt and fish inadvertently uncovered the first lode and appropriately named it the Trout and Fisherman. The townsite is about one fourth of a mile wide and little over a mile in length. Origin of the community's name was the anglicized form of the name of the great Ute chief. At various times it was pronounced Ule, Oo-lay, and Ure. Even the chief himself finally gave up and began signing documents with the contemporary form.

Prospectors came in from Lake City, Silverton, and Mineral Point. Soon, the Clipper and Cedar lodes were located in the basin and their claims actually ran through the present townsite. Ouray's first store was opened in 1876 by J. D. Crane, but they didn't build a school until 1883. Several newspapers were published in the town at various times. First to appear was the *San Juan Sentinel* in 1877. It lasted only a year. The year 1877 also saw the introduction of the *Ouray Times,* which was published until it was absorbed by the newer *Budget* in 1886. Its name was ultimately changed to the *Plaindealer.*

By far the most unusual of Ouray's newspapers, and probably the most unique in Colorado, was the *Solid Muldoon.* David Frakes Day, its founder, was a Union army veteran. The Muldoon Publishing Company came into existence on September 5, 1879, and the first issue of the paper corresponds to that date. The irreverent wit of Day made his editorship a peculiar one to say the least. It was not enough merely to publish "all the news that's fit to print," the *Muldoon* carried all the news, plus the salty, scathing, and frequently racy comments of the editor on the affairs of the world, state, county, local people, or what-have-you. Often libelous, always humorous, the *Solid Muldoon* kept Ouray and its environs in a state of perpetual agitation and apprehension.

When one of Colorado's United States Senators was campaigning for reelection in Ouray, the disrespectful Day reclined at full length on the grass in front of the bandstand. Finally moved by the editor's indifference, the politician inquired, "How long do you intend to go on lying down there, Mr. Day?" The inevitable answer was not long in coming. "As long as you keep on lying up there, Senator," replied the editor.

During the election of 1882, the *Muldoon* became a daily, but the small population dictated its inevitable return to weekly status. Early in 1892, it moved to Durango where it became a daily at last.

The facts concerning the move to Durango are not entirely clear. The following version was found among the records of an Ouray contemporary of that period. "The *Solid Muldoon* became one of the raciest organs that ever appeared in the West. It got to be so racy that the citizens of Ouray offered Day first $3,000 and then $6,000 to move away from the camp but he refused to go. Finally he left the hospital and Durango too and went back to Northern Ireland." The reasons for his hospitalization, if it actually occurred, are left to the conjecture of the reader.

The *Miner*, the *Pilot*, and the *Argus* were also published in Ouray at various times.

The winter of 1888 was a pleasant one in the San Juans. There had been a thaw in January, but Washington's birthday found the snow hard and compact and the weather was fine until the end of February. Some days were so warm that the snow melted a little, even on the tops of the mountains, but froze again from the cold; thus, the fear of snowslides was removed temporarily. The steep canyons surrounding the Ouray district made the entire area a particularly dangerous one for slides.

There were some remarkable instances in the history of Ouray County, however, which show that a man may fall a great distance into a canyon and not be killed. Two miners who had spent the night in town, left for Red Mountain on King's stage with Ike Stevens as driver. Ike enjoyed the reputation of being one who would stay with the horses to the last. It had been snowing a little, but it was a pretty fair morning when they pulled out for Red Mountain with a big load of eggs and general merchandise. The two miners occupied a back seat in the sleigh. Just as they were rounding the last dangerous point, before coming to the numerous small slides that always come down when it stormed, the accident occurred. On the cliffs above, there were two spires of rock that shot up for many feet. The snow had drifted in between these and down upon the road, forming a high bank over which Ike had the temerity to drive. Consequently, when the sleigh went down through the ridge of snow the box came loose from between the runners and started over the edge of the cliff. The horses plunged forward and Ike held tightly to the reins. Both miners, the eggs, and a large amount of merchandise went over the brink and fell straight down, nearly 250 feet into the canyon. Strange to say, not a bone was broken. The two men escaped with a few scratches and a big scare, but the sleigh was in splinters. It had been a sheer fall until they came within twenty feet of the bottom and then a tumble of about the same distance into the creek. The miners were in an India-rubber condition when they realized where they were and resolved the next time to go home before the regular bedtime.

Chief source of the mineral wealth that induced settlement in and development of Ouray was the Mount Sneffels district, nine miles south of the city. William Quinn and Andrew Richardson first found their way onto Mount Sneffels in the fall of 1875. Notwithstanding the extremely high altitude, they remained and worked their claim all winter. The presence of anyone other than Ute Indians was unsuspected. The founding of nearby Ouray was a circumstance unknown to them.

During the winter of 1875-76, the Wright brothers of Silverton climbed the forbidding heights on snowshoes and made a strike on what has since been known as the Wheel of Fortune Lode. Next to appear on the scene were a British metallurgist, William Weston, and his partner, George Barber. The pair staked out six claims which they worked, summer and winter, until 1881. Having driven over eight hundred feet of tunnels in solid rock, the latter two men sold out for fifty thousand dollars to a New York syndicate.

Outright sale to Eastern capitalists was a common fate suffered by many a poor prospector. More often than not, it was deep mining that produced the rich ores so much in demand; but deep mining was, and is, an extremely expensive undertaking. Lacking sufficient capital, the original discoverer of a bonanza usually had little choice except to sell out to an American or British syndicate. Not only did these outsiders assume little or no risk, but they were notoriously addicted to channeling their profits into Eastern banks rather than spending or investing here in Colorado. On the other hand, in all fairness, the syndicates did create jobs and did further the development of many districts. After all, the alternative to their way was not to develop the mine at all. Without their help, the financial history of many a San Juan mining town would have been an infinitely leaner one indeed. Available local money during those times was as scarce as hiccoughs at a prayer meeting.

Moving above the Camp Bird Mine, the farther you go up the canyon the wilder and more sublime the scenery becomes. Gradually the pine and the spruce disappear and you stand upon a desert of rock with here and there a little patch of grass kept alive in the scanty soil washed in by the rains. At Porters, which was the original name for the town of Sneffels, there was a valley of a few acres surrounded by pines. The earlier name came from one of the first settlers, George Porter, a photographer who operated a studio in the large, white, false-fronted building that is visible in the winter photograph. By far the greatest number of the older pictures of Sneffels used in this book were made by Porter. This town was then the end of the wagon road. Here was the celebrated Revenue Tunnel, cut into the mountain which rises to a height of over 12,500 feet behind the town.

The town of Sneffels grew up in this level meadow, on the slope of the mountain of the same name, at a point where Stony Peak looms up at the end of the val-

Courtesy Library, State Historical Society of Colorado
Sneffels in the winter of 1897. The background mountain is Stony Peak.

Collection of Robert L. Brown
Sneffels in 1960. The few remaining structures were built after the 1897 picture was made.

ley. The Revenue Tunnel was the center of the town's life and no miner employed there had any excuse for being late to work since the town actually grew up around it. It was an incredibly rich property and paid well during the years it was worked.

Owned by A. E. Reynolds, the Revenue was the first example of electric power being used for development of a mine. Instead of the more common alternating current, Reynolds used direct current and constructed a string of powerhouses all along the creek bed. At first the lines carried eight hundred volts but this was later cut to five hundred. Mules were killed frequently when they placed their noses against the trolley, and some accounts tell of men being electrocuted at Sneffels. The mine boardinghouse, still standing, had a problem with lights, since they were wired in series. At night, when a worker wanted to extinguish his light and go to sleep, instead of being able to switch it off, he put a can over the bulb.

In addition to the wealthy and productive Revenue properties at Sneffels, a smaller mine and mill combination named the Torpedo Cliffs came into existence. Actually, as in many similar cases, the mill was built to work the ores of other producing mines nearby with the hope of earning enough money to develop their own mine. As things turned out, the fickle smile of fortune failed to smile on the enterprise, the dream was not realized, and the mill never turned a wheel.

One morning, as one of Ashenfelter's packers was driving his train of mules down the steep trail to Ouray, he was stopped by a prospector named Andy Welch who inquired if Ashenfelter was prepared to handle his business too. The packer looked derisively at the unproductive hole behind the man and made appropriate remarks. Instead of being offended, Welch proceeded to tell the jack whacker, "Next shot I'll have her for sure." This general overoptimism was characteristic of pros-

Courtesy Library, State Historical Society of Colorado   Photo by George R. Porter
Sneffels, looking toward Camp Bird. George R. Porter took the picture from the front of his studio.

Collection of Robert L. Brown
Sneffels in 1962. The large building at the right is the old boardinghouse.

pectors generally, and its presence has frequently been noted as a factor in the development of other mining districts. Andy Welch, in fact, was so optimistic that he actually had cleared a road up to his claim just on the strength of what he expected to find there.

Almost on the apex of the range, in the Sneffels district, the Humboldt Mine was situated. From there, the mountains stretched away from it toward the south in the form of a vast amphitheatre until they reached Red Mountain. At that point they turn to the north, seeming to end in the giant peaks that rise up to the east of Ouray. A person's eye might easily have outlined this sublime scene from Sneffel's highest point, tracing the black curling smoke as it came up from the smokestacks at the Yankee Girl and taking in at a glance the whole country for miles around. Old Mount Abrams, gray and dull-colored from the heat and storms of thousands of years, towers above all of the others and appears to be but a rifleshot away from the Ouray toll road though in reality it is many miles distant.

The Humboldt property was exposed to all the rigors of the winters that raged on those lofty mountains. No trees or sheltering gulches broke the force of the intense blizzards which swept along those naked heights. To witness a snowslide within a short distance from the miners' bunkhouse was no rare occurrence.

The Humboldt was tunneled in at an elevation of, roughly, thirteen thousand feet. The mine gave employment to about one hundred and eighty men before the fall in the price of silver. Every day long trains of burros might be seen moving up and down the trail, bringing in supplies and carrying out the valuable minerals to the smelters down below at Ouray. At times the storms on top of the divide were so severe that even the most hardy miner dared not attempt a trip down to the town. On one side, the route led for a greater part of the way along the edge of an embankment, while on

Collection of Fred and Jo Mazzulla   Photo by George R. Porter

A winter view of Sneffels made by George R. Porter in 1890. Porter's studio was the white building with the false front.

Collection of Robert L. Brown

Sneffels now. Note foundations of old buildings across the creek

the other were high cliffs that extended to the summit of the range. During a severe storm the incautious traveler was apt to lose the trail and, wandering over the cliffs, ran the risk of being hurled to destruction.

One day a Swedish miner set out over the trail in a blinding snowstorm. Losing his way, he wandered for some time among the cliffs, vainly trying to find the trail. So filled was the air with thickly falling snow that it became impossible for him to know the direction in which he was going. He walked off into the abyss and fell down the jagged rocks for a distance of about five hundred feet. The rocks, being covered with frozen snow, afforded him no opportunity of clinging to the jutting crags; so that he shot down with almost meteoric speed. He lay at the bottom for many hours, suffering excruciating pain and nearly freezing to death. Some other miners who chanced to be passing saw his body far down in the gulch against the white snow. Using the greatest caution, and after much difficulty, they reached the spot. The man was in a state of unconsciousness, his skull fractured and his body a bruised and bleeding mass. Additional help was secured and the unfortunate man was taken out to the hospital at Ouray where he died in a few days.

One of the richest and best known of the Sneffels' properties was the Virginius, discovered by William Freeland in 1877. Located beyond the town of Sneffels, in the high twelve-thousand-foot valley looking toward Stony Peak, the mine was worked on several levels through a network of some three miles of tunnels. The Virginius is also said to have been the first Colorado mine to utilize electric lights in its underground workings.

From the south of Sneffels up toward the Virginius there was once a burro trail, so called because it was not usually wide enough for a horse, especially when the animal was going up the mountain heavily loaded. Swaying from side to side and stumbling now and again, the animals needed to rest every few yards, since the rarity of the atmosphere and the abruptness of the ascent were considerable. This zigzag manner of moving made the distance to the summit three times that of the line of sight. The snow was often very deep. If the horse stepped off the well-beaten track, he was sure to go down carrying the rider with him. Once on the roll, it was hard to tell where he would stop.

The Virginius was one of the richest silver properties in the world. Its shaft was down about 1,100 feet, with tunnels cut in every one hundred feet. The vein was a true fissure and it was presumed by some that it went down indefinitely. This tunnel was designed to cut the original shaft of the Virginius at two thousand feet or more and all the veins that lay in the course. Much expense was saved in this way, and ore was shipped with less inconvenience. It was the plan of the owners that by moving down the boardinghouses and by placing them on a level with the town, the dangers of the snowslides could be diminished.

Occasionally, accidents marred the progress of work at the tunnel. One winter morning, a telephone message came down to Ouray announcing that three men had been seriously injured in a mining disaster and were calling for the priest and a doctor. The road was in very bad shape, having been closed for some time. By using great care the two men got through the dark without injury and found the victims, one living, the second dead, and the third badly wounded. The three men, named Robinson, Maloney, and "Big Paddy" Burns, had been loading holes with explosives before retiring from their shift when an explosion occurred. The former two were over the holes and Paddy had just put down a box of dynamite at the opening of the tunnel when, without a moment's notice, the explosion went off, decapitating Robinson and exposing his lungs to view. Maloney was struck over the eye by a piece of rock which was forced through his skull and his brains were oozing out. "Big Paddy" Burns, who was standing at Maloney's side, was knocked down, receiving a shower of rock in the side of his head. He thought he was finished and bellowed lustily for the priest. The men who were around gave him a stimulant to keep him alive until the priest arrived. Paddy, however, bewailed his sad fate, keeping up his monotonous cry, "I'm dead, I'm dead, why did I not die at home with my father?" This was the clamor that reached the priest's ears when he arrived. Taking one look at the victim, he said, "There is nothing the matter with you." The strength of Paddy's voice convinced the cleric that he was far from being dead. That night he was removed to the hospital where he remained for six months, during which time a splinter of rock gradually worked its way out of his skull, to the great amusement of the nurses, his friends, and to the dismay of Paddy.

Many miners followed the unfortunate custom of taking giant powder into their cabins and holding it by the fire to thaw out. When frozen, it would not ignite, but when thawed it was one of the most dangerous and powerful of explosives. A miner named Billy Mayer was engaged in thawing powder at his cabin near the Virginius when eight sticks suddenly exploded. The stove was blown through the roof and the cabin was demolished. Billy was horribly mangled and his right hand was badly torn out of shape. All his clothing was ripped to shreds as the discharge hurled him under the bunk. His partner, who was washing their dishes at the time, was not hurt but did receive a painful shock and some slight injuries. Billy recovered sufficiently to whisper, "Wrap me in a blanket and bring help." It was only a mile to the Terrible Mine, but there were so many feet of snow on the ground that it was impossible to get there without snowshoes. Billy's partner, an Italian, knew nothing about these devices and, therefore, was unable to use them on his feet. Picking them up, he put his hands into the straps and set out to swim over the sea of snow. The trail was downhill most of the way, with obstructions hidden beneath the surface. When he encountered these, he "swam" around them, using the snowshoes to keep him on top and his feet as propellers. By 3:00 P.M. he arrived at the Terrible, having started from the cabin at about 7:30 that morning. A party of four was speedily organized to carry the mangled miner to Ouray. All had snowshoes, properly used this time; and the trip was made without serious trouble. Arriving at the cabin, they found Billy and his dog, side by side, in the splintered bunk. They hastily constructed a hand sled and placed Billy on it, covering him up as protection against the cold. Two of the party took the lead and two more kept behind, holding a rope fastened to the sled to keep it from tipping over. It was now growing dark and the wind had started to blow. Sometimes the location of the trail was lost and as the howling storm gathered about them, they became increasingly worried. One of the men broke his snowshoe and another was so worn out that he asked to be left behind. Just before entering the gulch, they heard the crash of a snowslide away to the right. Its sound, they said later, could easily be told from the explosion of dynamite since it came with a dull heavy thud, devoid of all resonance. At last, ready to drop, they arrived at the Terrible. Four other volunteers had agreed to transport Billy the additional three miles down the mountain to Porters (Sneffels); but, it later developed, they were lost in a snowslide. As the four men had failed to reach the Terrible, the original party of miners, fatigued though they were, resumed the task of bearing Billy toward the hospital at Ouray. Upon returning the following day, they saw the track of an awful snowslide along the way and knew at once the fate of the other four who had not arrived. Looking closely, they saw a hat on the snow. Following the track of the slide, they soon came to a hand, frozen stiff, protruding above the surface. They dug around it carefully and presently reached the head of a man. He was standing up as straight as an arrow with his hands thrown out, as if to ward off a crushing blow or perhaps to keep them free from the snow packing when the crunching mass had closed around him. There was a large cavity in the snow which had been thawed out by his warm breath, leading the men to believe that he may have lived five or six hours standing up in his snowy tomb.

The road to the Virginius was kept in good condition except in winter. Farther up the canyon, however, it was somewhat dangerous because of its closeness to the precipice. One false step and both horse and rider would be hurled for a drop of nearly two thousand feet below.

In the earlier period, all ores from the nearby Yankee Boy, Wheel of Fortune, and the Virginius as well, were shipped down, from above timberline, on pack animals and sent to Lake City for treatment. Only very rich ore could still show a profit after withstanding the thirty-five-dollars-a-ton cost for transportation. Some ores went to the smelter at Silverton where another charge of forty-five dollars per ton was assessed for processing.

Below Sneffels, just south of the road down to Ouray, is the great Camp Bird, one of the largest and most profitable of all San Juan properties. Geologically, Camp Bird is a misfit. With only a few exceptions, the San Juan camps were predominantly silver producers. The Camp Bird was a gold camp. Chronologically, it was out of step with our story, too, for its discovery and prime production period occurred after the collapse of the silver boom. Quite apart from these facts, its history is still considered a part of the San Juan saga, primarily on the basis of geographical proximity.

Another story in the Horatio Alger tradition figures strongly in development of the Camp Bird. This time the hero is an Irishman, Thomas Walsh, who, like Otto Mears, came to this country prior to attaining his ma-

Collection of Robert L. Brown
Teakettle and Potosi peaks from Yankee Boy Basin. Diana Brown
in foreground.

Collection of Robert L. Brown
A wide-angle view of Yankee Boy Basin showing the needles
formation.

jority. Like Mears, he, too, was a builder, being a carpenter by trade. But quite unlike the canny "Pathfinder," he was a prospector at heart. Strong prospecting tendencies had caused his inevitable gravitation to Leadville in 1879. During his stay in the Cloud City, Walsh operated the Grand Hotel on Chestnut Street. He later worked on a construction gang near Golden for a time and helped to build bridges for the Colorado Central Railroad. His first love, however, was mining and this led him back to working in Del Norte and in Gilpin County. He was also one of the original argonauts in the rush to Deadwood in 1876. He, like Tabor, made money during the Leadville and Rico booms and promptly lost it in the crash of 1893.

For a time, beginning in 1896, he operated the Walsh Pyritic Smelter near Silverton at the point where Cement Creek flows into Baker's Park. The primary purpose of this smelter was the treatment of the ores sent down from Red Mountain by the Yankee Girl and Guston mines. In 1894 Walsh had organized the company which put up this plant.

In 1895, while indulging his abiding passion for prospecting once more, Walsh entered the Imogene Basin, high on the slopes of Mount Sneffels above Ouray. There he dug out some silicious ores that assayed three thousand dollars to the ton in gold. Some say his partner, Andy Richardson, made the discovery; but Walsh's daughter details how her father did it himself. The Imogene Basin, incidentally, was named by Richardson for his wife. Most of the old-timers accept the version that has Richardson working as a scout for Walsh and making the Camp Bird discovery in the process.

A third version of the tale has Walsh busily sampling the huge dumps of the Camp Bird in 1895. In the process it is said that he found tellurium components that were rich in gold.

Still another, and by no means the only other, version

of the Walsh saga describes how, in the search for silicious ores, he investigated the mines of the surrounding country—not only those in operation, but also the abandoned prospects. He bought the Hidden Treasure Mine in the Imogene Basin. This was a low-grade silver property which had never done much. In July of 1896, he went up to see how the work was progressing. Quite incidentally, he noticed some pieces of pink spar among the debris scattered at the foot of the cliffs which formed the upper limits of the basin. The spar reminded him of Cripple Creek where he also had mined with some success. He made a mental note of this fact. The following September he visited the locality and climbed up into the old Gertrude Adit, from which he figured the pink spar had come. Taking some samples from each drift, he sent them at once to Ouray to be assayed. The returns indicated several ounces of gold per ton. More samples were taken and sent to Leadville. The results were confirmed, so he went to work quietly and began the steady consolidation of all adjoining property.

Most accounts also detail how he became so engrossed in his work that he failed to notice the Canada jays, or camp robbers, who stole his lunch. Anyone who picnics in our mountains will attest to the highly developed skill of this species in regard to the theft of food.

Following the decline in the price of silver, Walsh was able to purchase additional rights to surrounding claims for a purported twenty thousand dollars. The price included about nine hundred acres. Under his astute management, production at the Camp Bird rose until it was second only to the Doyle and Burns Portland properties at Cripple Creek. Total production has been estimated at between thirty and fifty million dollars, with twenty-five million dollars being taken out in the next twenty years alone.

Water pressure for the various hydraulic aspects of mining was always a problem. For example, when the

Camp Bird operated at full capacity, its pumping deprived the Barstow, on the other side of the range, of water pressure.

By 1902, without today's income tax structure, Walsh was a millionaire and had little need for the mine. Consequently, he sold it to a British syndicate for $5,200,000.

Aspiring to a career in politics, Walsh was elected to the United States Senate where he served Colorado with distinction. During this time he purchased the fabled Hope diamond for his wife, Carrie Bell, who subsequently passed it on to their daughter, Evalyn Walsh McLean. Mrs. McLean went on to become the reigning social hostess in Washington during the administration of President Warren G. Harding.

A steep, winding grade carries today's visitor up the canyon to Camp Bird and Sneffels. Several climbing switchbacks and a number of sections of ledge road with overhanging rocks have given this byway a well-earned reputation for trouble, particularly in winter. Since the actual grade is reasonably wide and quite safe, the problem lies in an optical illusion. There are no safety rails; the canyon is deep and its walls are extremely sheer.

In winter, however, the danger is very real indeed. The San Juans have actually spawned the greatest number of snowslides in the state. In 1909, the Waterhole Slide took the lives of four men and sixteen horses. During the winter weather, warm days and cold nights caused formation of long icicles along the edges of overhanging cliffs above the Camp Bird road. To assure protection from injury, when snow deposits fell, miners regularly indulged in the sport of shooting them down.

An early-day driver named Chauncey Mills frequently drove both stages and freight teams. One morning in 1893, he left Ouray headed for the Revenue Mine at Sneffels. When he arrived at Windy Point, one of his horses went off the road. While they were trying to get him back into the tracks, a snowslide came crashing down upon

*Courtesy Library, Colorado
State Historical Society*
Half of a mislabeled
stereo pair showing a section of the road above
Camp Bird, looking to-
ward Sneffels.

Collection of Robert L. Brown   *Photo by Evelyn M. Brown*
The great Camp Bird mill and town, with United States Mountain
in the background.

them and swept the entire outfit down the mountainside. Two of the men standing behind Mills were killed. Another, who was standing three feet from him, also lost his life. A third helper, standing fifty feet from him, was killed; but Mills himself happened to catch hold of a tree and was saved.

Eighteen six-horse teams were on the same road once when the big Waterhole Slide ran and killed twenty-three horses and five men. Drivers usually went over the tops of the slides with their pack outfits, not taking the time to shovel through them since they never knew when a new avalanche would run.

Hardly a winter passes even today without reports of slides and accidents on the road to Camp Bird. Many lives have been lost over the years. In 1936 a Denver man, a woman cook, and a blacksmith were swept off the grade to an icy-cold death in an avalanche. In the mine itself, a total of forty workers were sealed in for several hours by the same slide before rescuers reached them.

Because of its fortunate geographical location, Ouray became the logical social, cultural, and economic center for the several isolated mines and small camps to the west. Most Saturday nights saw its streets crowded with packers and miners down from the Virginius, Camp Bird, or Sneffels. Most came to spend the weekend, and most of their paychecks "seeing the elephant," and passing the time with a night and a day of riotous living. Some others spent their off hours at the Ouray Free Reading Room, and many remained to participate in religious services the following morning. Shortly after noon, the exodus started and the men began their long trek back up Canyon Creek, nursing their respective hangovers or enjoying their individual spiritual rejuvenation. For the next five days, life in the town returned to normal.

From the viewpoint of today's behavioral sciences, we now recognize weekends like those spent at Ouray as valuable and necessary safety valves. Such outlets provided a welcome and, for some people, an essential departure from a life of hard work, monotony, isolation, oxygen starvation, cold, and snowslides. The role played by Ouray, and other communities of its kind, cannot be overlooked in the overall life of any mining district.

~ 12 ~

Telluride and It's Neighbors

SAN MIGUEL COUNTY was originally the western portion of Ouray County. In February of 1883, the state legislature performed a bit of natural geographical surgery. Following the crest of the great mountain range that separates contemporary Ouray and Telluride, the new county was created and a geographically difficult administrative problem was eased. San Miguel County was divided into four mining districts, known as Upper San Miguel, Lower San Miguel, Iron Springs, and Mount Wilson. Its new name came from the nearby stream and mountain range, which in turn had been named for St. Michael by early Spanish padres who had come north from New Spain.

Fur trappers out of St. Louis in 1831 were the first Anglo-Americans to explore the region. Their search for beaver and other fur-bearing animals caused them to follow several of the more likely-looking streams far back into the high country. Since their fur gathering resulted in no permanent settlements, the area was literally forgotten until a detachment from Charles Baker's group penetrated it in 1860-61. Following the San Miguel River up the valley to Howard's Fork, they passed out over the range across what was later called Ophir Pass and returned to Baker's Park once more.

Placer mining caused the initial boom here, just as it had done elsewhere, with moderately productive results

Collection of Fred and Jo Mazzulla
San Miguel City had buildings along both sides of its single street
in the 1880's.

Collection of Robert L. Brown
The location of San Miguel in 1962. Telluride is far up the valley
at the extreme right.

in 1875-76. The following year saw about three hundred men working the gravel along the San Miguel River. It is not surprising that the first town to be founded was also given the name of San Miguel. Established in 1878, the settlement was situated about a mile out of present-day Telluride on the way to Placerville. The modern highway now bisects the old townsite where no part of the original community currently remains. Nearby is the old road across Boomerang Hill to Alta Basin and Ophir.

By today's standards it seems incredible, but a great mark of prestige for every mining community, no matter how tiny, was the acquisition of a post office. San Miguel was no different. Soon it put on further airs and called itself San Miguel City, and by 1880 it boasted a population of two hundred men and five women. A sawmill was erected very early in its life span and soon the inevitable hotel was in business, too.

Hydraulic mining was attempted also in 1877 when the Wheeler and Kimball Ditch was completed to carry water to the claims. During 1888 the San Miguel Gold Placer Company was capitalized at three million dollars to work the river and its tributaries. Here, in the midst of a great silver rush, was still another gold-producing region. In addition to the unusual amounts of silver, lead, and copper, gold is still found in some abundance even today.

Because of the great mountain range, which includes Mount Sneffels to the north and a tremendous bank of huge peaks to the east, this basin was virtually isolated from the other mineral-producing districts until Otto Mears pioneered his wagon road from the Uncompahgre Valley across Dallas Divide. Later, this same grade became the route of his beloved Rio Grande Southern, built in 1890.

In addition to San Miguel, a second community named Columbia was also started in 1878 although the townsite

Cable for the Nellie Tramway

Collection of Randy and Morine Baisch   *Photo by Moore Bros.*

This Moore photograph shows the cable for the Nellie Tramway on Telluride's main street. Note that each coil is continued to the next. Total length was 10,810 feet without splices.

Collection of Robert L. Brown

The main street of Telluride in 1964. Note absence of tower that once reposed on structure behind the "Drugs" sign.

was not surveyed and no plat was filed until 1883. Its
name was subsequently changed to Telluride. Around the
town on three sides are huge ledges of porous quartz, containing free gold, rising fifty to one hundred feet above
the face of the mountains.

Because Telluride was much closer to the rich mines
that were being opened up, the residents of San Miguel
gradually abandoned their own town and gravitated up
the valley to Telluride. Growth of the town otherwise
was rather slow due to severe transportation problems.
The real boom came during the nineties, after the Rio
Grande Southern had extended its tracks into the county.

When Telluride was in its prime, there were only two
important days on the calendar—Christmas and July 4.
There were many Cornish miners working in the district
and most of them came to town only on those days, unless it was to attend a funeral for one of their country-
men. They loved music and many of them were fine sing-
ers. Elaborate preparations were always made for the
Fourth-of-July celebration. The committee in charge had
each side of the long street decorated with rows of evergreen trees, colorful bunting, and flags. The Telluride
band usually furnished the music, helped out occasionally
by one of the outside musical groups. Platforms were
built in the street for the inevitable hard-rock drilling
contests. A racetrack was often constructed a mile or
so below town and here one could see exhibitions of calf
roping and bronchobusting. There were also Indian pony
races, as well as regular horse races. An amphitheatre
was built on the hillside from which the people had a
beautiful view of the town. The celebrating usually lasted
for three days and closed with a big ball during the final
evening.

There was no church building in Telluride until the
early 1890's. All such meetings were held in the local
courthouse. The first church to be constructed was the

Congregational. Later, Catholic and Methodist churches were also erected.

High in the Marshall Basin, above the town, was the rich Sheridan vein, discovered in August of 1875 by John Fallon. Both the Union and the Smuggler, two of Telluride's biggest producers, were located on this single formation. During July of the following year, one J. B. Ingram was prospecting in the basin. It occurred to him at the time that the Union and Sheridan claims exceeded their legal allowance. Taking his own measurements, he discovered that both had about five hundred feet of land that was not legally theirs. Putting down his own stakes upon the surplus ground, he named his property the Smuggler. This incredible bit of good fortune resulted in one of the region's richest mines. Its principal vein was fully a mile long and by the turn of the century it had something in excess of thirty-five miles of tunnels beneath the surface of the mountain.

To serve it and the other mines developed on this vein, a crosscut tunnel was made through the mountain. From its mouth, a tram was constructed to carry the ore down below to the Pandora Mill, built in 1888 to handle eighty tons of rock a day. Actually, a small town called Pandora had been started there in 1875, shortly after the Pandora Mine had been located. Chief source of income for residents of the town, however, was the huge Smuggler-Union, a gigantic flotation installation type mill that refined the ores brought down from high on the mountain.

Some distance north and east of Pandora was still another small community that, for a time, hoped for a rich ore discovery or some other condition that would justify its existence. This was the town of Old Dallas, located where Dallas Creek joins the Uncompahgre River. It was a thriving community with about twenty stores and saloons, well patronized by the freighters and cattlemen. Beyond these dubious marks of distinction, it had no claim to fame until the railroad arrived.

In the Gold King Basin, across Boomerang Hill, were the Alta and Gold King properties. A small community grew up there, too, complete with a large boardinghouse, a fine white school, and many private residences which are still standing. There was never a church at Alta. A forty-stamp mill, powered by electricity, was soon erected near the mine entrance. Overhead, the tram cables with buckets in place, may still be seen.

Alta was an example of a large, thriving mining camp that never actually became a town although it possessed all the requirements for formal incorporation. The Gold King Mine itself was discovered in the 1870's and was worked spasmodically up through World War II, except for a period of dormancy between 1924 and 1938. Within the camp, the Black Hawk Tunnel reaches back a reputed nine thousand feet into the earth to the St. Louis and Alta veins, which have produced between fifteen and twenty millions of dollars. Over the years, a total of three mills were constructed at Alta but all have since burned. The last was destroyed in 1945.

A third producing area was located up in Bridal Veil Basin, also above Telluride. The Tomboy, another rich producer situated high up on the Savage Fork of the Marshall Basin, was sold in 1879 to the Rothschild banking interests for a reputed two million dollars. Still another of Telluride's better known properties was the Liberty Bell, clinging precariously to a steep mountainside about two miles north of town. In all, the mines around Telluride are estimated to have produced close to a quarter of a billion dollars' total.

One of the dangers in San Juan milling and mining was, and still is, the snowslide. To a stranger the interruption and damage from this source would seem to present a very serious obstacle to the use of a tramway. It does, but to the same extent it affects all operations in a precipitous and snowy mountain region. The Smuggler-Union Tramway was stopped for several weeks as a con-

Collection of Randy and Morine Baisch
The Smuggler mills at Pandora, east of Telluride

Collection of Randy and Morine Baisch
The Liberty Bell buildings, high above Telluride. This entire group
is now gone, carried away by a snowslide.

sequence of the damage done by a slide. During the same season the Liberty Bell Mine buildings were swept away and their mill was idle for four months. In the latter case eighteen lives were lost and a majority of those belonged to rescue parties who went out to give aid to those who had been caught by the first slide. Successive avalanches entombed the rescuers.

As a rule it is possible to predict the track of snowslides because they commonly follow the line of destruction marked out by them in previous years. Great injury to life and property in the San Juans is often caused by the unexpected slide which takes an entirely unsuspected line of descent. Such was the case in the Liberty Bell catastrophe. The buildings had been erected at a spot confidently believed to be immune from such danger.

The destructiveness of a snowslide must be seen to be appreciated. Buildings and tramways are like toys in its path. Any men in its right-of-way are mere straws in a whirlwind. In reality, much of the damage done is due to a vacuum caused by the rapid motion of the mass of snow and the disturbance following in its wake. One on-the-spot observer described it this way: "Its thunderous noise first attracts one's attention and then you see the mass of snow gathering underlying rocks and uprooted trees, amid a quickly gathering mist of snow particles driven fiercely by the whirlwind in the rear. The rushing mass will not stop at the bottom of the slope, but its momentum will carry it some distance up the opposite side while all the forest trembles and the air is darkened with a snowy mist." In the cemetery at Telluride there are many large graves enclosing the remains of groups of unfortunate miners who were swept to their deaths by fateful avalanches. Their resting places are not marked by showy tombstones or epitaphs, but close by a white marble monument attracts attention with the inscription upon its face. It tells a startling story.

TOMBOY

Collection of Randy and Morine Baisch
The settlement at the Tomboy property, high above Telluride

Photo by Ronald F. Ruhoff
The same view of the Tomboy as it appeared in September of 1963

Just east of town and straight up the sheer wall of the cliff lies one of the most spectacularly located of the big mines. This is the Black Bear. The hanging cliff trail to the mine and beyond was reopened a few years ago by the Telluride Jeep Club 50. From the town it looks like a series of Z-shaped cuts going up steeply across the sheer face of this great rock wall and that's just about all it is. The trail, for it can hardly be called a road, starts from Pandora and sweeps sharply up along a narrow, rocky series of switchbacks. If you drive this one, use extreme caution since more than one Jeep has gone off over the side. What is more, it is usually necessary to back and turn your way around the switches. From on top, the view is indescribably beautiful with Telluride spread out far down below you. If you choose to go on past the Black Bear Mine, the road continues up over the divide and comes out close to the top of Red Mountain Pass on U.S. 550. Still another of the spectacular trails to Telluride begins on the Ouray side, high in the Imogene Basin at the Camp Bird Mine. The second level of the Camp Bird was at an elevation of 11,510 feet, and the place where the trail crossed the divide from the mine to Telluride was about 13,800 feet high. The trail was a good one in summer and people were not required to lead their horses except on the steeper portions of the rise and during the abrupt descent on the other side. When they reached the summit, a halt was usually called in order that they might take in the splendid view of the mountains. Looking back over the course just traveled, one would see the shadows covering the valley of Canyon Creek and the sheltered corner among the hills where Ouray lay concealed. Looking the other way, the grim desolation of timeworn summits and crumbling crags reached down into the gloomy gorge of the San Miguel River and into the sunlit valley of Telluride. The descent to Telluride was tedious, for it meant leading the animals most of the way—and some horses are particularly slow to be led, however willing they may be to be ridden. Besides, the drop from the top of the range to the valley is said to be just five thousand feet in the course of five miles. All the way down, one passed mines and mills. Of the latter, the new Tomboy Mill in Savage Basin always loomed most conspicuously through the dusk.

Labor wars shook the basin in 1901. At issue was the contract work system which would have reduced the daily pay of the workers. In July of 1901 the management of the Smuggler-Union introduced the system of working by contract, which resulted in paying a miner according to the amount of work done. It was directly opposed to the underlying principle of unionism and, of course, there was a strike. Members of the union refused to work but a large number of experienced miners accepted the contract system and remained at the mine.

When the operators continued working with nonunion labor, the incensed unionists surrounded the mines. On the third of July, a body of strikers attacked and shot indiscriminately in the bunkhouses, offices, and other buildings and succeeded in killing eight nonunion men. Herding the survivors of the fight onto a nearby hilltop, they invited them to leave the district. The hated contract system was abandoned and things returned to normal for a while. In 1903, the operators of the Tomboy hired a nonunion work force and raised the curtain for Act II.

A walkout by union members resulted in an appeal to Governor Peabody by the Western Federation of Miners. The governor, typically, passed the buck to President Theodore Roosevelt with a request for Federal troops. Teddy still remembered how his tailfeathers were singed in the Cripple Creek strikes and he was not anxious to go for seconds at this time. While serving as McKinley's Vice-President, Roosevelt had been mobbed at the Victor station and only narrowly averted a thorough mauling at the hands of some anti-McKinley miners. With this background, the President deftly fielded the "hot potato" back to the reluctant arms of the governor. Major Z. T. Hill was placed in command of the state militia and lost little time in taking over the mines and instituting martial law in Telluride during January of 1904. Union leaders were arrested, a few were beaten and sent, licking their wounds, out of the district.

Not about to take this one lying down, the federation brought up their heavy artillery in the person of Harry Orchard (real name B. F. Horsley), a professional assassin for the union whose accomplishments would have made the meager efforts of Alfred Packer look like child's play by comparison. Among his achievements one may find various dynamitings in the Coeur d'Alene district; the blasting of Governor Frank Steunenberg, of Idaho, to kingdom come with another well-placed charge; dynamiting the Vindicator Mine at Goldfield, Colorado, causing the deaths of two men; and the ruthless bombing of the Independence station near Cripple Creek, which resulted in nineteen deaths and many more injured. Possessed of all of the finer social instincts of a young timber wolf, Harry Orchard cut a bloody swath across the troubled pages of Colorado's labor history. His favorite weapon, obviously, was dynamite, set off by a windlass, acid vials, and giant caps. Only once did he deviate from his preference. On that occasion he tried poison but was so disappointed in the results that he returned immediately to dynamite, his first love, and never again departed from the true faith.

Since Governor Peabody was widely blamed for Telluride's labor troubles, Orchard was ordered to eliminate him. Two attempts were made to earn his fee under contract, the same system the union had so roundly condemned at the Tomboy. When Orchard failed to produce results, the union refused to pay. His first effort aborted when a newsboy ran down a path usually followed by the punctual Peabody on his way to work. Needless to

Collection of Fred and Jo Mazzulla
A burro train is loaded in the street at Ophir about 1890

Collection of Robert L. Brown
Ophir in 1962. Note the presence of three of the original buildings.
Ophir needles are above the town.

say, the boy was killed. Still determined to earn his stipend, Orchard planted dynamite in the front lawn of the governor's residence and arranged for it to go off when the front gate was opened. Mercifully, the wire broke and Orchard, under pressure of performing other needful activities elsewhere, forgot all about it for many years. Peabody eventually died a natural death, but Orchard's downfall was religion.

Becoming extremely devout, Orchard confessed all and spent his declining years within the Idaho State Penitentiary. One day, while talking with reporters who were attempting to add up his tally sheet, he suddenly recalled the Peabody interlude. When the startled residents of the former governor's home dug below a depression in their front lawn, they were somewhat more than mildly surprised to uncover one of Harry Orchard's infernal machines. What a way to learn about an obscure San Juan labor war!

When all else had failed, a union-organized army was formed and for a time they operated out of an abandoned mine near Telluride; but in the end their power was broken and the mineowners continued to operate—with nonunion labor. Since that time, the large output of the Telluride district has come chiefly from the mines of three large companies—the Liberty Bell, the Smuggler-Union, and the Tomboy.

Almost directly south, across the range, lie the Ophirs, New and Old. New Ophir is at the foot of the Ophir Needles and was once called Howard's Fork. Nearby stood the incredible Ophir loop, by which the Rio Grande Southern gained enough altitude to get up out of the valley. Two miles east, at the foot of Ophir Pass, is Old Ophir. Quite apart from the fact that this is actually the older of the two towns, the buildings here are far better preserved. Fine structures of dressed lumber, many obviously of twentieth-century vintage, still line the main street.

Collection of Fred and Jo Mazzulla
Ophir, as photographed from Silver Mountain. Building at extreme left was the school.

Collection of Robert L. Brown
Ophir in 1962. Waterfall Creek comes down from the high valley at the left of the central peak.

The town is situated in the small valley between Yellow and Silver mountains. Through this valley flows Howard's Fork, a branch of the San Miguel River. From the center of the town, numerous prospects and at least a dozen claims can be seen. Ophir was first laid out and the initial log houses were built in 1878. During that year, the Gold King Lode was discovered. The pocket of rich ore taken out of this claim exceeded the richness and the quantity of that taken out of the Osceola. The year 1889 promised to bring the boom that every young mining camp apparently has at some time.

Early in the season over five hundred prospectors were at Ophir. Five saloons were distributing "forty-rod," and everything indicated that the boom had arrived. Just at this time, however, the carbonate excitement started at Rico and that settled the boom. Prospectors wanted carbonate, galena, and gray copper. The result was that the boom didn't develop and Ophir had to wait.

There were several popular routes in and out of the basin which are no longer used today. North of Telluride, Blue Lake Pass went over the top at an altitude of 12,600 feet and came down at a point just south of Mount Sneffels. Imogene Pass was 13,365 feet high and started beyond the upper Camp Bird Mine. Southeast of the Upper Camp Bird and northwest of Imogene Pass was Richmond Pass, a less well-known crossing that topped the range at an elevation of 12,640 feet.

Although a large number of closely situated mines contributed to the overall employment picture in Ophir, some income was also derived from the freighting business that resulted from the nearby pass.

Originally opened as a toll road in 1881, Ophir Pass now consists of a series of narrow ledges cut from the abundant slide rock. The grades are steep and suitable only for four-wheel-drive vehicles, horses, or hikers. From the top, one may enjoy a superb mountain panorama out across the green San Miguel Valley. Following

Collection of Fred and Jo Mazzulla
Ophir Pass as it appeared in the late 1880's, while it was still a
toll road.

Collection of Robert L. Brown
At the top of the Jeep road over Ophir Pass, one may pause to
enjoy this panorama of the Mount Wilson group of peaks.

the old pass down the other side, to the east, will take you to U.S. 550, a few miles north of Silverton, out of San Miguel County and away from Telluride and its neighbors.

Collection of Robert L. Brown
Looking west across the Howard Fork from on top of Ophir Pass

Collection of Robert L. Brown
Author and family on top of Ophir Pass

～ 13 ～

And This Too Shall Pass Away

IN 1893 THE SHERMAN SILVER PURCHASE ACT was re-
pealed, an act that rang out the death knell for San Juan
mining.

Early in 1963 a small amount of adrenalin was pumped
back into the tired old veins when some mining men
began to show a renewed interest in reopening some of
the old San Juan silver mines. Most of the resurgence
of interest was attributable to the fact that Uncle Sam
finally quit the market and ultimately stopped selling
silver for ninety-two cents an ounce. Logically, such
action resulted in an increase for the market price of
silver to $1.25 an ounce, as of this writing. Time only
will tell us whether or not the current jubilation of some
Colorado mining interests was justified.

During the seventy years that separated these two
events, the final acts of our drama were played out on a
stage at Washington. The fate of the San Juan camps
was but a small pawn in the imminent struggle of the
titans who sought to establish the preeminence of gold
over silver. The events that followed not only evacuated
a cluster of mining camps in southwestern Colorado;
they also gave a new sense of direction to the United
States as a great world power.

The currency system of the United States had been
based on bimetallism since the days of George Washington. Bimetallism simply means the use of both gold and

silver in legal coinage. The role of silver in the development of the American West and its status in relation to the national economy as a whole is a curious phenomenon indeed. The presence of silver in Colorado's high country had been detected well before the first rush of 1859, but it was more difficult to mine and mill than gold and was worth only one-sixteenth as much. Our monetary system in the West also suffered because of its inelasticity. The nation's money supply, instead of increasing when the need was greatest, actually declined. In order to alleviate this shortage, the Westerner saw more money in circulation as the most desirable and logical answer. The silver dollar, coupled with controlled quantities of bullion from the mines, seemed an acceptable medium for circulation along with gold coins. A ratio of sixteen to one was utilized—sixteen times as much silver in silver dollars as there was gold in gold dollars. This worked well until the California Gold Rush of 1849 when such quantities were mined that the value of gold was reduced. Gold then became less valuable in relation to the white metal, and silver dollars began to disappear from the market as people melted them down for commercial uses.

The miners themselves soon got into the act, too. Instead of bringing their silver to the mint to be coined, they sold it directly to silversmiths and bypassed the middleman.

In 1873 the Congress terminated all coinage of silver dollars and placed the country on a gold standard. Actually, in 1868 the production of gold in Colorado was valued at two million dollars; while silver, worth $1.326 an ounce, produced a total of only a quarter of a million dollars. A scant quarter of a century later, there was a complete turnabout. By this time, gold production had reached $5,300,000, while silver mining now turned out a total value of $20,880,000. The figure is even more startling when one realizes that the price of silver during this same period had shrunk to a scanty eighty-seven cents an ounce.

Then came the great silver strikes in the San Juans, at Leadville, in Summit County, and those in Nevada and Arizona. Silver suddenly became so plentiful that the roles were again reversed, and its price started a gradual decline in relation to gold.

The mineowners demanded that the government continue to purchase at the old ratio of sixteen to one, and they called the demonetization of silver "The Crime of 1873." Western farmers and debtors joined them in their appeals. Being deprived of their needed cheaper currency, Western mining interests secured passage of the Bland-Allison Act in 1878. Senator Richard P. Bland of Missouri introduced the bill during the first Congress of President Hayes. It was vetoed by the President but was passed over his veto by the Congress. Provisions of this new piece of legislation instructed the Treasury to purchase not less than two, nor more than four million dollars' worth of silver each month, such metal to be made into silver dollars. Actual practice, however, kept the purchases more in line with the minimum figure, and the basic problem remained unsolved. The net result had the government buying twenty-four million dollars' worth of silver every year, to be coined into silver dollars which, in 1878, were worth less than ninety cents in gold. This was fairly good business for the San Juan camps, but not for the nation as a whole. Westerners next favored completely free and unencumbered coinage of silver at the same old ratio of sixteen to one.

The political implications became distressingly evident in 1885 when Grover Cleveland entered the White House. The new President was blindly opposed to the doctrines of free coinage of silver. Western newspapers thundered in its favor. During 1885 a silver convention was held in Denver and the Colorado Silver Alliance was formed. In 1889 the National Silver Convention met at St. Louis.

Silver now became the burning political issue with both of the established parties and a shadow of white crept across the land.

Meanwhile, strike after strike followed and silver literally poured from the mines around Leadville, from Summit County, the San Juans, and elsewhere. The various ranges of the Colorado Rockies apparently held a nearly inexhaustible supply of the white metal. Horace A. W. Tabor once boasted that there was enough to build a solid wall of silver forty feet high and four feet thick all along our eastern boundary. Posterity does not reveal by what stroke of modesty Tabor was restrained from building such a wall.

Our Free Silver exponents worked through a variety of political organizations. Here in Colorado it was the Populist or People's party. Feeling ran so high in the silver camps and in the state as a whole that a Populist candidate, Davis H. Waite, of Aspen, was elected governor. This was the only time in the history of Colorado that a minority party was able to put its man into the Statehouse. Nationally, the Populists infiltrated the Democratic party.

When faced with disaster, Governor Waite said, "It is infinitely better that blood should flow to our horses' bridles rather than our national liberties should be destroyed." From that day on he was known as "Old Bloody Bridles" or "Bloody Bridles Waite." His answer to the problem would have Colorado purchase the entire output of its silver mines for shipment to Mexico. After it had been coined into "Fandango Dollars," it would be returned to the state for use as legal tender. The prosperous eighties drew to a close with silver production still miraculously holding in the neighborhood of twenty million dollars per year.

By 1890 the Congressmen from the Western silver-producing states became so powerful that by voting in a bloc they were able to threaten passage of the McKinley

Tariff unless Congress granted them free coinage. The
outcome was still another compromise. In order to secure passage of the McKinley measure, the President ap-
peased the "silverites" by agreeing to purchase four
and one-half million ounces of silver each month. This
was made possible by Congressional passage of the Sherman Silver Purchase Act of 1890. The Sherman Act
rocketed the price of silver up from eighty-four cents to
one dollar and fifty cents per ounce. This new figure was
more than double the amount allowed by the Bland-Allison Act and resulted in the Treasury storing an ever-
increasing stock of silver bullion that was constantly
decreasing in value. This act partially precipitated the
panic of 1893, through the resulting lack of confidence
in governmental fiscal policies. The real causes of the
slump were more psychological than actual. Our gold
reserves were reduced because the McKinley Tariff cut
down Federal revenue. Fearing the worst, people started
to hoard gold. Financial reserves slipped below the
$100,000,000 mark; people were out of work; banks
closed; and workers marched on Washington.

Capitalists feared that such large purchases under the
Sherman Act might cause the gold dollar to be replaced
by a depreciated silver dollar. Business grew still worse,
banks called in their loans, some shopkeepers were forced
to close their doors. When investors rushed to redeem
their securities in gold, the reserve in the United States
Treasury dropped to $70,000,000, far below the danger
point.

On August 7, 1893, President Cleveland called the Congress into special session and asked for an immediate
repeal of the Sherman Act. The House passed it at once,
but the Senate fought over it until October. The Silver
Senators were supported by the Populists and South-
erners. The final vote was forty-eight to thirty-seven
for repeal and a subsequent end to San Juan mining.
Quite apart from the seriousness of the repeal, another

excellent market was also closed when India, a valuable customer for the white metal, curtailed its production of silver coins. Most Republicans had voted for repeal, and most Democrats voted against it.

Mines and smelters closed in silver camps all over the state as the price of silver dropped from eighty-three cents an ounce to sixty-two—less than half its set price—in a single four-day period. Eureka, Animas Forks, and Sherman began to look like deserted villages. In one three-day period ten banks closed in Denver alone.

The battle for "Free Silver" was not over. Although the corpse was in the coffin, it was a real struggle getting the lid down. In 1896 the Republicans, in convention, came out with a plank favoring gold in their party platform. Senator Henry M. Teller, of Colorado, led a delegation of thirty-four Westerners out of the party at the St. Louis convention. It was expected that the Democrats would follow suit in their plank, but this expectation was premature and failed to reckon with recent Populist infiltration into the party.

William Jennings Bryan, an attorney and defeated Congressman from Lincoln, Nebraska, swept aside the pre-convention favorites and received the party's nomination through a dramatic piece of moving campaign oratory. This was his notable "Cross of Gold" speech, still a favorite in high school declamation contests. Actually, the address was not new. Bryan had delivered and polished it several times before; but in the days prior to overexposure on radio and television, it was new to the Democrats and turned the trick.

The "Battle of Standards"—silver versus gold—was the prime issue in 1896, one of the most bitterly contested elections in history. The fate of the San Juans and other Western silver camps once more hung in the balance. Dirty politics was the rule rather than the exception in this one. Employers used wage cuts and threats of layoff to force workers into the Republican camp. Wage earners in some Eastern factories were paid off on the Saturday night before election day with a notice that they would not be needed further if Bryan was elected.

Sixteen ounces of silver were worth only about eleven dollars in 1896, while an ounce of gold would bring $20.67. It is likely that our country would have lost its credit abroad if it had used a debased currency. There was a prevailing fear in Europe that if Bryan became President, America would try to pay off its debts in silver, which was not worth as much on the international market as in the United States Treasury. What is more, the supply of gold at that time was not sufficient for carrying on the business of the country.

Senator Edward O. Wolcott, of Georgetown, often described himself as a Silver Republican. In an effort to placate France and England and to promote "International Bimetallism," Wolcott made a trip to Paris and London. He tried to persuade those governments to agree to bimetallism in exchange for tariff favors from the United States. However, none of the European countries then on the gold standard was willing to abandon it. His mission was a failure.

Bryan's opponent in 1896 was the reactionary William McKinley, of Ohio. The result of all these circumstances and conflicting factors was an election-day plurality of six hundred thousand votes for McKinley, who carried the most populous states to rack up an electoral vote plurality of 271 to a mere 176 for Bryan. The popular vote was much closer with percentages of fifty-one to forty-nine. A Gold Standard Act was adopted in 1900 and sounded the death knell for the last holdouts in Colorado's silver camps. Following its demonetization, the market price of silver dropped an average of one to four cents an ounce as each succeeding year passed.

As the artificial pegs were removed, one by one, from beneath the price of silver, many of the San Juan towns began to fade slowly out of existence. The noises of drilling and blasting gradually gave way to a pervading atmosphere of unproductive peace and quiet. All too quickly the population dwindled as people drifted away to other camps or to return to their former homes in the East. For a time the trains and stages continued to run in an effort to put up a front and save face, but the number of passengers, as well as the pay load, decreased. Business declined, jobs grew scarce, and a small-scale financial panic enveloped the San Juans. The silver barons fought a good and a brave fight, and certainly in the light of history they cannot be blamed if they mistook temporary relief and a false prosperity for victory.

Shortly after the turn of the century, Colorado's silver production plummeted below ten million dollars for the first time since the great silver boom of the seventies. The pure silver camps never recovered. Deep within the innumerable, almost isolated, pockets that are the essence of the nearly vertical topography of the San Juans, gloom and pessimism were everywhere. The exodus from these silver camps was now becoming almost as rapid as the rushes that had resulted in their original creation. Since many of the mountain roads were still little better than horse trails, the emigrants departed, carrying their most treasured possessions. The accumulated property of several years and the numerous loads that had gone up on the backs of burros, could not be removed in a day, or even in a week, by the same means. Tragically, much of value necessarily remained behind.

Even after the decline, there were those who refused to give up the fight, steadfastly believing in the virtues of a way of living that was gradually becoming an empty dream for most. In late September, 1896, a party of Italian miners opened up a rich vein of gold-bearing quartz running over five thousand dollars to the ton. The find was located in Deer Park, on the same mineral belt as the Montana, Quail, and other rich properties that were discovered in that locality. The Montana people sank a shaft on their property and the vein carried a high grade of gold ore. Although they encountered a great amount of water, the ore more than paid the expense of driving the tunnel. Forty-five feet down, the vein matter at the bottom carried sufficient free gold to warrant further depth.

Even at the turn of the century, when most San Juan mining men had conceded the loss of their battle, there were still a few hardy souls who insisted on giving it one more try. The Pride of the West on Green Mountain again began active operations in January of 1900 after having been closed down since the previous July. This mine had been one of the big shippers and was once the largest producer in Cunningham Gulch. When the mine and mill were in full operation, their combined output added considerably to payrolls in San Juan County. Some one hundred men were employed directly at the mine alone. The product was heavy lead ores, carrying forty ounces of silver and one to four ounces of gold.

At present the empty towns still sit there, remote, nearly forgotten relics of a colorful past. Scattered among their crumbling walls are discarded boots, coffeepots, stoves, bits of harness, school books, cooking utensils, and other pathetic examples that point unmistakably to the acceleration with which the abandonment progressed. For the pure silver camp, it was all over. Some went to Cripple Creek, while others left the state to try their luck again on the latest bonanzas—which, in their turn, would also wither and die.

Those camps like Telluride, Alta, and Carson, where some gold was found, too, rode out the crisis more easily for a time. Luckily for Colorado's shattered finances, one of the world's greatest gold camps had been discovered in the crater of an extinct volcano in 1891 at Cripple Creek.

Notwithstanding the decline in its financial importance, the history of the San Juan silver era is slow to die. Even today an occasional newspaper story stirs up the memories of some people with post-mortems involving great names. One such story served as a grim reminder of the tragedy written in the white vastness of winter near the rooftop of the world. It was uncovered in January of 1952 by members of the San Juan County snowplow crew opening the Cunningham Gulch Road northeast of Silverton. As their plow topped a rise near the Green Mountain Mine, nine miles out of Silverton, the crew expected to sight the mill and other buildings of the Highland Mary Mine. Instead, they saw a vast void of white with a large blackened patch where the mill had stood no longer ago than the previous Saturday. The famous Highland Mary Mill, the blacksmith shop, boardinghouse, and other structures were gone; and it was evident from a distance of only three quarters of a mile that fire had swept the buildings causing a possible property loss of one quarter of a million dollars.

Belated recognition of the importance of the San Juan rush was extended by the United States Department of the Interior in 1962 when Silverton was designated as a National Historic Landmark. Only two other Colorado communities, Leadville and Central City, had been so honored at that time. The same designation was awarded to Telluride in July of 1964 in recognition of its impact on the mining frontier by producing more than sixty million dollars in precious metals.

After the great influx of prospectors, miners, and town builders had passed, there ultimately came into the mountains a group of settlers who were attracted by the broad, fertile lowlands in some of the valley bottoms. Here, hay, grain, and vegetables for home consumption could be produced. This later stage in the settlement and development of the San Juan region has produced a permanent population with every indication of prosperity. But deep in the mountain fastness, high up among the great peaks, the curtain of uncertainty has been drawn across a great era—and a fascinating period in Colorado's history has come to a close!

Index

Western
Americana
F
782
S19
B87

Brown, Robert Leaman, 1921-
An empire of silver; a history of the San
Juan silver rush, by Robert L. Brown.   Caldwell,
Idaho, Caxton Printers, 1965.
328p.   illus., map (on lining papers) ports.
22cm.   index.

Includes bibliography.

1.San Juan region, Colo.-History.   2.Silver mines and
mining-Colorado.   3.Colorado-History.   I.Title.

3(3370

University of the Pacific Library

3 5132 00238 4774
University of the Pacific Library

550 RIDGWAY

LEOPARD CREEK

PORTLAND

62

LOTUS

CAPITOL CITY

FALL CREEK
SAW PIT

SNEFFELS

OURAY

ENGINEER PASS

ROSES CABIN

145

VANADIUM

SAN MIGUEL

CAMP BIRD

MINERAL POINT

CINNAMON PASS

TELLURIDE

PANDORA

IRONTON

ANIMAS FORKS

WHITECROSS

SHERMAN

RED MTN. PASS

GUSTON

RED MTN.

SUMMIT

EUREKA

CO. RE.

TROUT LAKE

OPHIR

CHATTANOOGA

GLADSTONE

HOWARDSVILLE

MATTERHORN

BURRO BRIDGE

WALDHEIM

145

SILVERTON

ARASTRA

STONY PASS

DUNTON

550

MOLAS LAKE PASS

RIO GRANDE RESERVOIR

RICO

HINSDALE COUNT

ELECTRA LAKE

EMERALD LAKE

ROCKWOOD

LA PLATA COUNTY

CUMBERLAND

VALLECITO RESERVOIR

LA PLATA CITY

HERMOSA

550

HESPERUS

ANIMAS CITY

160

FORT LEWIS

DURANGO

BAYFIELD